W9-AAJ-010

THE POLITICS OF DECEIT

SAVING FREEDOM AND DEMOCRACY FROM EXTINCTION

GLENN W. SMITH

WILEY

JOHN WILEY & SONS, INC.

Published by John Wiley & Sons, Inc., Hoboken, New Jersey.
Published simultaneously in Canada.

For general information on our other products and services, or technical support, please contact our Customer Care Department within the United States at 800-762-2974, outside the United States at 317-572-3993 or fax 317-572-4002.

Wiley also publishes its books in a variety of electronic formats. Some content that appears in print may not be available in electronic books.

For more information about Wiley products, visit our web site at www.wiley.com.

Library of Congress Cataloging-in-Publication Data

Smith, Glenn W., 1953 Sept. 30–
    The politics of deceit : saving freedom and democracy from extinction / Glenn W. Smith.
        p. cm.
    Includes bibliographical references and index.
    ISBN 0-471-66763-3 (cloth)
        1. United States—Politics and government—2001–   2. Political culture—United States.
3. Manipulative behavior—United States.   4. Mass media—Political aspects—United
States.   5. Political participation—United States—Psychological aspects.   6. Political
psychology.   I. Title.
    JK275.S55 2004
    306.2'0973—dc22

                                                                                    2004007666

Printed in the United States of America

10   9   8   7   6   5   4   3   2

To the memory of my father, Al Smith, and to my mother, Bunny Smith, who taught me reverence for the past and respect for those with whom I share the living present.
And to my daughter, Katie McLean Smith, who teaches me daily about our responsibility to the future.

CONTENTS

FOREWORD

This book is both so thoughtful and so useful that I am a little startled and even slightly awed to find it written by my old friend Glenn Smith. Not that I've never had anything but admiration for him, but sometimes when you have known someone for a long time—"good ol' so-and-so"—you tend to take that person for granted, and this is what I've done with Glenn Smith. I've known him as a reporter, a political consultant, a caring Dad—even a beer-drinking buddy. Good ol' Glenn—he's always right on the mark about politics and, like the rest of us Texas progressives, eternally engaged in some losing cause.

What I had really expected was a smart, funny book full of how-to, like something that James Carville, Michael Moore, or Jim Hightower might write: handy tips, lots of partisan cheerleading, and so on.

Lord knows I've spent enough time gnawing at the question *why?* in today's political climate. Is it the candidates? The rules? The media? The money? What's *wrong* with American politics? When you watch it at the state and local level as Smith and I do, it's hard to miss how wrong we get it. Setting aside political ideology, the bad guys win and the good guys lose far too often—I'm not talking about who is right or wrong on the issues of the day, but about candidates' integrity, competence, and the ability to think about something besides their own reelection. We are losing superb Republicans and gifted Democrats to candidates with good hair and fatuous platitudes.

Many people I know in both political journalism and consulting have become cynics over the years. I remain optimistic to the point of idiocy, but this is in part a strategy of self-preservation. Glenn Smith has taken to the consolations of philosophy and, I admit, has made it much further than I have. I read widely, but Smith has foraged so much more deeply and so much further afield than I have that I sometimes have trouble keeping up with him. He moves backwards and forwards in time, from writers highbrow to lowbrow, all the while informed by a merciless knowledge of marketing gained through long experience.

What I find fascinating about this book is Smith's expertise in marketing—he analyzes focus groups, how they work, and how they are applied to politics. Not that much of it is new to me, but Smith's first-person accounts are invaluable. This is a guy who has spent years selling you candidates as though they were deodorant or dishwashing liquid. He sees what's wrong with this arrangement in a way that no one who hasn't "been there/done that" ever can.

As a professional optimist, I'm especially pleased that Glenn Smith, a realist with substantial cause to despair, sees signs of hope for democracy. Most of us who covered the primary in 2004 concluded, "Holy cow! There really is 'something happening here/What it is ain't exactly clear.'" Smith believes the Internet, the first interactive form of mass communication, has the potential to bring people back into politics. I will let him explain.

I suspect this book will get more serious attention from right-wing publications and perhaps will even be read by more conservatives than liberals. I say this because I believe the Right in recent years has been better about taking ideas seriously than the Left. Smith's contribution is so much larger than the usual liberal mantra of "We're right, and anyone who can't see it is an idiot." From straight out of the frontline trenches of political warfare, Glenn Smith gives us some genuinely original thinking, a few laughs, and a glimpse of a better world.

We can't ask for more than that.

Molly Ivins
Austin, Texas

ACKNOWLEDGMENTS

What insights I might have into the nature of freedom and the health of our democracy have been learned in part from those public servants whom I have been lucky enough to counsel over the years. I would especially like to acknowledge former Texas Lieutenant Governor Bill Hobby, whose commitment to democracy is matched only by his intelligence and compassion for the least fortunate among us.

Years ago I was taught to view my employers, colleagues, allies, and opponents as teachers, and I have not suffered from a lack of instruction from some of the best political minds of our time. Many of them may disagree with my conclusions, but all of them helped shape my thinking.

I must offer a special thanks to George Lakoff, linguist, cognitive scientist, and progressive political thinker and activist. George opened my mind to new ways of thinking, and his steadfast and optimistic commitment to progressive change is inspirational. He has spent countless hours talking politics and philosophy with me, and I will be forever grateful. Also, the late neuroscientist Francisco Varela graciously gave his time to help me understand his phenomenological approach to ethics and human life. Cognitive scientist Shaun Gallagher devoted his time to help me clarify the relationship between human consciousness and freedom. Needless to say, the conclusions are my own.

I learned the importance to democracy of spiritual expression and religious freedom from the profound writings of Reinhold Niebuhr and Czech philosopher Jan Patočka. I must also acknowledge the influences of theologian Paul Tillich and of Eric Hoffer, the self-taught "longshoreman philosopher" and author of *The True Believer*. I read the books of these last two thinkers in high school and, while much of it was over my head at the time, I have never forgotten the spirit of their work. I would also like to acknowledge the teachings of two friends, the late Reverend Clark Lennard and Lama Surya Das, who taught me that political reform and social justice begin with the human heart.

I would like to thank Molly Ivins for her generous foreword to the book. I would call Molly a national treasure, but the term is used mostly for those whose best work lies behind them. In Molly's case, her thinking and writing is more vital and important than ever. Thanks, Molly, for your amazing loyalty to your friends and for your insight into the tragicomic troubles of our time.

Wes Boyd and the rest of the team at MoveOn.org helped me understand the history-shaping possibilities of Internet activism.

Special thanks to Geoff Rips, Cyndi Hughes, and Melanie Ferguson, three friends who read the manuscript and offered new insight and approaches to some of the issues discussed. My partner, Margie Becker, and her mother, Nancy Becker, also gave their time to the project. Margie's patience and support made the book possible.

I am grateful for the support and encouragement of David Pugh, my editor at John Wiley & Sons. In addition, I must acknowledge the contributions of production editor Alexia Meyers and copy editor Matthew Kushinka for their skillful and attentive editing.

A heartfelt thank you to Rick Pappas, my lifelong friend who just happens to be one of the country's best literary and entertainment lawyers.

All the friends and colleagues who have helped me before and during the writing of this book are simply too numerous to mention. To all of them I say thank you.

INTRODUCTION

"**A** long habit of not thinking a thing *wrong*, gives it a super-ficial appearance of being *right*, and raises at first a for-midable outcry in defense of custom. But the tumult soon subsides. Time makes more converts than reason." So wrote Thomas Paine in the opening of his revolutionary pamphlet, *Common Sense*. Paine was urging his countrymen to join in the struggle for American independence. Just because the colonists had lived with English rule for decades did not mean that rule was not oppressive—nor did it justify continued allegiance to the British crown.

We find ourselves in a circumstance similar to that of our fore-bears, though what threatens us does not come from across an ocean but from within ourselves. The tyranny we face is one built upon contemporary political practices that devalue responsibility and par-ticipation—both personal and communal—while life-and-death political discussions and decisions are limited to a virtual world of illusion and coercion. The presidency of George W. Bush represents the dangerous triumph of the cynical and the manipulative. While claiming to advance the cause of freedom throughout the world, the political practices of the Bush administration are nothing less than a war on freedom and democracy.

Just because we have become accustomed to the politics of manip-ulation—a reliance on paid advertising, elitist control, and popular disinterest—does not make our political practices *right*. It is argued in the following pages that our political customs threaten democracy and freedom with extinction. Further, *contra* Paine, we may not have the luxury of waiting for time to accomplish what reason can-not. Nothing short of a revolution in the way we practice politics in America will keep freedom and democracy from disappearing behind

1

the mirrored curtain of our self-absorbed, vain, and impoverished political customs.

Eastern Europeans who struggled for decades behind an iron curtain understood the devastating consequences of a demoralized public in a mass civilization. The dissociation of the people's freedoms and needs from the mechanisms of authoritarian control is the way of tyranny. Such was Vaclav Havel's point when he warned the West that we shared many "post-totalitarian" qualities with those nations that once struggled under Communist regimes. He spoke of "the general unwillingness of consumption-oriented people to sacrifice some material certainties for the sake of their own spiritual and moral integrity" and described this condition as "living a lie."

The political scientist Wendy Brown recently made a complementary point: "Many of the least defensible elements of twentieth-century communist states, leaving aside overt and routinized political repression, have lately made their appearance in ours: overgrown state size, power, and reach; groaning apparatuses of administration intermixed with a labyrinthine legal machinery; expensive and extensive welfare systems that routinely fail their client populations; inefficient and uncontrolled economies; lack of felt sovereign individuality; and chronic urban housing shortages." All these symptoms arise from living within our lies.

I have worked for many years within this lie. As a journalist and political consultant, I—like so many others—underestimated the significance of the mirrored curtain that separates the people from democratic institutions and mechanisms of power. The dissociation is, of course, of great benefit to the Bush dynasty and the right-wing ideologues who prop it up. They are enemies of truth who skillfully construct illusions of freedom while building for themselves an ever more impregnable and authoritarian fortress on a hill. In fact, the expert propagandists of the Bush administration have so refined the techniques of dissociation and manipulation that any act of resistance may seem inadequate to the task of restoring freedom and democracy. As a long-time Democratic consultant, I erred in thinking I could further progressive policies by exploiting better than

Republicans the tools of our contemporary political practices. I played into the hands of my opponents by helping advance inherently conservative rules of engagement—the power of money over argument in the public sphere, the disproportionate spending on advertising over grass roots recruitment, and the reliance on suspect instruments of opinion measurement. This is the complete reduction of politics to marketing.

Unilateral disarmament in the realm of political communications is not a possibility. Today, a candidate or party that did so would simply forfeit the race. But we must recognize that our contemporary political practices are the instruments of authoritarian-style government. Sure, Democrats win now and again. But it is no accident that progressive policies make few real gains. There is seldom a mandate for any substantive reform, nor can there be so long as all parties and candidates rely on millions of dollars in advertising to convince voters they are committed to, say, protecting the environment. With all this visible commitment, it is easy for voters to assume the environment has been saved.

In 2001, after George W. Bush had become President but before September 11, I had occasion to conduct an extended series of focus groups in diverse settings throughout the state of Texas. Focus groups consist of 12 to 15 voters, recruited by professional marketing consultants and each paid $50 or more to spend an hour and a half discussing whatever issues the sponsors would like to discuss. The sponsor's strategists sit hidden from the group behind a two-way mirror, all the better to scientifically analyze the responses without actually engaging in dialogue with voters. It is not unusual that in the same marketing facility a group of consumers tastes a new cereal while next door another group discusses (it's much easier to pick a favorite cereal) the politics of health insurance or education.

Bush had been governor of Texas from 1995 to 2001, when he ascended to the White House. We asked our focus group participants what they had liked about Bush's gubernatorial years. Without hesitation, Texans from all walks of life in all parts of the state said the same thing: Bush's commitment to education was laudable. Later in the sessions, we asked what kinds of problems Texas faced. Once again, without hesitation or understanding of the inherent contradiction, these same participants said, in effect, that public education in Texas remains a disgrace. They were perfectly comfortable looking with favor upon Bush's well-crafted appearance of concern for education while understanding from their daily lives that public education remained in pitiful condition.

Democracy will not long survive this kind of voter dissociation. Political consultants defend such research tools as focus groups by pointing out that they are, after all, talking with real voters about real concerns. In a typical political focus group, however, a candidate's strategists are looking for the best language, image, or advertisement to sell an already chosen candidate or policy. They are not looking for guidance from voters on what should be sold. Such political technologies as the focus group perfectly illustrate the mirrored curtain. Voters see only themselves in the wall-sized looking glass that separates them from the policymakers. Political decisions are made behind the mirror, not in front of it.

When you place Bush's obsession with secrecy next to his assault on the rights and freedoms guaranteed by the Bill of Rights that protect us from unwarranted search and seizure or imprisonment, it becomes clear how the focus group symbolizes the technology of tyranny. Bush and his strategists sit in the dark behind a two-way mirror. They get to know everything about *us* while we are allowed to know nothing about *them*.

Once the correct coercive message is extracted from the experimental subjects, consultants craft television advertisements. This is all done while the candidate works the phones and travels the country to raise from the monied interests the funds required for advertising. The ads run and, lo and behold, opinion changes. This is usually done in competition with an opposition candidate; in these scenarios, somebody loses. For the loser, enough minds have not been changed. But that does not change the coldly manipulative nature of the entire enterprise. Advertising and marketing scholars such as Harvard's Gerald Zaltman now tout recent studies showing that advertising, especially television advertising, does more than persuade, coerce, or inform. It actually alters the memories of viewers. It can and often does change what we believe happened to us or around us. Consequently, to the extent that our sense of individuality is dependent on memory, it changes *who we are*. Rhetoric has always been about persuasion. But this is beyond rhetoric. This is radically different from what Aristotle, Enlightenment thinkers, and our nation's founders thought about rationality and speech. In the 2002 elections, viewers in the top 75 television markets in America saw four times more paid political advertising than broadcast news stories about politics. Four times. By any sensible measure, this is insane.

What do the defenders say about the proliferation of political advertising? They say that if it were not for the ads, voters would not get any political information at all. The proof that this is not the case is that in the nineteenth century—when 80 or 90 percent of eligible voters actually voted—there was no radio or television advertising. There was plenty of political hogwash, to be sure. But there was also real, meaningful, face-to-face discussion (and the occasional fist fight) over issues, candidates, and concerns.

We have eliminated, consciously or unconsciously, many of the old ways we had of exchanging political stories, ideas, or beliefs with one another. Political parties are little more than bank accounts, logos, and sponsors of televised studio events called conventions. In their zeal to eliminate the excesses of ward politics, reformers in the early years of the twentieth century began an assault on human political organizations that today robs us of an authentic public sphere.

An insidious consequence of the "virtualizing" of the public sphere is the elimination of human tragedy from the tableau. Real human beings get sick and die, unprotected by health insurance and sentenced to second-class medical care. Underprivileged children are abandoned to a dark, dangerous world of violent schools, poor educational opportunity, and bleak futures. Of course, no society can ever eliminate human tragedy. Behind the mirrored curtain, however, people are not called to respond to tragedy because there is no real presentation of tragedy. Local television news is awash in crime stories. The faceless victims become like cartoon characters, flattened to the concrete but popping up again, resurrected to become tomorrow's faceless victims. Yes, the news tells us over and over again, bad things happen. Part of our addiction to this kind of news, however, stems from its unreal nature. There is a hole in our culture's heart. We consume these stories to fill the void opened by our inability to rescue the less fortunate with understanding and true compassion. When an unexpected and horrible tragedy does intrude upon our consciousness—September 11 or a natural disaster—Americans respond with a remarkably heroic spirit of fellow-feeling. Why are we unable to summon this spirit to address the daily tragedies of our common life?

Bush has mastered the virtual presidency. When he leans forward at the podium, nods his head toward the camera, and summons that caring (and, he believes, daring) look to his eyes, we believe he really is something called a compassionate conservative. He makes us feel that he is addressing the tragedies that afflict our families, friends, and neighbors. But the talk itself is disconnected from those who will suffer or succeed depending on the effectiveness of his persuasive force. The public's general absence from any political discussion runs parallel to the absence of the victimized from the public's consciousness. This is a circumstance in which only the right wing can succeed—the right has created an environment in which the consequences of their policies are invisible. There is no suffering. There are no victims. This is why they lead the fight against every kind of political reform except those that widen the divide between the rich and the poor, the powerful and the powerless. Karl Rove knows the handicap facing Democrats, who by and large want to address the tragedies of contemporary American life. Before Democratic solutions can be sold, however, Democrats first have to convince a somnolent public that there are any tragedies at all. Democrats are asking people to vote for the Buzz Killers.

When we wonder why politics seems so polarized, why so many politicians gravitate to what may seem to us as extremes (I think the distance between political contestants is dismally small, but their shouting is extreme), it is due in part to the fact that candidates no longer have to negotiate their positions with a real public; dialogue is no longer necessary with a public beyond the focus group chamber. Worse still, in today's celebrity culture, skilled journalists' professional standing is determined more by playing along with elitist propaganda than by stepping to the voter side of the mirror to speak to (and for) those of us not dining at the best restaurants in Washington, D.C. Too often, these same journalists turn every important issue of contemporary political life into a punditized television circus in which the only thing really communicated is that all views are equally banal.

I fear that seeking legislative campaign reforms to revitalize democracy may be about as effective as pre-revolutionary colonial petitions were in changing the policies of King George III. Reforms would have to be approved by incumbents elected through the very political practices that must be overthrown, which is not likely. There has never been a time in our history when one political party so dominated the mechanisms of power. Until 2004, Democrats became competitive by masquerading as Republicans. Bush's extremism has made it easier to draw distinctions. The right wing will not be persuaded to loosen its stranglehold by appeals to human rights or democratic theory. Still, reforms should be demanded. We must go further, however, and revolutionize our democracy from the bottom up and from the outside in.

There are already steps in this direction. For instance, a new kind of Internet activism is just entering its adolescence. Cutting edge organizations are altering the political landscape. I have worked with one of these groups, MoveOn.org, and can attest that its members are courageous and hardworking and may be leading the way to a new and more democratic future. Millions of Americans who yesterday found few avenues for effective political participation are today involved in public discussion. But few of their lives (like this author's) are marked by the poverty, hunger, second-class educational opportunity, or dangerous working conditions that plague the lives of those they seek to help. In this regard we are like members of an earlier American progressive movement. So far, there have been no missteps. But we should take a lesson from some of the Progressive Era failures (Prohibition, for instance), because they resulted in part from a paternalism that was sometimes blind to the real needs and wants of the less fortunate Americans on whose behalf they struggled.

Our political practices also obscure deeper troubles that threaten our freedoms and our democracy. The progressive theologian Reinhold Niebuhr, a tireless defender of human rights and dignity, said many years ago that "Modern democracy requires a more realistic philosophical and religious basis." In this regard, we do not see the risks and failures of our political practices because we have lost our vision of what freedom and democracy mean. Moreover, we cannot get a strong and vital understanding of these terms because our political practices have debased them. Contemporary philosopher Jean-Luc Nancy wonders whether it is possible even to speak of freedom any longer, so lost are we in our efforts to define what we mean by the term. Determinists have carried the day, with some, like cognitive scientist Daniel C. Dennett, telling us there is no such thing as free will but that there is a limited kind of freedom. He tells us, like a scolding parent, that we should be thankful for what we do have. The lack of a more realistic philosophical and religious consensus with regard to freedom and democracy has led us into a cultural and political *cul de sac*. Without such consensus we are left with a shrugging acceptance of freedom as the choice between Burger King and McDonald's and democracy as something professionals take part in while the people shop.

Freedom in a democracy is precisely the recognition that the number and variety of choices, paths, and opportunities available to me is entirely proportional to the number and variety of choices available to you. I cannot make myself more free by constraining the rights and freedoms of others, if for no other reason than I must lose the use of at least one of my hands while I hold on to the chains of those who are bound.

Progressives in the West have all but ceded spiritually-based language of value and ethics to the manipulators on the right. As I argue later in the book, spiritual expression is essential to the discovery of personal—and interpersonal—freedom, although an admittedly cruel paradox exists, given the disgusting human rights excesses, excuses, and excommunications of many religious institutions. This freedom is found in those moments of prayer, meditation, or communal ritual in which our hearts and minds are flooded with possibilities hidden from us just moments before. The problem with religion, however, occurs when the joys of these moments become dominated by institutional bureaucrats who learn to exploit both our desire for this infinite opening of possibilities and our fear that it will forever be closed unless we follow their commands and their institutional rules.

It is not a coincidence that every great progressive reform movement in American history involved profound and publicly expressed spiritual elements. The Civil Rights movement comes to mind, as does the Abolitionist movement. For that matter, the immigration to early America was obviously a religious movement in part, and the American republic itself was strengthened by a deep and abiding respect for freedom of religious practice.

The consequences of the Left's failure to understand human spirituality are twofold: People to whom progressives want to speak cannot understand what they are saying because the reformers often talk an austere, wonky, secular language that ignores much of what the would-be audience believes make us human. Even more troubling is that without an understanding of the spiritual nature of man there can be no real understanding of human freedom. In other words, too many of us do not even know what we are fighting for. Separation of church and state does not mean the eradication of all spiritual expression from public life. Such an erasure is not possible, even if it were desirable. Democracy will be much healthier when we understand that there is a place for religions of all kinds and types. If any one of us possessed the Truth (as some people believe they do), there would be no need for democracy. But because there is no such thing as the all-encompassing Truth, we must have democracy to make sure each of us and each of our children can pursue the smaller truths available to human beings.

To be sure, contemporary political sound bites often include religious language. President Clinton spoke of a New Covenant in his 1992 inaugural address (it proved to be a covenant in style more than substance). Like President Carter, Clinton understood the potential of shared spiritual narratives and mythologies. Both offered alternatives to the dominant, right-wing Christian Millennialism employed so skillfully by President Reagan (and now taken to new extremes by Bush II.) Clinton abandoned his covenantal approach when right-wing attacks forced him to focus on the preservation of his presidency. Democracy and freedom will not survive so long as we continue to live within our lies. Eastern European dissidents such as Havel spoke of "living within the truth" as a way for authentic, human movements to oppose authoritarian rule. The notion was that we are able to controvert—in conversation, in writings, in daily interpersonal behavior, and in small and large ways—the visible and invisible mechanisms that rob us of an opportunity to be fully human. In this way, our views can be heard and understood in a public sphere that's darkened by no curtain, iron or mirrored.

As a political professional who has struggled for years within the rigged terms of engagement, I try to give an insider's perspective on what shape these acts of resistance and revolution should take. Most of those I have worked with in politics are honorable, well-meaning, dedicated professionals. Not one of them could or should be expected to change the rules of the game in which they are engaged. It is up to us—the voters and thus the popular commissioners of politics—to revolutionize political practices that threaten the future of liberty.

We need to reemerge into a public sphere that is open to all people and to all views. We need revitalized political parties. We need more neighborhood activists and more civic engagement. We need to recognize that in today's America it is often not just government that intrudes on our freedom, but the very practices by which our leaders rise to power. We need also to understand that political freedom is put at risk by selfish elites, people who threaten our livelihoods if we speak against their interests and who assume that they somehow merit extraordinary shares of our finite monetary and natural resource wealth. Meanwhile, the vast number of Americans are left with little money and our natural resources are depleted.

We need to rip away the mirrored curtain and take back democracy.

We need a revolution.

And for a few short months or years, we may still have the freedom to begin one. We may not have the time Paine believed would eventually persuade others to freedom and self-rule. But we have the reason.

1

THE MADNESS OF KING GEORGE III AND OUR CONTEMPORARY POLITICAL DILEMMA

There is something exceedingly ridiculous in the composition of monarchy; it first excludes a man from the means of information, yet empowers him to act in cases where the highest judgement is required.

Thomas Paine
Common Sense

On the morning of November 2, 1920, a young African-American named July Perry cast his ballot for President of the United States in Ocoee, Florida. His vote cost him his life. A friend, Mose Norman, tried to vote later that morning. He was turned away, and the anger of racist whites at his and Perry's boldness turned to murderous rage. Before dawn of the next day, Mr. Perry was dead, shot full of holes and hanged from a tree. Five hundred African-American residents of Ocoee were driven from their town. An undetermined number were killed.

When the first shots were heard, 12-year-old Armstrong Hightower and his two siblings ran and hid in a nearby orange grove as fire roared through their neighborhood, burning a church, a lodge, and two dozen homes. The three children climbed into the trees to sleep that night, fearful of wildcats and Klansmen. It was Armstrong's sister Annie's birthday. The next day, the children walked seven miles to a nearby town and were reunited with their parents. None but Armstrong ever returned. When he did finally go back 81 years later, he was 93. On that visit, he said he missed his childhood friends. He remembered November 2, 1920, as the night "the devil got loose." He glanced at the Ocoee of 2001, transformed as it was by the presence of Disney World thirty minutes away.

But he said he could still smell the fire.

In 2000, the year before Armstrong Hightower returned to Ocoee, Republican election officials in Florida, in what one activist called "lynching by laptop," purged thousands of qualified African-American voters from the rolls through a complicated and error-prone computer program. Others were intimidated into not voting. Still others had their ballots thrown out. In all, some 200,000 voters, a large percentage of them African-Americans, were denied a voice in the 2000 presidential election. Paid GOP operatives, recruited from around the country by email, raced to Florida to stage mock protests for the television cameras as Democrats tried to force a recount and rectify the injustice. Republican state Senator Daniel Webster, who hails from Ocoee, helped lead the fight to block the recount. It had been 80 years since the Ocoee conflagration. But the smell of it remained in the air.

That same election night in 1920, while Armstrong, Annie, and Josephus Hightower clung to the branches of orange trees and scanned the grove for predators, KDKA radio of Pittsburgh, Pennsylvania, broadcast the presidential election returns to a national wireless audience. It was the first such national broadcast. In a wooden shack atop a Westinghouse plant, chief engineer Donald G. Little and announcer Leo Rosenburg sat in the cramped quarters, took phone calls from the *Pittsburgh Post* where workers relayed the vote count, and announced the running totals into "the ether." As a storm raged outside their shack, the radio men reported on the presidential contest between two newspaper men, Republican Warren

Harding (who won handily) and Democrat James Cox. Throughout the night Rosenburg frequently asked listeners, "Will anyone hearing this broadcast please communicate with us, as we are anxious to know how far the broadcast is reaching and how it is being received."

The birth of commercial radio was attended by—and, many historians believe, contributed to—a spiritualist craze that gripped the nation after World War I. Radio itself seemed magical, as voices from far away could be heard in a listener's headset (loudspeakers took a while to perfect). It was an eerie, and, some people thought, probably occult phenomena. "Sounds born of earth and those born of the spirit found each other," wrote art historian Rudolph Arnheim. To journalist Walter Lippmann, what radio carried was not the broadcasts of ghosts, but broadcasts to ghosts.

In his 1925 book *The Phantom Public*, Lippmann fumed and fulminated against progressive reformers who thought it prudent in a democracy to include the voices of as many citizens as possible in elections. A public of "perfect" citizens is a phantom of the idealistic imagination, Lippmann wrote. "[T]here is not the least reason for thinking, as mystical democrats have thought, that the compounding of individual ignorances in masses of people can produce a continuous directing force in public affairs," he stormed. Paradoxically, he argued for more public debate, not because it would enhance deliberation and reason in public decision-making, but because it would reveal the self-interest of dominant public conversationalists—that is, of special interest groups.

These ideas of Lippmann's (he was considered a liberal pundit) continue to beguile conservatives. The book was republished in 1994 by the Library of Conservative Thought. And the idea of elite democracy it recommends has been fully reincarnated by a conservative jurist and academic, Richard A. Posner, who argues that increased participation in democratic processes might harm the economy by distracting Americans from their primary private duty: consuming the goods and services of the capitalist economy.

Phantom citizens or not, a large portion of the public let KDKA know that they had heard the broadcast. But there was nothing mystical about that. And although it is believed that July Perry marked a ballot in Ocoee, Florida, it is doubtful that his vote remained among those counted and reported by the national broadcast. It is hard to imagine that the racists of Ocoee counted their victim's vote.

In the 1920 election, 75 years of struggle had brought the franchise to women. Many believe that Charlotte Woodward Pierce, the last surviving signer of the famous 1848 Declaration of Sentiments and Resolutions passed by the Seneca Falls women's rights conference, voted that year. African-Americans died trying to vote, however, as they would continue to do throughout the century. Their heroic efforts shame Lippman's dismissive attitude about broad participation in the public sphere. But such an attitude is still with us and, unfortunately, it is winning.

KDKA radio is now owned by Viacom. It broadcasts Rush Limbaugh's right-wing radio show. It is one of the largest media companies in the world and competes with Disney, which owns ABC and Disneyworld, the latter located just up the road from Ocoee. It also competes with Rupert Murdoch's News Corporation (which owns Fox News). In 2000, a Bush relative working at Fox on election night prematurely called Florida for Bush. It helped establish the legitimacy of the Bush victory even before the full scale and scope of the election controversy was known. During their election coverage, none of these media giants needed to ask viewers to call in to see how far their signals reached. They reached far, indeed.

Thomas Paine said, "Freedom hath been hunted round the globe," and the hunt has come back to America. In 1776, the year America was founded, there were portents of a new age, just as there are at the turn of the twenty-first century. That year Paine wrote *Common Sense*, a slender volume published anonymously. He referred to those heady days as "the seed time of continental union, faith and honor." We are now in such a seed time, and much can be gained by revisiting Paine's themes and purposes. There is no monarchy to oppose. But in many ways the subtle bonds of "corporate democracy" and the practices of politics themselves—the power of money in elections, the demise of political parties as vehicles for public participation, the overwhelming reliance on manipulative advertising and other marketing techniques, diminished voter involvement, the debased language of political and policy discussion—provide contemporary analogues to the difficulties and dilemmas faced by the early Americans under colonial rule.

The Public and Porphyria: Are We All King Georges Now?

It is not an ocean but a sea of information—and disinformation—that separates Americans from their leaders and from one another. It is not by force of arms (at least, not yet) that America is driven toward a new kind of tyranny. Many have a sense that something has gone terribly wrong. Too many of us are forced to the safety of the orange groves, hiding, watching for predators we recognize and predators we have never seen before, as events that will forever alter our lives happen in the kind of impenetrable darkness that surrounds a community on fire.

In *Common Sense*, Paine spoke of the isolation of King George III, whose disconnection from real intelligence about affairs in the colonies contributed to the impasse that ultimately led to American independence. The King also suffered from a physical ailment that was symbolic of his political isolation. It's called porphyria. His peripheral nerves could not communicate with his central nervous system, causing dementia. Similarly, the central nervous system of the Kingdom—the King—was separated from the world he ruled.

In many ways contemporary Americans, too, suffer from porphyria. Pursuing our dissociated individual fulfillment, we are unable to come together to address common difficulties. Our contemporary political practices exclude citizens from obtaining meaningful information while pretending to empower us "to act in cases where the highest judgement is required." In the film *The Madness of George III*, Willis, a physician summoned to retrieve the sovereign's sanity from this malady (and thereby forestall the regency of George IV), remarks, "The state of monarchy and the state of lunacy share the frontier. Some of my lunatics fancy themselves kings. He's the King. Where shall his fancy take refuge?"

Driven from the public sphere just as Armstrong Hightower, his family, and others were driven from Ocoee in 1920, we have taken refuge not in the orchards of democracy but in isolation from one another, in a magic kingdom of illusion and private interest, dissociated from the fate of others and fearful that public participation in the political decisions of our time may destroy what little solace we find through our private, personal, and commercial pursuits.

To remain where we are would be, as Willis said, lunacy. But our porphyria is treatable. The political practices that reinforce the pathology are ones that we have adopted. They may be practices that have evolved through some misunderstandings of democracy and freedom, through a laziness of the citizenry, or through a drive for power of the elite, but they are not too large to handle. We have to find a way back to one another, to a restored sense of a shared democratic community in which it is understood that the freedom of one is connected to the freedom of all.

The year 1920 is an appropriate year to begin an examination of freedom and democracy in the America of today, to begin an analysis of our political condition, and to explore solutions to the crisis of democracy. The 1920s were a turning point in American history. Although the shift in public consciousness we examine was not abrupt and involved complex economic, cultural, political, and technological forces that had been under way for many years, the twenties marked a tipping point, a time when Americans' prevailing idea of freedom changed.

Of 1920, Nathan Miller wrote, "The public mind was diverted by a whole host of new fads, fashions, and concerns. The popular song of the day was 'Yes, We Have No Bananas.' Prohibition and the new-fangled radio soon replaced the threat of Communism as the chief topic of conversation..." Americans were interested in buying cars, procuring an illegal drink, or purchasing a crystal radio set. Historian Michael McGerr believes the emphasis on personal expression led to the demise of the Progressive Era. "The emphasis on individual freedom and the pursuit of pleasure, especially among the young, left aging progressives disappointed and even aghast." But even Progressive reformers share responsibility for emphasizing the private over the public and finding permanent detours around avenues for citizens' participation in politics and government.

In earlier decades, Americans tended to view freedom as the absence of authoritarian control. Philosopher of freedom Isaiah Berlin would refer to this as "negative freedom," or the elimination of external restraints on individual or group experience. But the rise of consumer culture and a mass audience created through advertising and professional public relations brought with them a new emphasis on another kind of freedom: the freedom to exercise one's will. This was a form of what Berlin called "positive freedom," and he believed that in its exclusive pursuit lay the seeds of totalitarian rule, which is the ultimate expression of will and the imposition upon others of the desires and wishes of a strong leader, nation, political party, race, or religion.

"Socialised forms [of positive freedom], widely disparate and opposed to each other as they are, are at the heart of many of the nationalist, Communist, authoritarian, and totalitarian creeds of our day," Berlin wrote in 1958. Berlin saw his words twisted by right-wing anticommunists of the 1950s, who viewed negative liberty as the absolute description of freedom in America and positive liberty as that pursued by godless communists. These beliefs prevailed even as they imposed new limits on political expression, thereby attenuating the very negative liberty they claimed to champion.

Two Kinds of Freedom

The difference in these two approaches to freedom can be expressed the following way. Positive freedom, which might better be termed *freedom-to-will*, entails an expression of personal will that can ignore or even impose restraints on others. An emphasis on negative freedom, which I call *freedom-to-experience*, focuses on the elimination of such restraints. Responsibility to others remains central to its practice. Freedom-to-will is a much more private concern than freedom-to-experience. Freedom-to-experience does not dismiss or proscribe others' freedom of individual expression, so long as the expression does not trample the liberties of others. Freedom-to-will ignores this broader context, though. Only the restraints on one's own will are noticed. Freedom-to-will is less relational and more egocentric than freedom-to-experience.

We should not confuse freedom-to-experience with passivity and freedom-to-will with activity. In fact, inattention to the freedoms enjoyed by others in favor of a hyper-individualist ethos ultimately produces in the individualist the very passivity he or she may believe has been overcome. The broad conception of freedom considered here was embodied by the Civil Rights movement and articulated by Dr. Martin Luther King and others who combined concern for personal, private freedom with the elimination of external barriers.

There is more at stake in our efforts to solve our democratic crises than our future at home. It is unclear whether our own seed time will witness the full blossoming of global democracy or the demise of freedom and the worldwide victory of autocracy, technocracy, corporatism, and blind consumerism. It was no non sequitur when, in the days after September 11, 2001, President Bush and then New York City Mayor Rudolph Giuliani urged Americans to go shopping, go to the movies, and go to ball games in order to show the world that we remained undeterred in our passionate pursuit of the consumption experience we call freedom. It is this *exclusive* conception of freedom we try so mightily to export to other nations.

This is not meant as just another anticonsumerism polemic. It is the misconception of freedom that needs correcting. It is not a case of "either/or." Freedom-to-experience includes within it a less authoritarian freedom-to-will—including even a consumerist orientation in which shopping helps form one's identity and recognition—so long as that pursuit remains subsidiary and does not unduly restrain the experiences of others. Human nature allows us to recommit ourselves to the ideal of true liberty while we pursue and acquire the products of our imperfect civilization.

In the 1990s, conceptual artist Barbara Kruger's witty poster highlighted the slogan, "I shop, therefore I am," an obvious twist on Descarte's *cogito ergo sum*, which remains one of two philosophical expressions that have obtained pop culture currency (the other is "God is dead"). Sociologist Sharon Zukin noted, "America has become, more than ever, a nation of shoppers. In 1987, the country had more shopping malls than high schools." But there are important reasons to focus our attention on the dominance of private interest over public interest rather than engage in a knee-jerk attack on consumerism. The first is a realistic understanding that the marketplace has been central to human culture since there was something we could call culture. Buying and selling have an important role in the development of individual and group identity.

The second is that anticonsumerists who demand that others conform to their own code of behavior swerve suspiciously close to an exaggerated expression of freedom-to-will. There is little doubt that the condescending, holier-than-thou scolds that pushed Prohibition led to a backlash that helped kill the progressive reform movement in the 1920s. A similar problem plagues some of today's environmentalists. Their private identity becomes so wrapped up in their advocacy that they forget to listen to others.

How does the pursuit of either kind of freedom lead to tyranny and oppression? Berlin explains that the drive for liberty can be confused with a similar but distinct human drive: the need for recognition. "It is only the confusion of desire for liberty with this profound and universal craving for status and understanding, further confounded by being identified with the notion of social self-direction, where the self to be liberated is no longer the individual but the 'social whole', that makes it possible for men, while submitting to the authority of oligarchs or dictators, to claim that this in some sense liberates them," he wrote.

When the desire for liberty is limited to the pursuit of freedom-to-will, especially in a consumer society in which we are at risk of purchasing a superficial self rather than living an authentic identity, recognition and belonging are consumable products, although they must be consumed over and over again. External bonds are forgiven, if they are noticed at all, as the price of belonging. In America, we too often consume to belong. The anxiety raised by possible social or economic exile is exploited by commercial and political advertising. The positive freedom to consume is seen as an ultimate expression of freedom-to-will. So long as we may belong, the state of our real freedom, the absence of external restraint, becomes a secondary consideration. When this ethos dominates, it is not hard to project one's desires onto dominant leaders or cults, onto something or someone that will express our freedom-to-will and consume for us, even if it is human lives that they consume.

This also helps explain how those who consume the most, those in the highest income brackets, can remain passionately opposed to national programs aimed at helping the less fortunate. President George W. Bush's wealthy friends justify and receive huge tax breaks because every tax dollar sent to the government is a dollar that they do not get to spend conspicuously. Thus it is that donations to charity (usually a pittance of what could be afforded) remain popular among some of the wealthy opponents of taxes. In this way they are able to express themselves in perfect "freedom" while they purchase the esteem of their peers for their generous spirits—a two-for-one sale. Even charity given anonymously has a self-satisfying advantage over taxation. The giver knows he or she signed the check.

Just as importantly, government expenditures on the less fortunate imply that there are external barriers to freedom the government programs will eliminate. But such barriers are irrelevant to those driven by the need for recognition and individualist expression. All one needs is a strong will to express oneself. Inadequate health care delivery, millions of children living with hunger and poverty, a public education system slowly strangled by those who resent the taxes it takes to keep the schools going—these are not barriers or restraints on an individual's liberty. They are natural and unfortunate consequences produced by the unwillingness of the weak to go to the American Economic Gym for a good workout.

The consequences of a focus on freedom-to-will are even more apparent when it comes to the natural environment. The freedom to belch deadly chemicals into the air and water outweighs the concerns of those who view such poison as a restraint on their own—and future generations'—freedom-to-experience. Conservatives assail environmental safeguards as illegitimate attacks on their freedom-to-will that will ultimately prevent consumers from buying what they need to fully indulge their own private desires.

Corporate Democracy and Private Interests

The ascendancy of private interests (freedom-to-will) over a shared freedom from coercion (freedom-to-experience) began long before post–World War I America, although there was a turning point in the 1920s. Posner promotes the benefits of "elite democracy" and believes a true public sphere in which informed citizens engage in meaningful ways is unnecessary and even dangerous to the pursuit of private, commercial endeavors. Posner argues that the movement to positive freedom is analogous to the Reformation.

"This change in emphasis enlarged the space for commercial and other private activities, spurring Europe's emergence into modernity. Representative democracy is to participatory democracy as Protestantism was to medieval Catholicism. It is a system of delegated governance. The participation required of the people is minimal. They are left free to spend their time on other, more productive activities, undistracted by the animosities, the polarization, and the endless inconclusive debates of an active political life," Posner wrote. In Posner's universe, politics is a poor cousin to economics and the commercial transaction far more beneficial and productive than political engagement. In fact, Posner argues that urging people to become more involved in local, state, and national decision-making might have an adverse effect on the economy—because, I suppose, they will not have quite so much time to shop.

Posner is a learned and articulate spokesman for, in his own words, "corporate democracy." But his portrait of contemporary life in America is chilling to those of us who oppose the forced abdication of citizens from a rightful place in society and who believe in preserving for humanity freedoms that go beyond the decision of which fast food restaurant to patronize. Astonishingly, Posner argues for this inhuman state of affairs. Here are a few of his remarks:

- "[A]n increase in democracy would probably have to be purchased with a reduction in liberty, the importance of which to a commercial culture can hardly be overestimated."

- "The United States is a tenaciously philistine society. Its citizens have little appetite for abstractions and little time and less inclination to devote substantial time to training themselves to become informed and public-spirited voters."
- "But it is doubtful whether political deliberation would today have fruitful spillovers to private or commercial life, and, if not, the reallocation of time from private and commercial activities to the political realm could reduce social welfare."

It is interesting to note that Americans tend to turn furthest from the public sphere and the pursuit of the freedom-to-experience in the years following wars (the 1920s, the 1950s—complicated somewhat by the Cold War—and, following Vietnam, the 1980s and 1990s). It is also true that these periods were marked by great advances in technology, especially communications technology: radio in the 1920s, television in the 1950s, and the Internet in the 1980s and 1990s. Each of these technologies was immediately commandeered by corporate America for commercial purposes, although the Internet may yet prove itself a resilient subversive force. It seems that the combination of war weariness and the availability of new commercial avenues of expressive individuality and freedom-to-will is a deadly combination for those committed to the more profound and fragile freedom-to-experience, or the freedom from tyranny.

Posner himself speaks to the debilitating consequences of our contemporary political practices. He simply does not think that they get in the way of what really matters: the pursuit of private, especially commercial, interests. He thinks we can live with them, but I think they foreshadow the end of democracy.

"The increasingly sophisticated techniques employed in public-opinion polling and political advertising have made political campaigning manipulative and largely content-free," he wrote. "Fear of giving offense to voters causes politicians to shy away from acknowledging hard facts. More, it causes them to flatter the people and exaggerate the degree to which the people actually rule. Political rhetoric is deeply hypocritical."

I could not have said it better myself. But this is from an advo-
cate who sees only danger in political reform. In his world, it is not
just the voters who are disenfranchised; so are the political leaders.
The real decisions are made by a very small meritocracy that gets to
decide who has merit and who does not. Reformers are unrealistic.
Hey, he says, this is "simply what American democracy *is*."

Posner's corporate democracy also requires political candidates
to adopt qualities better suited to the corporate than the democratic:
"The role of the politician tends to elude the understanding of the
political theorist. The qualities requisite in a statesman or other
leader are closer to those of a broker, salesman, actor, or entrepreneur than to those of an academic," he wrote. Posner is not alone in
his thinking. He is a very honest spokesman for a Hobbesian world
view (shared by Leo Strauss, the Chicago philosopher-king of our
so-called neo-conservatives like Paul Wolfowitz and Richard Perle)
that has little faith in the goodness of human nature. Self-rule is
anarchy, according to Posner.

To sum up this view, we might say the American public sphere has
been almost emptied of meaning. Meaning is now better expressed
through commercial transactions. Apologists for the status quo argue
that most people are not intelligent enough to make constructive contributions to society. Selfish, private concerns trump public, selfless
activity. All of this guards against precipitous political change that
might put the meritocracy at risk and—horror of horrors!—distract
Americans from their duty to buy, buy, buy. This is a triumph of the
freedom-to-will.

Living within the Truth

A remarkably similar characterization of our withering democracy
was made many years ago by Vaclev Havel, in an essay published in
a 1979 book by a group of Czechoslovakian writers who had determined that "living within the truth" was the only effective personal
and collective way the Communist tyranny then in place could be
exposed and ultimately overcome. After the fall of Communism in the

former Soviet Union and Eastern Europe, Havel became president of the Czech Republic. Havel and other dissidents committed themselves to reviving the spirit and dignity of humanity from within a repressive regime. We have much to learn from their efforts. We may live in less overtly brutal and oppressive societies, but the threats to true freedom and democracy are just as real. Here, in light of Posner's defense of corporate democracy, it is worth comparing his description of contemporary America to Havel's insight that our democracy and others might already be—or headed toward becoming—an oppressive social order of the type he and his colleagues sought to undo.

"Is it not true," Havel asked, "that the far-reaching adaptability to living a lie and the effortless spread of social auto-totality have some connection with the general unwillingness of consumption-oriented people to sacrifice some material certainties for the sake of their own spiritual and moral integrity?" This unwillingness has erased the opportunity for an authentic life of integrity and dignity. Havel referred to Communist Czechoslovakia as "post-totalitarian," meaning it had added more subtle methods of control to the usual means of political imprisonment, torture, and murder. Examining these more subtle and manipulative methods, Havel recognized his nation as "just another form of the consumer and industrial society, with all its concomitant social, intellectual, and psychological consequences." He saw similarities to what Posner calls corporate democracy.

"Between the aims of the post-totalitarian system and the aims of life there is a yawning abyss: while life, in its essence, moves towards plurality, diversity, independent self-constitution and self-organization, in short, towards the fulfillment of its own freedom, the post-totalitarian system demands conformity, uniformity and discipline. While life ever strives to create new and 'improbable' structures, the post-totalitarian system contrives to force life into its most probable states," Havel wrote. Posner seems to be saying the latter is a good thing. "This is what American democracy *is*," he says.

In a critique of the kind of liberty we are calling freedom-to-will, Havel quotes Alexander Solzhenitsyn, who called illusory those freedoms not based on responsibility (an earmark of freedom-to-experience). We in the West may enjoy many personal freedoms and securities unknown in Communist Eastern Europe, Havel said. In the end, however, we are victims "of the same automatism" as the victims of Communist oppression. We are not capable of "transcending concerns about [our] own personal survival to become proud and responsible members of the *polis*, making a genuine contribution to the creation of its destiny."

Posner is okay with our absence from the polis. Any widespread attempt to add meaning back into the public sphere might, he says, have negative consequences for commerce. His is not an isolated view. It is an adept articulation of a worldview shared by most of those in charge, and sadly, by many Americans not in charge.

Let's look again at this picture. A learned U.S. appeals court judge and well-known conservative academic carefully describes and promotes corporate democracy, the traits of which are looked at with eerie understanding and alarm by dissidents who battled against totalitarian Communism. Solzhenitsyn was a hero to the Right in America. Ronald Reagan's supporters give the former president credit for defeating Communism and consider themselves allies of Havel, Solzhenitsyn, and other dissidents. Posner himself applauded the work of Havel and Solzhenitsyn. He derided such writers as Paul Erlich and the late Edward Said as "our Havels and Solzhenitsyns, writ small." I assume this to mean that Havel and Solzhenitsyn loom large in his esteem. Posner admired them for the risks they took in the struggle for liberty, but not, apparently, for the kind of liberty they sought.

When respected conservative intellectuals can mount what seem like reasonable arguments favoring the exclusion of the majority of Americans from the democratic process we can see with stark clarity that something is dangerously wrong. But how can we make it right? How do we live within the truth as Havel recommended?

The late Italian writer Italo Calvino gives us a wonderful metaphor for living within the truth. He retells a story about Guido Cavalcanti from Boccaccio's *Decameron*.

[Guido walked] as far as San Giovanni, which was a favorite walk of his because it took him past those great marble tombs now to be found in Santa Reparata, and the numerous other graves that lie all around San Giovanni. As he was threading his way among the tombs, between the porphyry columns that stand in that spot and the door of San Giovanni, which was locked, Messer Betto and his friends came riding through the piazza of Santa Reparata, and on seeing Guido among all these tombs, they said:

"Let's go and torment him . . ."

Finding himself surrounded, Guido promptly replied:

"Gentlemen, in your own house you may say whatever you like to me."

Then, placing a hand on one of the tombstones, which was very tall, he vaulted over the top of it, being very light and nimble, and landed on the other side, whence having escaped from their clutches, he proceeded in his way.

"Were I to choose an auspicious image for the new millennium, I would choose that one," Calvino said. It is not hard to see why. In the story, Cavalcanti is cornered among the porphyry—there is that word again—columns by an elite band of bullies angry at his refusal to conform. But rather than play their game, Cavalcanti changes the rules of engagement. He "raised himself above the weight of the world, showing that with all his gravity he has the secret of lightness, and that what many consider to be the vitality of the times—noisy, aggressive, revving, and roaring—belongs to the realm of death, like a cemetery for rusty old cars."

What is called for is just such a refusal to endorse and play along with the existing rules of engagement. Isolated from a true public sphere, we need to respond with the inventiveness and courage of Cavalcanti. We do not have to accept our political practices as inevitable consequences of modern life. There is nothing inevitable about them. We need to recognize that it is freedom-of-expression that should take precedence over freedom-to-will. We need to recognize that our virtual politics of mass marketing and minimal public involvement leaves us wandering alone, unable to recognize with any depth the sorry circumstances of our lives. But this does not take a new constitutional convention or some radical change in human consciousness. It simply requires us to respond as Cavalcanti did.

If we are to be cured of our porphyria, our collective inability to talk with one another in a revitalized public sphere, we can do so simply by refusing to live within our lies. We must reach a new understanding of freedom. We must recognize how our democracy is distorted by political practices that place a premium upon marketing techniques while devaluing the participation of the vast majority of Americans. We must see that the reason we value democracy is because it can guarantee individuals from diverse faiths, interests, and backgrounds the freedom to become what they wish without inhibiting the freedoms of others.

What will our leap to freedom look like? What are the political practices that must be changed? We need to find ways of increasing the number of citizens who can make an authentic contribution to discussions in the public sphere. This means a new emphasis on grass roots organizations like MoveOn.org, a web-based activist group that has given millions of Americans a new voice in our national political debates. National, state, and local political parties need revitalizing. We explore these and other possibilities in subsequent chapters.

How much value do we place on political participation when, in the early months of the 2004 Democratic presidential race, political pundits all but picked a winner (in error) before a single vote had been cast or counted? There is good news and bad news here. The bad news is the distance between the voters and the political elite. But the good news—and it is very good news—is that Howard Dean got the early frontrunner nod from the experts precisely because he had identified new ways of involving people in the process. His innovative, Internet-based grassroots strategy gave real people a voice in the campaign and a new role in the public sphere. Of course, Dean also took advantage of progressive discontent with the policies of President Bush. As the first to stand in strong opposition to these policies, Dean put his rivals at an initial disadvantage that he then capitalized upon with his skillful web-based campaign. His early success points the way to future practices that could restore some vigor to our democracy.

Other symptoms of our political porphyria are evident in the attention paid by the media to the amount of money raised and its probable effect on future advertising as well as a candidate's chances of electoral success. The winning candidate, of course, must be competitive in fundraising and be able to communicate to the largest possible mass audience through advertising. Because political contests are competitive contests there are always winners and losers, even when all of the candidates play by the same rules, have equivalent dollars, and passable, adequate advertising. This is often taken to mean that democracy is not challenged by the reliance on money and marketing over the involvement of people. After all, the candidate with the most money and the best advertising does not always win. Somehow it is imagined that the wisdom of the people prevails, regardless of how few participate, regardless of the manipulative excesses of the process, and regardless of the seemingly inexorable rise of a kind of nineteenth-century Victorian class divide. This divide is one in which a few stuffy gentlemen—yes, most are men, though far from gentle—hide their personal foibles (William Bennett's gambling, Rush Limbaugh's drugs) while insisting the rest of us should follow an antiquated "virtue" that never meant anything more than a demand that those of us who are less favored acquiesce to their selfish pursuit of power and money.

These are the bullies that find us at San Giovanni. Like Cavalcanti, we should leave them to their sport among the dead (he did abandon his tormentors in the graveyard, referring to that locale when he granted them the permission to speak as they wished "in their own house").

As the Bush administration banged the drums of war in advance of the invasion of Iraq, millions of Americans were joined by even greater numbers from other nations in public protest. Bush dismissed them as nothing more than a "focus group." He would not listen to such rabble. The irony of his remark is sweet. Remember that the president benefited from daily polling and focus grouping around the country to find the best way to package his policies. (Do not let the administration pretend otherwise. Bush strategist Matthew Dowd is a former colleague of mine from the days when he was a Democrat. Karl Rove drafted Dowd onto the Bush team because he is very skilled in the analyses of data produced by contemporary opinion research techniques.) Then, when many of his countrymen refused to remain locked safely behind a two-way mirror in the focus group facility and instead marched into the sunlight to decry the President's wishes, he derides them as, yes, a focus group.

The antiwar marches of 2003 were somewhat different from the Vietnam protests of the 1960s and 1970s, and they may be a signal that Americans and others around the world have begun to emerge into something like a new and relevant public sphere. The recent marches in which I participated were attended by people of all ages, races, religions, and economic backgrounds. There were grandparents and young parents with children in strollers. There were clergy and shopkeepers. The homeless marched beside many well-to-do citizens who live in gated communities. They made a beautiful rabble.

And the attitude, as Calvino recommended, was serious but light. There was not much realistic belief that Bush would be deterred from his fool's errand. But there was much hope that something new was becoming visible. Participants were heartened to find that so many from such diverse backgrounds would find common purpose and willingly articulate that purpose to the nation and the world. How far this is from the sterile world of opinion polling, focus groups, and advertising. It is no wonder the right wing attacked the patriotism of the Dixie Chicks and all those who opposed Bush. Such unprincipled assaults on legitimate protest are made by those bullies left behind by the new spirit of political life, which, as Havel says, "moves towards plurality, diversity, independent self-constitution and self-organization." The deadening demands for "conformity, uniformity and discipline" have been recognized for what they are. Like those left behind by the freedom-loving Cavalcanti, the champions of corporate democracy are threatened by the smallest sign that the greater public is beginning to understand their awful ruse.

In 1920, American political and cultural life was undergoing radical change. A mass audience was born as radio found its ethereal audience. Conservatives were back in charge and a new concept of freedom, the freedom-to-will, with its emphasis on the personal and private over the public, was beginning to dominate political consciousness. Eight decades of struggle had led to the full enfranchisement of women, but African-Americans in the South were murdered for exercising their right to vote. More than eighty years later women's rights are once again under assault, the politics of race is still with us, wealth is once again concentrated in the hands of the few while the great majority of working Americans are left to fret about their jobs, their bills, and their children's educational opportunities. The entrenchment of regressive political practices may make these seemingly intractable problems tougher than ever to solve. Their very persistence is disheartening. How, many of us ask, can I possibly do anything personally to help improve the state of my country and of the world?

We must share the perspective of Armstrong Hightower in 2001. Returning home to Ocoee, he could still smell the fire. It still burns, but it burns like the torch of liberty, lighting the way forward, not backward. We may take the first steps with simple gestures of living within the truth, and leverage this private and personal commitment into a more public freedom-of-expression that will improve our lives, strengthen our freedoms, and honor all of those—Charlotte Woodward Pierce, July Perry, Mose Norman, Armstrong Hightower—and the many millions of Americans who sacrificed or risked their lives for freedom and democracy.

A better understanding of just what freedom we seek will help guide us. For too long we have labored without a shared understanding of a possible human freedom. Pragmatic political practices have inhibited its growth. Philosophical misunderstandings have obscured its meaning. What we seek in the next chapter is an elucidation of freedom that is defined as a maximization of human choices in ways that support individual freedom and communal well-being.

2

FREEDOM

O ye that love mankind! Ye that dare oppose, not only the tyranny, but the tyrant, stand forth! Every spot of the old world is over-run with oppression. Freedom hath been hunted round the globe. Asia, and Africa, have long expelled her... O! receive the fugitive, and prepare in time an asylum for mankind.

Thomas Paine
Common Sense

On the morning of September 22, 1692, Samuel Wardwell was taken from the Salem, Massachusetts, prison, placed in a cart with seven others convicted of witchcraft, and delivered to the gallows. Wardwell was the son of William Wardwell, who was exiled from the Massachusetts Bay Colony with Ann Hutchinson when they refused to abandon their religious beliefs in capitulation to their religious leaders. Samuel was a carpenter in the Salem-Andover area. Some believe he helped build the home that Hawthorne later made famous in *The House of Seven Gables*. Wardwell, during his initial interrogation, appeased his inquisitors with an elaborate tale of his involvement with the devil. Two weeks later, he recanted, certain the recantation meant death. But complicity in the web of deceit woven by the Salem witch hunters was more than his conscience would bear. Samuel Wardwell chose the freedom of living within the truth. He was the last man hanged on charges of witchcraft in American history.

As the cart carried him and the other convicted consorts of the devil up the hill to the gallows, it was momentarily delayed when one of its wheels lurched into a rut. Choking on the smoke from the hangman's cigar, Samuel coughed out his last words. Both were taken as signs of the devil and signs of his guilt. The signs are easy to read for those with a need to justify inequitable actions or salve their own consciences.

Two hundred and eighty-five years later in Prague, Czechoslovakia's most accomplished twentieth-century philosopher, Jan Patočka, died of a brain hemorrhage after 11 hours of brutal interrogation by the Communist authorities. He was being questioned about his role in the Charter 77 protest. Charter 77 was a document signed by Vaclav Havel and other leading Czech dissidents. It accused the Communist regime of human rights violations. Patočka coined the phrase *life in truth*, subsequently taken up by Vaclav Havel in his concept of *living within the truth*. The terms point to human dwelling within the essential freedom and dignity of our shared existence. Living within the truth was the only course open to those enslaved by oppressive regimes. Dissenting in word and action when faced with the lies of oppressors restores freedom to the dissenter and diminishes the insidious reach of the state. In such circumstances, the stance is often dangerous. Wardwell and Patočka decided some things are worth dying for.

Our constitutional democracy is supposed to guarantee to all *life, liberty, and the pursuit of happiness*. It is supposed to promote and protect those who live within the truth. Juxtaposing the deaths of a Czech philosopher living under an authoritarian twentieth-century regime with the persecution of a seventeenth-century New World colonist allows us to focus on the unique character of the American promise of freedom. Wardwell and Patočka lived outside the reaches of our current democracy, the former living before the American Revolution and the latter living in Czechoslovakia. Betrayers of human freedom from any era always stand violently opposed to those who live within the truth. Within the frame of our democracy, Americans are supposed to be free to *live* within the truth. But how can we measure our success at living our ideal when we cannot agree on the common characteristics of freedom?

Contested Concepts of Freedom

Different definitions of freedom can lead to dramatically different political and policy conclusions. "Rather than seeing freedom as a fixed category or predetermined concept, I view it as an essentially contested concept, one that by its very nature is the subject of disagreement," wrote historian Eric Foner. President Bush claims to be defending freedom while his administration openly challenges freedoms that the Bill of Rights guarantees all Americans. Some see through Bush's deceit and understand his cavalier reference to freedom. But without a more widely shared and understood idea of freedom, such sound bites are effective manipulations of the facts.

"Freedom is the president's favorite foreign policy term these days, an all-purpose word he employs to define a high purpose, defend action on the ground or parry awkward questions," says foreign policy journalist Peter Slevin. Slevin says Bush's use of the term is intentionally vague. "The precise meaning he leaves to the listener, giving the word a warm fuzziness and creating a cause beyond rebuttal." As Slevin indicates, Bush successfully employs the term "freedom" to cast social and political conflict in black-and-white terms.

"Freedom itself was attacked by a faceless coward," Bush said after the attacks of September 11, 2001. "Freedom and fear are at war. The advance of human freedom—the great achievement of our time, and the great hope of every time—now depends on us," the President said. Freedom becomes the positive side of a duality that fails to paint the whole picture. Bush thus casts himself on the side of freedom, and terrorists—and anyone that opposes Bush at home— are left on the dark side among freedom's enemies. This simple-minded, good-and-evil equation allows listeners to make of freedom what they will, so long as they know Bush is its champion, whatever freedom is.

Bush's real rhetorical goal is to present himself as the very image of freedom. Oppose Bush and you oppose freedom, albeit a warm and fuzzy definition of freedom. This fuzziness helps disguise a cold and sharp-edged selfishness that grants an almost divine status to the "free" market, that is, Bush's corporate contributors. Meanwhile, the poor and middle class are stripped of the kind of life and liberty the framers of the Constitution believed should be guaranteed to all citizens. Admittedly, the authors of America's founding documents used a limited definition of "citizen," excluding slaves, women, and the non-propertied class from full political participation. But they were sincere in their devotion to a political concept of freedom as self-determination, guaranteed protections from overbearing government intrusion, and, more importantly, a vision of freedom as a social state that also recognized its embodiment was possible only in the individual personality.

Libertarians who champion freedom for the individual often miss the social aspect of freedom. Could I be called free if every other person on earth disappeared, and I found myself alone? Collectivists who subordinate the individual to the group often fail to understand that freedom is nourished by its social circumstances while taking root in the individual personality. Dr. Martin Luther King recognized both qualities of freedom when he said, "None of us is free until all of us are free."

Freedom is essential to our very humanity. It involves the shared recognition that by maximizing the choices and opportunities for thought and action on behalf of individuals, the choices available to others are also increased. The obvious corollary is also true. When the group's choices are increased, individual freedom is also enhanced. Freedom is possible only when humans take up the problematic nature of our being, as individuals and as groups, and move beyond the concern of merely surviving. How then do our contemporary political practices threaten our freedom when it is seen in this light?

Our political practices, from television advertising to brief presidential appearances on the deck of an aircraft carrier, privilege the manipulative over the informative. Even Adam Smith, the eighteenth-century philosopher and darling of free market conservatives (who ignore much of what he wrote), pointed out that speakers should make their words "maximally usable" to the listener. Rather than narrow the listener's possibilities, the ideal communication multiplies the listener's possibilities for new insights, actions, or rebuttals. In a public sphere that has devalued interaction in favor of one-way communications, it can be said that the ideal contemporary political communication is *minimally* usable.

The art of rhetoric was developed by the Greeks as a consequence of their democracy, and so we may say that the ability to persuade others in the public sphere is a key characteristic of the successful democratic citizen. But the principles of rhetoric assume equal status among the participants in the given circumstance. A successful citizen was assumed to be able to persuade, but also to *resist* the persuasive attempts of their peers. When Bush uses the word "freedom" dozens of times in a speech he has gone beyond persuasion. He attacks his listeners' abilities to resist.

This is the unspoken goal, then, of existing political practices: to break down voters' abilities to resist the message.

The political press usually prefers to concentrate on the skillfulness of the manipulations rather than enhance the "usability" of the words or issues at hand. The meanings and values of political utterances are seldom explored in depth. For instance, on the night of the 2004 New Hampshire Democratic primary, the commentators concentrated on the growing communication skills of John Kerry, Howard Dean, and John Edwards, rather than the substance of their post-election comments. (To his credit, Chris Matthews of MSNBC's *Hardball* was a notable exception. He repeatedly tried to bring the discussion back to substantive issues of the campaign.) Reagan, Clinton, and Bush are praised as "great communicators" able to overcome obvious personal or political liabilities. The focus is upon the narrative trajectories of the players—who is winning, who is losing, and why—as is the case in most successful storytelling. This is only exaggerated in a celebrity culture such as ours. To make matters worse, many are reluctant to admit that this circumstance exists.

Few consumers want to admit their choice of, say, an automobile, is effectively determined by the power of a particular brand's message, even when all involved in the transaction admit the winning message was designed around demographic research models employed to diminish the target audience's ability to resist the message. Instead, we talk about the merits of our choice and the good terms we negotiated with the dealer. Similarly, we like to believe we are making free, rational decisions in our choice of a political leadership. In many ways, though, we are not.

When success in politics depends upon reducing voters' abilities to resist messages, what incentive remains for the victors to develop social, economic, and education policies that might help restore citizens' participation in formulating those policies? There are many people—Richard Posner, for example—who believe that the complex issues of today's world remain beyond the intellectual and moral reasoning abilities of all but a self-selected elite. If this is truly so, let's all admit it and move on. At least we could dispense with the hypocrisy, if not the autocracy.

Because today's political practices are designed to break down our abilities to resist messages, a loss of freedom ensues. The loss of freedom is followed by transformations of democratic institutions that reinforce the practices employed by those who have succeeded in taking the helms of those institutions. When freedom as we define it here becomes irrelevant to the machinations of government, why would government take steps to protect freedom? As expected, we find that elected leaders exaggerate the symbols and rhetoric of freedom while individual liberties are curtailed. American flags fly at every political event. Bells of liberty ring, patriotic music plays. While we are distracted, the political pickpockets go to work.

Bush uses the word "freedom" more than any other word. His attorney general, John Ashcroft, uses the language of the Constitution as the name of a U.S. Justice Department website (www.lifeandliberty.gov) that carries nothing but propaganda for the Patriot Act, the post-9/11 law that, among other things, suspends habeas corpus for anyone the administration believes might be connected to terrorists.

The strategy here is clear: If we say we are taking these steps on behalf of freedom, it will hide the fact that the steps are intended to diminish freedom.

In terms of resisting the power of one-sided political communications, one of the more hopeful developments of the last few years is an increase in interactive, internet-based political communicating. Involvement in the public sphere has been greatly increased through internet activism and the enhanced availability of information relevant to our shared social, political, and economic lives. The Internet is a tool that is fast becoming maximally usable to its users. This renewed participatory sphere is restoring citizens' abilities to *resist*. It is resuscitating democracy and freedom. When citizens are engaged in conversations with one another about, say, the pros and cons of the Patriot Act, it is less likely that the manipulations of one leader or party will be as effective as they otherwise might be.

A Common Understanding of Freedom

Is it possible, then, to reach a common understanding of freedom while acknowledging that it will always remain a somewhat contested concept? Can we approach a shared understanding of freedom that will help us restore a sense of community to our political lives? These are not idle questions, nor are they of purely academic interest. It is arguable that no concept unites the peoples of democracies more than the concept of freedom. But when political figures distort and misuse the concept, when political scientists and philosophers fail to provide adequate and understandable definitions, when the possibility of human freedom is questioned by hard-bitten realists or positivists who insist that such concepts are meaningless since they are historically contingent, what ideal remains for us to collectively endorse?

It is true that most of us do not know with any certainty that freedom is even a contested concept. We take the term for granted. Freedom is something we have that our enemies lack. They resent our freedoms and want to take them away. Asked what freedom means, many Americans would answer that freedom means not being imprisoned or executed for one's religious or political beliefs. But human freedom means much more than avoidance of extreme oppression. We might also call freedom a higher stage of being human, a stage in which we are aware that we have the power to increase or decrease the possibilities of our lives. Until we recognize this, however, we stand little chance of restoring a sense of shared purpose to public life. Obscure academic and scientific skepticism about the possibility of human freedom—from age-old arguments over free will to realpolitik or pragmatic assumptions that security, not freedom, should be our first priority—affect the public consciousness. Well, we say, we may not achieve a perfect freedom but at least we can achieve a safe and secure lifetime.

In the public sphere, especially in an attenuated public sphere, talk of security seems always to take precedence over talk of freedom. The means of establishing the security of a population lies with the economic and political elite. Their power is consistently enhanced by every step taken to make their constituents "secure." In other words, there are clear pathways to profit and power in the endless drive for security. Issues of security easily capture the public imagination because the locus of the debate is fear. Security measures seem wonderfully concrete, while freedom remains a vague ideal. A true freedom of the many seems to threaten the financial and political security of the few, or at least this is so in the view of the powerful few—hence the constant tension between security and freedom. The simple recognition of the advantage enjoyed by security over freedom is the first step in reformulating a shared concept of freedom.

Freedom faces what is perhaps a more formidable obstacle than those who exploit human weakness for their own gain. We sometimes fear freedom, preferring security to the uncertainties and responsibilities that come with liberty. History has repeatedly witnessed a willingness to forego freedom for safety and security, for freedom *from* freedom. These fears also make it possible for us to settle for fewer freedoms or to mistake private, personal satisfactions for freedom of some kind.

The anxiety of responsibility for ourselves and for others is greatly reduced when others make decisions for us. There is no doubt that many citizens, even in a democracy, feel little commitment to true freedom. But it is important to remember that those who prefer comfort, security, and relief from the anxiety of responsibility to the rigors of the freedom-to-experience are already under the sway of some individual, institutional, national, or religious authority. It would be a mistake to attribute to human nature an aversion to freedom. The aversion is rather the product of cultural, economic, and political forces that create instability and anxiety and lead people to be ready to give up freedom for stability and security.

Roosevelt's "Four Freedoms"

One of the most articulate statements of freedom by an American political leader—Franklin Roosevelt's famous "Four Freedoms" speech to Congress in January 1941—was a speech intended to rally support for military opposition to totalitarian and imperialist regimes in Germany, Italy, and Japan. In a State of the Union address primarily devoted to national security, Roosevelt spoke of "a world founded upon four essential human freedoms." They are: freedom of speech and expression, freedom of religion, freedom from want, and freedom from fear. Each of these is contestable. Each is packed with possibility. And each is under assault in contemporary America and in developed and developing nations throughout the world. The moral schism could not be greater between Roosevelt's remarks and George W. Bush's plea that we shop our way out of terrorist threats. Roosevelt's words also give us another good entry into the exploration of freedom. Are we doing enough, then, in our pursuit of Roosevelt's Four Freedoms?

Freedom from fear may be the most primal of Roosevelt's four freedoms, at least in the sense that fear can so often lead to a loss of the other three. So it is disturbing that fear is the method of choice in political communications. Few successful politicians shrink from using fear—of terrorism, crime, economic uncertainty. My friend and former colleague Paul Begala, now cohost of CNN's *Crossfire*, used to reluctantly concede this point in campaign contexts. Nothing motivates voters like fear, Begala said, recognizing at the same time that the right wing was much more inclined than Democrats to manipulate with fear—and much more able to take advantage of it. Fear of strangers, especially those who can be identified easily by different skin color, speech, or other superficial characteristics, is often a subtext of much political advertising and public relations, especially the campaigns of the Right. Think of the first President Bush's famous "Willie Horton" ad, which led voters to believe his 1988 opponent, Michael Dukakis, wanted to empty the prisons of dangerous black men to prey on innocent white Americans. Of course the ad was not that explicit, but no analyst has viewed it any other way. Fear is the companion of those who sell us security. Without fear, why would we buy what they are selling? Political leaders have little reason to free us from fear because it is through our fear that their power flows.

How about freedom from want? The current gap between the richest and poorest Americans now challenges the Gilded Age for sheer selfish indifference and cold-hearted malice toward those gathered below the top of the economic ladder. Today, the richest 10 percent of Americans own close to 80 percent of the wealth; the richest one percent own almost half. Ongoing tax breaks for the rich, the elimination of the social safety net, the termination of low-income housing programs, the millions of children without homes or access to adequate health care, the loss of American jobs to cheap and easily exploited overseas labor—all these are conservative initiatives or the consequences of their initiatives. In today's America, freedom from want is guaranteed only to the wealthy. The rest of us are left in a kind of Darwinian, survival-of-the-fittest swamp that the privileged tell us is a natural and unavoidable part of life.

This is not simply a question of how many possessions we have, although it is undeniably true that there is a small percentage of our population who lives without any material want whatsoever. The picture grows even more alarming when we understand that the wealthy promote material possessions as the Holy Grail of human life. The less affluent are left to fret about what it is about *themselves* that leaves them wanting. Sadly, the prosperous do not hesitate to let the poor know what they think of them. The poor can come to think that it is their fault, that there is something un-American, even inhuman, about their condition. It is not just that the jobless and the working poor are often without health care, adequate diets, and educational opportunity. The alienation, loneliness, lack of family and community support, feelings of shame, fear, and worthlessness all contribute to poorer health and shorter life expectancy. Today the citizens of twenty-five countries are healthier and have longer life expectancies than Americans. As the Washington physician Stephen Bezruchka points out, the poor die younger than the rich. Period. But the poor do not die from a lack of material possessions. Their health suffers because of the stress placed upon them by their wealthy neighbors.

How are things on the freedom of religion front? Luckily, our government is not yet the handmaiden of any orthodox religion, although the Republican corporatist alliance with the religious right comes dangerously close to an ad hoc theocracy of a sort. A growing number of Americans feel justified in forcing upon other Americans the moral viewpoints of their private religion. There are no Samuel Wardwells hanged as witches, but there is plenty of religious coercion in the public sphere. In addition, Republican efforts to replace public education with a system of private school vouchers is little more than an effort to turn over to religious institutions the education of our young—at least our white, suburban young. Since the economy has little need at this moment for millions of newly educated workers at home (they are much less expensive to hire in Mexico and India, for instance), the corporatists sees little practical necessity in educating any but their own.

And freedom of speech? For the moment, our constitutional protections remain reasonably intact. But Bush and his radical right (and more moderate conservatives who follow the party line) leave little doubt about their disdain for open and honest political conversation. Such discussions are anathema to control freaks, and ultraconservatives value control above all else. Alternative versions of the truth may raise questions that make conservatives squirm. So Bush derides demonstrators as meaningless "focus groups" and brags that he does not have to listen to anybody. Yet people have to listen to him—he is the President. Speech, however, has become a function of money. Without wealth, one has difficulty being heard in a virtual public sphere, for the entry fee is incredibly expensive. Only a fool would believe that a middle-class professor, truck driver, or nurse has the same ability to be heard as, say, Rupert Murdoch or Bush. We may think that no one in America is arrested and imprisoned for saying something the government does not like. But the Patriot Act allows just such practices. Fortunately, even conservative jurists have special regard for political speech. Without the courts, some of the freedom would have been stripped from speech long ago.

Roosevelt's practical, political, and economic freedoms carry an implicit message. Freedom is a relational concept. It does not and cannot exist in isolation. One's freedom is intimately tied to the freedom of others. This brings us back to themes regarding Isaiah Berlin's positive freedom (which we called "freedom-to-will") and negative freedom (which we called "freedom-to-experience"). Positive freedom, or freedom-to-will, bears little resemblance to the political and economic freedoms Roosevelt promised America and the world. In fact, as Berlin noted, obsession with freedom-to-will often led to the sort of totalitarian control that Roosevelt sought to eliminate from the world.

Freedom-to-experience does not preclude more private freedoms. It carries with it an understanding of responsibility to others. The legal, political, and economic norms developed and maintained by viable democracies are intended to help us negotiate these responsibilities. We are social beings and freedom-to-experience recognizes this essential fact. For example, automobiles greatly enhanced individuals' freedom-to-experience. But roadways are relational constructions. We must negotiate our way through traffic with the aid of our regard for others, marked lanes, traffic signals, and so on, and hope to avoid collisions. Freedom-to-will seeks to impose one's own "rules of the road" on all other travelers. At the extreme, the driver obsessed with personal freedom-to-will is a driver prone to road rage. Maybe we should think of road rage as a kind of down-home, personal version of Bush's preemptive military strategy.

Freedom and Human Possibility

Freedom is a topic little discussed in contemporary political campaigns, although candidates often bandy about the word. In early 1990, one year after the fall of the Berlin Wall, I wrote a radio advertisement for Ann Richards' gubernatorial campaign in Texas. I was lucky enough to have former Congresswoman Barbara Jordan lend her majestic voice to the spot, which simply extolled the value of freedom and the possibilities for its enhancement. It was one of the few ads in which freedom, as such, was the "message." Once again, I am not talking about the mindless repetition of the term, but of straightforward political communications that speak of freedom as a primary value, communications that at least attempt to describe what is meant by the term. Political professionals are extremely impatient with ambiguity. It is much better, they believe, to talk of a chicken in every pot rather than hunger. It is even better to raise voters' fears by saying one's opponent is stealing the chickens from their pots, a practice that one's own candidate will with great courage and determination bring to an end. Needless to say, our current political discourse is debased.

Jan Patočka, the Czech philosopher who inspired Havel and other ultimately successful dissidents, writes that human freedom was born simultaneously with history, politics, and philosophy. Prehistorical humans, Patočka says, lived only for survival, unconscious of the possibility of freedom and the troubling mysteries of Being. Building on the work of Hannah Arendt, Patočka, perhaps more than any other twentieth-century thinker, found justification for a postmodern, post-Nietzschian, concrete conception of freedom as the very essence of the human. Freedom was not contemplated in prehistory, when the why of the world was not questioned. Using Hannah Arendt's conjecture, before history, philosophy, and politics, human beings were limited to living only for the sake of survival. In

essays written to inspire political action, Patočka said, "... political
life in its original and primordial form is nothing other than active
freedom itself (from freedom, for freedom). The goal of striving here
is not life for the sake of life (whatever life it may be) but only life
for freedom and in it, and it is understood, that is, actively grasped,
that such a life is possible." Freedom is born in the recognition that
we can have more or less of it, and that it is our responsibility to seek
greater human freedom. As Patočka said, we need to understand that
a life of true freedom and responsibility is possible.

Our contemporary malaise is due in part, I believe, to doubts
about the possibility of freedom. These doubts are not new. True
freedom is realized only when doubts of its possibility are recognized,
confronted, and overcome. The enemies of freedom are quite content
with a demoralized public. Our political practices—from overtly
manipulative one-way political communications of advertising and
marketing to the impossibly high entry fees into a virtual political
sphere of the elite—reinforce our skepticism. But freedom (and I am
speaking here of freedom as something like freedom-to-experience)
was born with the opening of the public sphere, as Arendt and
Patočka point out. When social groups grew large and complex
enough that the traditional household-centered organization proved
inadequate for negotiating social challenges, humans stepped beyond
life as mere survival, questioned the nature of being, and opened a
public space for negotiations. History is the record of these negotiations. Philosophy is the constant challenging of admittedly temporary, nontranscendent solutions to the problems of being.

Politics is, or should be, the very action of human freedom in the
world. Our emergence into the society, or the public sphere, allows us
to negotiate with one another the inevitable conflicts and competing
opinions that arise among us. No one should be excluded by law, custom, or habit. But even in our democracy, politics is not viewed as
fully participatory. Instead, citizens have become consumers of political products.

Edward F. Findlay says Patočka seeks to demonstrate "that the
essence of human freedom and possibility, that is, the realization that
humanity could break the chains of its bondage to the order of work

and the household and begin to live freely, first took form with the development of the idea of the polis." Born with the creation of the public sphere, freedom is now threatened by the political practices that dominate this sphere.

It is almost as if we are threatened with a return to the prehistorical, to the ancient time when humanity was focused only on daily survival. This is indeed not far from Marshall McLuhan's speculations on a media-saturated global village, although his was a more optimistic vision. Driven from the polis, our concerns for the world shrink, our responsibilities to others (and hence ourselves) are forgotten, and life becomes the *work* of survival as opposed to the *production* of a truly human future. Failing to heed the warnings of Havel and others who saw the similarities between the "post-totalitarian" (remember, he used the term to point to the use of subtle but no less totalizing means of control) regimes of Eastern Europe and the corporatist, consumer-oriented regimes of the West, we have entered what Havel termed "the world of general demoralization."

In Patočka's analysis it becomes clear that the historical movement into freedom carried with it an overwhelming sense of the social nature of being. It became necessary to seek answers to questions about the whole rather than the simple particulars of the day-to-day work of individual survival. This meant that from its beginnings freedom has been linked to *responsibility*, yet another argument against positive freedom or freedom-to-will that, in the end, produces selfish, isolated individuals. When life is linked to "something free, something capable of accepting responsibility and respecting responsibility, that is, the freedom of others," Patočka writes, politics becomes the vehicle for our collective journey to freedom.

When the polis becomes a remote dwelling for an elite to make choices on our behalf, the possibilities for freedom are greatly curtailed. The deprivation is greater, however, when we consider Patočka's regard for the *spiritual* nature of freedom. It is instructive to compare Patočka's vision to that of American philosopher Richard Rorty. Rorty takes Patočka to task for refusing to eliminate the metaphysical quest from our public and private lives. According to Rorty, freedom is only a contingency, and recognizing this leaves us ultimately free from metaphysical baggage, baggage that is always in error (because it points toward unachievable transcendentals) and is usually detrimental to equality and justice.

For Patočka, however, metaphysical yearning is a distinct and inescapable part of being human. When human beings emerged from the private into the public sphere and concern for the social and environmental world replaced a limited concern for immediate survival, being was opened to a world of value and fact, doubt and uncertainty. Says philosopher Peter Lom, "Patočka argues that attempts to get rid of metaphysics are futile, first of all, because moral evaluation is inescapable, and second, because every kind of moral evaluation always has a metaphysical component." Patočka did not believe metaphysics or spiritual pursuits would succeed in finding a foundational or transcendental ground upon which all values could be based. Rather, he believed it philosophy's duty to continually seek such answers. This is the Socratic "care for the soul" that Patočka discusses. In other words, Rorty holds to a kind of metaphysical belief that there is ultimately nothing metaphysical to believe in. Patočka has already grasped that contradiction and instead holds open an important—maybe ultimately important—place for honest and truthful spiritual pursuit.

Lom writes that Patočka's "most valuable lesson is that spirituality may be joined with skepticism and modesty, in a model of Socratic skepticism informed by humility that strives for a nondogmatic openness to the possibility of transcendence." This deserves careful consideration. Patočka is concerned with a pragmatic political philosophy that returns to the flesh-and-blood circumstances of human life. He felt that these circumstances always included the spiritual pursuit of the transcendental. To ignore care of the soul is to ignore the full possibility of freedom. Once again we are threatened with a return to the prehistorical. Clearly, the dangers of dogmatized spirituality are many, for an imagination seized by a single vision or belief is an imagination closed to new possibilities.

It is tragic that this essential human search is so often distorted into close-minded hatred of those who have arrived at different questions or different answers. Writes Lom, "Metaphysics has a bad name in the history of political thought less for not delivering on its promise of certainty than for the human suffering associated with it, first through the conflict and oppression carried out in the name of the absolute dogmas of the Church and, second, through the excesses of the secular dogmas of all modern ideologies." Spiritual expression is ultimately a way of increasing human choices. But so often our need to seek is exploited by those who want our seeking to end in their own power.

But it is no less tragic that in a nation in which 90 percent hold to some metaphysical belief or other, in a nation that guarantees religious freedom, secular political practices that seem so well separated from the spiritual threaten to deprive us of the very freedom our spiritual lives help strengthen. It is no accident that the Right is skillful in the use of religious-based language and values. For the Right, especially the Christian Right, the use of such language is a win-win situation. With a little luck they may succeed, at least informally, in establishing their moral view as a quasi-state religion. At worst, the secular Left appears the culprit in the devaluing of spiritual pursuit. Here, the Right's political gain is guaranteed.

Throughout this discussion we see that freedom is a thoroughly social phenomenon, precluding attachment to the kind of isolated, freedom-to-will that is promoted so highly within a consumer society. Rather than mourn the passing of an authentic freedom-to-experience, we should consider that Havel's and Patočka's ideas were born within a post-totalitarian system much more oppressive than our own. Their recommendation is that we must live within the truth. It is necessary to redefine freedom because the politics of deceit demoralizes us all by substituting false idols for human freedom, by driving too many from the public sphere, and by creating a virtual polis inhabited by oppressors who masquerade as liberators.

Freedom and the Politics of Deceit

As Havel points out, however, totalizing regimes soon become captive to their own lies. "The post-totalitarian system touches people with its ideological gloves on. This is why life in the system is so thoroughly permeated with hypocrisy and lies..." For instance, it is impossible for the Bush administration to admit it lied about the presence of weapons of mass destruction in Iraq. Why? Because the regime's first duty to itself is to guard against truth that would reveal its deceptive foundation. Havel presents us with a catalog of post-totalitarian deceits. Among them: "the expansion of imperial influence is presented as support for the oppressed; the lack of free expression becomes the highest form of freedom; farcical elections become the highest form of democracy; banning independent thought becomes the most scientific of world views; military occupation becomes fraternal assistance." In other words, there arises the need to disguise the real aims of totalizing regimes in acceptable ideological splendor: We are the freest nation on earth; the greatest democracy in history; the greatest champion of human rights around the world; no child will be left behind; we will liberate Iraq; our enemies hate us for our freedoms.

"Because the regime is captive to its own lies, it must falsify everything. It falsifies the past. It falsifies the present, and it falsifies the future," Havel said. This necessary deceit is greatly facilitated by political practices that remove the great number of citizens from an authentic public sphere. This makes it even easier for the Bush administration to undertake the greatest assault on civil liberties since passage of the Bill of Rights in order to protect our freedoms. The preposterousness of this lie is lost in the fabric of deceit that shrouds us. As Havel concludes, "Individuals need not believe all these mystifications, but they must behave as though they did, or they must at least tolerate them in silence, or get along well with those who work with them. For this reason, however, they must *live within a lie*. They need not accept the lie. It is enough for them to have accepted their life with it and in it. For by this very fact, individuals confirm the system, fulfil [sic] the system, make the system, *are* the system."

What is necessary to preserve such a system, however, is also the system's greatest vulnerability. This is why it lashes out with such vengeance at those who seek to live within the truth. Marginalizing all dissent is an absolute priority. Still, the system remains vulnerable to the smallest acts of resistance. Prohibited from publishing essays critical of the regime, Czech dissidents practiced "writing to the desk," that is, circulating their work among friends and neighbors in small, private gatherings. In time, the truth pierced the fabric of deceit. When circumstances were such that the lies could no longer be maintained, the regime toppled in a bloodless revolution. In today's world, the Internet provides an even more profound way of writing to the desk. It is why organizations such as MoveOn.org deserve such praise. Their efforts to live within the truth are truly heroic and historic. Operating outside the system and not reliant on traditional one-way political advertising, millions of activists have access to information at almost no "transaction cost"—that is, they have access to perspectives, facts, and competing values with little cost in dollars or time. More importantly, they are heard. Through the Internet, millions of people who were once alienated are reemerging into the public sphere.

Their reappearance in the polis revitalizes freedom, pierces the rotten diction (to paraphrase Emerson) of the system, and renews the possibilities of freedom first born with history, politics, philosophy, and true human being. It is a small beginning, but no less heroic for its modest beginnings. These new avenues of resistance will be mocked by conservative pundits, attacked as radical by the system's conservative shills, and presented as a danger to the very freedom the activists seek to reawaken in our world. By living within the truth, though, each of us can help make freedom a possibility for everyone.

We have seen, then, that human freedom is freedom-to-experience, a freedom that lives in the individual personality but that remains dependent on the freedom of others. It is intimately connected to responsibility, for it is possible only within the context of concern for the whole, for the world in which we live, and for those who share the world with us. Ultimately, freedom means increasing the number of choices available for human action. While it may seem that my own room to move may be enhanced by restricting yours, such a view is gravely mistaken. My choices actually increase as yours increase. The mere requirement that I enforce limits I would impose on others creates demands upon me that limit my choices. Most importantly, freedom is realized in individuals, not in totalizing systems of any sort. Freedom is therefore always the possibility that life for the sake of something grander than mere survival will prevail.

"Between the aims of the post-totalitarian system and the aims of life there is a yawning abyss: while life, in its essence, moves towards plurality, diversity, independent self-constitution and self-organization, in short, towards the fulfilment [sic] of its own freedom, the post-totalitarian system demands conformity, uniformity, and discipline," Havel wrote. "While life ever strives to create new and 'improbable' structures, the post-totalitarian system contrives to force life into its most probable states."

Beyond Determinism

Another obstacle to the emergence of a new, shared concept of human freedom must be addressed: determinism. For modern science resolved long ago that determinism trumped our naïve concepts of free will. The principle that events in the physical world are open to exploration because they are caused—or determined by previous events or circumstances—has served science well. But the question of whether human behavior is determined has dogged philosophers and theologians for millennia. If all human actions are determined by our prior actions and the prior actions of others, of what use is it to extol the merits of human freedom that, after all, may be nothing more than a lucky and beneficial illusion? The issue is not irrelevant to considerations of political freedom, as the seemingly distant and arcane debate over free will has a substantial impact on the public consciousness. Fatalism, cynicism, and nihilism creep into our worldview when the dominant intellectual community tells us that even human behavior must be governed by the deterministic laws of science. Isaiah Berlin, concerned with articulating a viable conception of human freedom, called "the frontier between freedom and causal laws...a crucial, practical issue; knowledge of [the frontier] is a powerful and indispensable antidote to ignorance and irrationality." If we are to stir a revolution in the struggle for freedom, the issue of free will must be addressed.

But science itself, specifically cognitive science, may give us a way around this dilemma. There is substantial new evidence that the brain employs mechanisms intended to open the mind to new possibilities and new choices, choices not strictly determined by past thoughts or actions or any observable "state of the brain." Neuroscientists have known for many years that temporary assemblies of neurons throughout the brain mark our moments of conscious thought and action. Each cognitive act is accompanied by synchronized sets of neurons. Think of these synchronized neural assemblies as connect-the-dot drawings. Certain dots (brain cells) are connected briefly when we think of, say, our lover. Another set of dots is connected when we reach for a beer. The phenomenon is known as *phase synchrony*.[1]

More recently a group of researchers has discovered a pattern to the brain activity occurring *between* conscious moments. This they call *phase scattering* or *active desynchrony*. The lines connecting the dots are temporarily relaxed, allowing for the possibility that new dots will be connected in the next conscious moment. The lines are not thrown into chaos or randomly scattered. Rather, *learning*, or habits—our previous thoughts and actions—appear to help shape the desynchrony of neural assemblies. Otherwise, the total disruption of neural patterns would lead to extremely disconnected thinking and acting. Nonetheless, this active phase scattering provides consciousness with neurological pathways to constrained but undetermined creative choices in our cognitive acts and perceptions. Active desynchrony constrains but does not determine subsequent conscious acts. This neatly avoids what is known as the Epicurean conjecture on the problem of human freedom in a causal world, which calls upon the chance "swerving" of atoms to eliminate strict causation. Random, uncaused variation cannot enhance our ability to cause change. Neuroscientist Michael Breakspear summarizes the relevant role of

---

[1]The author was greatly assisted in this discussion by conversations with the late Francisco Varela, Shaun Gallagher, and George Lakoff. Their work in neurobiology, neurophenomenology, linguistics, and other cognitive sciences was instrumental in my understanding of this critical issue. Any error in interpretation remains my own.

the active desynchrony of neural assemblies this way: "Desynchronization may allow the brain to switch flexibly between one coherent state and another...nonlinear desynchronization facilitates the brain's flexible and adaptive behavior."

It would thus appear that our conscious, attentive decisions and behaviors leave their mark on a neural process that separates one cognitive moment from the next, although they also open indeterminate alternatives for action. This reciprocal process is the natural basis for the concept of free will theorized by Robert Kane, who writes that "some of the mental events or processes involved [in our acts and perceptions] must be *undetermined*, so that the causation by mental events may be nondeterministic or probabilistic as well as deterministic." Keeping in mind that experience does constrain these flexible moments of freedom, it once again becomes clear that freedom is not a private matter. We learn from our social experiences. The brain works to increase the pathways for action, and our social interactions can facilitate or debilitate these pathways. We can learn that there are multiple possible reactions to a given stimulus, or we can learn hidebound habits that limit our choices. Such is the nature of freedom.

The early information theorist Heinz von Foerster once imagined a personified Metaphysics asking her little sister, Ethics, what she should recommend to her protégés. Ethics answered: "Tell them they should always try to act so as to increase the number of choices; yes, increase the number of choices." This is just what the neural correlates of freedom appear to accomplish. When we act to increase the choices of others, our own possibilities increase as well.

Freedom is not some elusive ideal, nor is it a lucky fiction invented by humans. Cognitive scientist Daniel Dennett suggests that, like money, the concept of freedom is a valuable creation of our minds. But freedom is not just an illusion that helps humans survive but that has no real basis in a deterministic universe. To the contrary, we appear to be wired for freedom. The philosopher Siobhan Nash-Marshall said, "Freedom is one of the defining characteristics of human beings. It touches on nearly every aspect of human life, from the religious to the civil, from the public to the private." She then described how differing concepts of freedom can and do play a significant role in our political and social lives. For instance, one of the reasons creationists oppose theories of evolution with such vehemence is that evolution appears to leave no room for human freedom. In theories of evolution, she wrote, "Freedom is not a biological fact." Some kind of freedom is, of course, necessary in the viewpoint of most Christians. It is fundamental to their religion that humans be able to choose good over evil. But what if there is a basis in human neurobiology for freedom? It would be much easier for creationists—at least those who are not Biblical literalists—to embrace evolution, a theory that comes with overwhelming evidence.

The framers of the Constitution designed our democracy such that freedom be viewed as the primary value. Nash-Marshall made this point, as do many others. It may seem as though freedom has its own prerequisites. We must be alive, and we must be rational, thinking beings. Government, then, should first guarantee our safety and security, and promote its citizens' rational capacities through education. These goals, however, rarely make good bedfellows. History is full of examples of security taking precedence over freedom. We are living in such a time right now. But freedom—true human freedom—should remain our paramount value; it is, after all, the foundation upon which our country was built. This means that during times when security and freedom come into extreme conflict, freedom deserves special weight in our policy deliberations.

Anthony Lewis, in his essay "Security and Liberty," recounted a remarkable conversation with Viet Dinh, a Vietnamese refugee who came to America in 1978 at the age of 10 to escape the excesses of the Communist regime in his home country. Dinh became an assistant attorney general under John Ashcroft and has played a significant role in designing the nation's new security policies in the aftermath of September 11. Lewis asked Dinh if he did not, in effect, design security plans on behalf of the Bush administration that approach something like the totalitarian practices he escaped by increasing government secrecy and threatening long-cherished civil rights. Dinh saw no parallel. "We see our work not as balancing security and liberty. Rather we see it as securing liberty by assuring the conditions for true liberty... What we're trying to do here is protect authority so the liberty of law-abiding people can flourish," Dinh answered. (Since his interview with Lewis, Dinh has left the Justice Department and is critical of Patriot Act excesses).

Dinh gave an accurate and open assessment of just what the Bush administration has decided is its primary goal: To protect authority, namely, its *own* authority. When efforts to protect authority take precedence over the protection and promotion of freedom, freedom becomes more than just a contested concept. It become malleable, its definition tweaked to meet the criteria necessary to protect authority. And that is exactly what the Founding Fathers designed our constitutional democracy to avoid. Unfortunately, however, we have played into the hands of those who value authority over freedom. By limiting our own definition of freedom to a private freedom-to-will we came to believe that we are able to maintain its avenues—purchasing what we deem necessary for personal expression, for instance. But we lost sight of the far more profound freedom-to-experience, which carries with it a responsibility to others. It does not seem to many of us that provisions of Bush's Patriot Act limit our civil liberties because our liberties are defined in such a way that our political organization hardly affects them at all.

This dissociation can and must lead, as Patočka has shown us, to a politics of deceit. Truth becomes a measure of the efficacy of statements in protecting authority, not in promoting freedom. Exaggerated or invented claims about Iraq's weapons of mass destruction are not lies, then; they are truths because the elimination of Saddam Hussein, even though unjustified by factual considerations, certainly serves to protect the authority of those who took him out. The American imperium is now in charge of Iraq, and Bush's cronies are in charge of its oil. If considerations of our freedom had been given priority by the administration, however, much more thought would have been given to taking steps that diminish the anger Islamic fundamentalists feel against the United States. Diminishing this anger, and the motivation to harm us in some way, would eliminate the pressure to curb civil liberties here by diminishing the threat to our security. But if maintaining authority—not guaranteeing freedom—is your first concern, why not take the easy way? Perversely, making the world a more dangerous place works to the advantage of those who seek first to protect their own authority.

According to *Dallas Morning News* senior political writer Wayne Slater, who with James Moore authored *Bush's Brain: How Karl Rove Made George W. Bush Presidential*, Rove is a devotee of Niccolo Machiavelli. Machiavelli advised Lorenzo de' Medici in *The Prince* to remember that the great number of people are always more interested in appearance than reality. So it follows that deception, as Patočka and Havel have noted, becomes the necessity of those dedicated to perpetuating their power over the freedoms of those they rule. Machiavelli wrote that "a prince must take great care that nothing goes out his mouth which is not full of the above-named five qualities, and, to see and hear him, he should seem to be all mercy, faith, integrity, humanity and religion." Pretending to these qualities makes it all the easier to rule with their antitheses. Kevin Phillips, in his book *American Dynasty: Aristocracy, Fortune, and the Politics of Deceit in the House of Bush*, quoted this very passage and then said, "...twenty-first-century American readers of The Prince may feel that they have stumbled on a thinly disguised Bush White House political memo."

We have developed a theory that holds that freedom is central to our very humanity, that freedom carries with it a responsibility to others, and that freedom is enhanced by our responsibility to others. Additionally, we recognize that

- One is not truly human unless free.
- One is not free if others are in chains.

The recognition of the possibility of freedom arose simultaneously with the creation of the political sphere, with the notion that humans had the capacity to look beyond mere survival to the mysteries of life and our own mortality, produce a future more meaningful than our past, and assist others in finding true freedom. This was the thinking of Adam Smith when he wrote that our words should be so constructed as to be "maximally usable" by the listener. Nash-Marshall makes essentially the same point when she explains why freedom must take precedence even over religious precepts. The Founding Fathers were careful to protect religious freedom and the separation of church and state not simply to protect against the abuses of organized religion (which were many), but to guarantee that our conversations with ourselves and—for believers—with God, were maximally usable. "Faith . . . is a conversation between a believer and God," Nash-Marshall wrote. "Like all meaningful conversations, it changes the conversers. It makes them see their life and the world through the eyes of the person with whom they are conversing, to some degree. And this gives the conversers a new understanding of their life and the world that surrounds them. It makes them see themselves and the world with startling novelty." To insist that others, under threat of death or punishment, adopt any normative "conversation with God" is to destroy the possibility that others will come to any new understandings at all.

During the Salem witch-hunt era, Samuel Wardwell chose to live within the truth and face the gallows rather than kneel to those who used fear and calculated deception to enhance their own power. Jan Patočka did the same when he stood up to his Czechoslovakian oppressors. We can see how their decisions to live within the truth, to choose freedom over authority, can enhance the freedom of others. By choosing freedom even in the face of death they serve to remind the rest of us just how central freedom is to being human. Our choices are increased by their recognition that freedom, embodied in individual human beings, is manifest only in our relationships with others, even those who live long after we are gone.

We can also see how debilitating our political practices are to the realization of freedom. One-way political communications, the importance of money over people, and the demise of a true public sphere all conspire to manipulate rather than inform. In a sense, the goal of a contemporary political campaign is to make its communication *minimally* usable. A candidate needs potential voters to be herded in a particular direction. It has even become standard practice to win by making one's opponent an unacceptable choice. This is the power that negative political messages wield. We have come to a time in our history that Kevin Phillips called "a Machiavellian moment." Our political practices themselves seem designed to aid and abet those who would govern by deception, by valuing authority over freedom, by exploiting the power of appearance over reality. When the relaxing of environmental regulations can be called a "Clear Skies" initiative, when an effort to turn over public education to private schools can be called "No Child Left Behind," when a president can define himself as a "compassionate conservative" while raising the tax burden on the poor and middle class and lowering taxes of the very rich, we find that that we have become dangerously accustomed to living within our lies.

But once we recognize that our very humanity depends upon freedom and our willingness to fight for it, we see that the only way to challenge the emerging authoritarian and antidemocratic autocracy is to make our voices heard. We must reenter the public sphere whether the powers that be like it or not. And this is why such seemingly insignificant developments like internet activism can make such a significant difference. Through such activities, millions of Americans have turned what was a one-way conversation into a true dialogue. If those in authority are going to lie, we must make them lie to our faces, and not to an abstract audience of political consumers. Because we have stepped within the public sphere, we will not accept their lies; rather, we will speak the truth to power. The politics of deceit will not survive a revival of a true public sphere. Freedom demands the truth.

3

SHAKING BUGS BUNNY'S HAND AT DISNEYLAND

Democracy Will Not Be Televised

And however our eyes may be dazzled with snow, or our ears deceived by sound; however prejudice may warp our wills, or interest darken our understanding, the simple voice of nature and of reason will say, it is right.

Thomas Paine
Common Sense

In Ann Richards' successful campaign for governor of Texas in 1990, Mark McKinnon (then in his Democratic phase—now he is one of George W. Bush's media directors) and I decided on a simple, if hackneyed, campaign slogan: "The New Texas." The idea was to present Richards as the candidate of change. A slogan is not a message; it is just a catch phrase intended to help identify a candidate or cause with positive feelings. We had a poster produced that included the phrase with a striking and emotional picture of Richards holding her granddaughter. The slogan also was used in television advertising.

The future governor was less than impressed. After McKinnon and I presented the concept, she gave us a withering look, threw her hands in the air, and said, "What does it mean?!?" We were stumped. The slogan, of course, did not *mean* anything. Richards was absolutely right in her criticism. Contemporary political communications are banal; while Richards is a consummate politician, she always sought to be more than that. McKinnon and I were just following our instincts, of course. Richard Posner, while wrong about many things, is right about the nature of political messages. "The increasingly sophisticated techniques employed in public-opinion polling and political advertising have made political campaigning manipulative and largely content-free," Posner said. On Richards' behalf, we were driven to adopt a slogan that was appealing but neutral. Even those enamored of the old Texas could support a "new" Texas, so long as it was presented in a non-threatening, warm, and saccharine manner. It is not really so different from Bush's "compassionate conservative" campaign, which is also content-free. Posner, as we noted earlier, also described the qualities of a successful leader as "closer to those of a broker, salesman, actor, or entrepreneur than to those of an academic." Richards is all of these things. But she had also come of political age during the years in which the dominant officeholder in Texas was a Democrat named William P. Hobby, Jr. While Hobby could be described as an entrepreneur—his business interests are considerable—he is neither a salesman nor an actor. Rather, he has the bearing of a big-hearted academic and the intelligence to back it up. Hobby enjoyed "sound bite" politics about as much as a trip to the dentist. He had come to the office in 1972, well after media politics began to dominate America but long before its full manipulative force was felt in Texas. I had worked for Hobby before joining Richards' campaign, and I knew she greatly admired Hobby's intellect and his "antipolitician" style. As much as she understood the demands of contemporary political campaigns, she longed to rise above them. That was part of her magic. To her, the emptiness of "The New Texas" was appalling. In the end it worked well enough, although Ann's victory in 1990 had less to do with any slogans or messages McKinnon and I designed for her. She won because of her perseverance in the face of stinging personal attacks and the self-destructive campaigns of her opponents.

The slogan was passable, however, because television is the dominant political communication venue in politics today. Such empty phrases resonate well in a medium that might better be termed "Banali TV." Television ads eat up 60 percent or more of campaign budgets. Every part of a contemporary campaign is designed around its advertising. Managers must make the ad budget the absolute priority. Every other consideration is secondary. Ann's media consultant was the late Bob Squier, the dapper and energetic Democratic consultant who spent years sparring with GOP consultant Roger Ailes on NBC's *Today*. In his last years, Squier joined an effort to diminish the impact of television advertising on politics by helping the Alliance for Better Campaigns gain support for a series of live "mini-debates" among candidates. He once likened the simple-minded approach to political advertising as an inept marriage proposal. "You're beautiful, you're wonderful, I want to marry you," says the eager young beau. "Well, that's very interesting," the object of his affection responds. "What else have you got to say?" The young man responds, "You're wonderful, you're beautiful, I wanna..." After a few minutes of this, the young lady is ready to call the police, Squier laughed.

If only this transformation of politics amounted to little but the rise of the vacuous and the fatuous. Instead, the domination of politics by television advertising amounts to a virtualization of the public sphere that structurally reinforces the conservative status quo, reduces complex issues of life-and-death importance to dumbed-down, black-and-white trivialities and, through its high cost, limits effective participation in politics to the rich. Make no mistake about the domination of TV ads: Squier used to say that in non-presidential races, 90 percent of the information voters receive on an election comes from televised ads. It makes one wonder why there are so many heated conversations among the political elite regarding the so-called press bias (conservatives think reporters are liberal, while liberals think they are conservative). In the end, we appear to be satisfied with receiving 90 percent of our political information from sources that are proud of their bias: the candidates who approve, produce, and buy the airtime for the ads. It is unlikely that the most noble and fair-minded candidate would waste money paying for ads that anyone could call even-handed.

Incidentally, while the national political press does play a more significant role in presidential elections, diminishing slightly the overwhelming direct-to-voter power of advertising, the influence of the press, too, has been diminished by the abandonment of political party politics in favor of sequenced, state-by-state primaries which help turn even national elections into statewide contests dominated by television advertising. Political ads also help shape the opinions and mindset of the press that assesses the candidates in the national general election showdown. Since Lyndon Johnson's infamous "Daisy" ad against Barry Goldwater in 1964, ads targeted only to reporters run frequently. Johnson's ad raised fears that Goldwater would blow up the world with his militaristic, pro-nuke sentiments. It ran once. But it drove press evaluations of Goldwater. It is a myth that journalists are somehow immune from the persuasive power of ads. They are human, and there is substantial evidence that television advertising is nearly irresistible. As we noted in the previous chapter, when it is understood that the goal of contemporary political communications is to break down voters' resistance to a candidate's message, television appears to be the ultimate weapon of mass deception. Reporters, despite their training, are no harder to deceive with advertising than the rest of us.

According to a respected 2000 study by Gary Noggle and Lynda Lee Kaid, "visual literacy"—knowledge of the deceptive techniques possible in television ad production—had no impact on subjects' responses to the ads. We will discuss this study more in a moment. For the time being, suffice it to say that journalists have not reached some above-it-all privileged position that renders them immune to modern manipulative techniques. What this means is that the next best venue for receiving political information has already been poisoned by the dominant venue. In a coffee shop many years ago, I ran into a reporter with knowledge of a campaign that was under way. In an offhand conversation, she repeated words and messages from the television advertisement as if they were her own, unaware that she had absorbed our message perfectly.

Television and the Demise of the Public Sphere

The German philosopher Jürgen Habermas, in a 1962 book that was based on his postdoctoral thesis, tracks the history of the public sphere in the West and concludes that it has all but vanished. "The extent to which the public sphere as an element in the political realm has disintegrated...is measured by the degree to which it has become a genuine publicist task for parties to generate periodically something like a public sphere to begin with," Habermas wrote.

> Television has played a key role, perhaps the key role, in the final stages of the disintegration of a public sphere in which citizens participate in rational conversations about public policy and the future of their community. Writes historian J. Harry Wray, "The virtue of capitalism, as its theorists see it, is that individuals have the ability to make well-reasoned decisions about what is best for them and ought to be allowed to do so. As capitalism has developed, however, events have conspired to make its moral foundation tenuous. Advertising, which begins as an ally of reason in that it provides information necessary for consumers to make rational choices, has become increasingly concerned with subverting reason. This development flows out of the internal logic of capitalism."

Wray's observation is that mass marketing required advertisers to make emotional claims about their products, to attach their products to human sentiments (sexual desire or social acceptance, for example) that have nothing to do with the products. "The rational individual, the foundation of capitalism, becomes the problem—the entity that must be undone." This is precisely the observation made earlier. Political advertising is aimed at tearing down our resistance to the message. The true ability to choose is the enemy of contemporary political campaigns. Part of the problem, of course, is that the image of the individual as a "sovereign consumer" making rational choices was an invention of capitalism in the first place. In fact, we have noted that the rise of mass marketing and the turn to positive freedom, or freedom-to-will, in the 1920s was key to the deterioration of the public sphere and the diminished concern for a shared freedom-to-experience. So it is interesting that in our "post-totalitarian age," as Vaclav Havel would put it, successful capitalist marketers have had to launch an assault on the mythic sovereign individuals they helped create in the first place.

The truly unsettling thing here is that capitalism still requires an ongoing belief in the possibilities of satisfying the desires of the private individual. Like a god, contemporary hypercapitalism giveth and taketh away. We are given a sense that we are isolated, individual, sovereign, rational beings, and then that sense is "undone," as Wray said, by irresistible marketing strategies. What is taken is our sense of self. Is it any wonder that even those of us who enjoy material luxury remain anxious?

The drive to privatize freedom, to create the exaggerated myth of the isolated individual in the political and commercial sphere, sometimes is made explicit by corporate capitalists. A business marketing trade group, the Ad Council, on July 4, 2002, ran a newspaper ad that extolled private choices over shared freedoms. "Read This Ad. Or Don't," read the headline on the ad. "By deciding to continue reading, you've just demonstrated a key American freedom—choice." It continues with a clear and concise argument for the private over the public: "Because while rights like freedom of speech, freedom of religion and freedom of the press get all the attention in the Constitution, the smaller liberties you can enjoy every day in America are no less important or worthy of celebration. Your right to backyard barbecues, sleeping in on Sundays and listening to any darned music you please can be just as fulfilling as your right to vote for president. Maybe even more so because you can enjoy these freedoms personally and often." In an editorial published in the

American Prospect the following month, the writers expressed out-rage at The Ad Council's admission. "If we lose our liberties as Americans, it will not be via a coup, but through small, incremental accretions of mindlessness. An America that defines freedom as the right to eat at either Wendy's or McDonald's—while the right to trial by jury erodes into obscurity—is not having a very glorious Fourth."

Distorted Communications

Habermas traces the history and transformation of the public sphere over several centuries. As we saw in Chapter 1, social, economic, political, and technological developments in the first decades of this century were themselves products of earlier trends. According to Habermas, the public sphere emerged from the dominant social organization model of the Middle Ages. The king, the only "public" person, represented himself before an audience of spectators. The separation of ruler and ruled has been reincarnated to some extent by television and modern marketing techniques: a candidate appears before us in our living rooms as we play the role of docile subjects. The rise of capitalism and expanded trade in products (and, not inci-dentally, news and information) helped create a new idea of a public sphere in which citizens participated in rational debate, checking the domination of the state. The public sphere developed out of the pri-vate institution of the family, evolving in much the same fashion that Patočka identified as the beginning of politics, history, and philoso-phy centuries earlier. Patočka linked freedom to responsibility in this historical movement, making clear the social nature of freedom at its root. Habermas has much the same in mind in his conception of the later development of the public sphere.

But the public sphere is altered by the rise of institutionalized political parties, intermediaries of the press, and government bureaucracies. "The parties," wrote Habermas, "are instruments for the formation of an effective political will; they are not, however, in the hands of the public but in the hands of those who control the party apparatus." As we will see in a moment, this intermediate step was clearly evident in nineteenth-century America. It is a step that distances individual citizens from full participation. (And Habermas was speaking primarily of parliamentary democracies rather than representative democracies such as we have in the United States.) Still, Habermas overstated the negative consequences of the rise of political parties. They are human organizations that provide a means for collective action. The public sphere, though altered by these mediating organizations, remains viable as the meeting place for rational discussion.

In the public sphere's final collapse, political parties—and the influence of the press as representative observers—fall victim to the reach and scope of the mass market. The press, like party organizations, served in the intermediate stage as information representatives. Like party organizations, journalists were the intermediaries as the possibility of full citizen participation (always a utopian dream) began to deteriorate. "Within the framework of the manufactured public sphere the mass media are useful only as vehicles of advertising," Habermas said.

Last year, in a conversation with Giovanna Borradori, Habermas linked the deterioration of the public sphere to breakdowns in communication. Violent terrorism is a kind of ultimate expression of alienation, frustration, and human isolation. "The spiral of violence begins a spiral of distorted communication that leads through the spiral of uncontrolled reciprocal mistrust, to the breakdown of communication. If violence thus begins with a distortion in communication, after it has erupted it is possible to know what has gone wrong and what needs to be repaired," he said. Maybe we could say the public sphere is replaced by the *public's fear*. Although fragmented and fragile, Western societies maintain some channels (legal suits, psychotherapy) to ease the pains of communicative breakdowns. Such channels are unavailable in the international arena. We can see here just how high the stakes are in restoring the public sphere.

The historical trajectory that Habermas elucidates can be seen in the transformations of American politics during the last two centuries. As Richard Perloff tracks it, the Founding Fathers and other elites in post-revolutionary America were skeptical of the public's ability to resist solicitations and overtures from unscrupulous politicians. The American Revolution was, after all, a revolution of the American gentry who had enlisted the support of tradesmen in overthrowing their masters from across the ocean. But despite efforts to build protections against the scornful and contemptuous campaigns for votes (the electoral college was one such innovation), democracy proved uncontrollable. We can see this antipathy to campaigns reflected in the language of politics at the time. Presidential candidates were to "stand," not "run" for election, for instance. For all the preaching against campaigning, "the practice of politics was different," Perloff said. "The American frontier spawned values such as individual liberty and popular democracy. The reality was that candidates had to get elected, and to get elected they had to persuade their brethren to vote for them."

In 1800, "standing for election" meant that both Thomas Jefferson and John Adams spent the campaign season on their farms. Nonetheless, those who worked for them were busy scurrying about the country, spreading the good word on their candidate and the bad word on their candidate's opponent. And, as Perloff notes, "the major weapon in the campaign arsenal was the partisan press, whose editors made no bones about their staunch support for one of the candidates and who engaged in 'no holds barred' attacks on the opposition."

It was in the late 1820s that the spirit of aloof republicanism gave way to more popular democracy. The Age of Jackson saw such novel inventions as "party platforms, nominating conventions, and national campaign committees," according to Perloff. "The reforms significantly increased democracy in that they gave the public a greater voice in the nomination process." The ideal public sphere as envisioned by Habermas never existed, which he was quick to recognize. But what is interesting to note is the restlessness of Americans and their constant striving for more popular democracy, a striving all but silenced in the modern era. America moved from an elite democracy to a popular democracy, although institutions arose almost immediately to mediate among citizens, candidates, and elected leaders. In the 1840 presidential election between Whig William Henry Harrison and Democrat Martin Van Buren, popular democracy took off in earnest. By 1840, there were 1,577 newspapers, all of them choosing sides in the contests. Political parties grew in stature, effectiveness, and—most importantly—membership. The country was awash in promotional giveaways, campaign jingles, and crafty deception. Harrison posed as a down-home, log-cabin rustic. In truth he was the aristocratic son of a prominent family. "The 1840 election," wrote Perloff, "marked the official burial of the age of elite politics."

The next half-century was a veritable carnival of popular politics, with rallies, torch light parades, military-style marches, and the formation of political clubs from communities of interests. As Perloff says, "During the Gilded Age, politics was a major leisure time activity." People spoke of their party affiliation in the same tones as they spoke of their families and religions.

The Passing of Politics as a National Pastime

According to Perloff, six factors contributed to the weakening of politics as a national pastime:

1. Progressive reformers, fueled at the end of the nineteenth century by a new faith in the social sciences, fought hard for reforms that would replace popular politics and its tendency toward corruption with what they hoped would be more dispassionate, sober, and deliberative reflection. Most of these early progressives were elites themselves, and their reforms—such as creation of the civil service to end patronage and diminish some of the motivation for getting involved on behalf of a candidate— sought to clean up the messiness of what they felt was out-of-control public participation.

2. As the Civil War fell further into the past, the public lost its taste for campaign spectaculars such as military parades.

3. Increased class division drove a wedge between the wealthy and the working class who had earlier set their economic status aside and worked together as equals on behalf of a candidate or party.

4. Progressives established business practices that seemed to promise a modicum of ability to manage the corruption they abhorred.

5. New leisure activities such as baseball and vaudeville came into popularity. Here we see the beginnings of the cultural changes that gained such momentum several decades later, changes, as noted in Chapter 1, that emphasized private freedoms over shared freedoms.

6. The press became increasingly independent from its partisan moorings. We will explore this further in an upcoming chapter, but it should be noted here that the press, following the lead of progressive reformers, also sought a dispassionate distance from the hurly-burly of popular partisanship in favor of an allegedly unbiased, independent, above-it-all perch where they would put fact and truth ahead of partisan argument. This also was fueled by a new business orientation in journalism. A newspaper's potential audience could include partisans of all kinds so long as it was not viewed as the mouthpiece of a particular party. A diverse readership was much, much larger than a narrow, partisan readership. The new journalists calculated that as they rose above partisanship, their profits would rise, too.

McKinley and Bush

In the 1896 presidential election, we see all these changes reflected in William McKinley's campaign. His manager, Mark Hannah, "systematically applied the principles of modern business to presidential campaigns. He employed more experienced workers at campaign headquarters, used up-to-date bookkeeping practices, expanded polling operations, relied on the telephone to keep track of campaign developments, and brought campaign finance into the modern age," Perloff said. Karl Rove models himself on Hannah and has consciously attempted to reestablish McKinley-era, business-friendly, elite rule. McKinley's campaign shows us the politics of deceit in its infancy; Rove's 2000 and 2004 efforts on behalf of Bush show us the politics of deceit in its full, manipulative maturity. Technology has, of course, played a key role in the ascendancy of political market-ing—manipulation at a distance rather than up-close participation. Many of the advertising and marketing principles so refined today, however, were present in the McKinley era. Their use grew steadily. By 1904, the *New York Times* would write that "campaigning is only a political name for advertising."

By 1920, cultural trends and marketing innovations in politics were reinforcing one another. The birth of radio and the availabil-ity of new leisure diversions and mass-marketed products allowed Americans to fall more deeply into a privatized conception of free-dom. The public sphere of an informed citizenry became an audience of isolated individuals. The transformation has profound implica-tions for freedom and democracy. But the change has been gradual. The evolution of our political practices and the technologies that helped them develop seem so benign, however, that it is difficult to gain a perspective from which the dangers are apparent. And of all these technological innovations, television has had the most pro-found effect.

Virtual Politics

In the 2002 midterm elections, local television news carried four times as many paid political spots as political news stories, according to a study released by the University of Southern California's Annenberg Lear Center Local News Archive in collaboration with the University of Wisconsin-Madison. In terms of viewing time, view-ers saw more than one minute of paid advertising for every 39 seconds of political news. Advertising records were set in the Iowa caucuses and New Hampshire primary in 2004, too. Politically speaking, Americans live in a virtual world created by partisan con-sultants who are skilled at the manipulation of reality. It must be granted that selfless honesty has never been a hallmark of political communication. The thinking goes that Americans see through the bunkum. They are rational actors, after all, and can tell the difference between sense and nonsense, solid information and twisted propaganda. This is not the case, however, and we admit as much in other circumstances.

Why, for instance, do we forbid cigarette advertising on television? Because we fear such advertising is irresistible. Why do we fret over televised violence? Why do we get so angry with broadcast (and print) reporters when we feel their coverage is biased against our own views? In these cases we believe that other viewers are being misled in ways they can't resist. It is common for many of us to believe that others suffer from the irresistible influence of the media, especially television. Not ourselves, of course! We are smart enough to see through it. But this is where we are mistaken. None of us wants to admit that our choices are anything but our own. And certainly we bring experiences, beliefs, and habits of thought to the party (although even some of these may have been determined in ways beyond our control).

Part of television's power is that the medium appears invisible. That is, it seems to viewers that they are simply getting a view of reality through a transparent window on the world. "The inherent properties of television are such that its essence is obscured. The deceptiveness of television is that it imparts a sense of 'being there,' of observing events firsthand instead of having them mediated," wrote Wray. Television, however, is anything but neutral or transparent. Television is opaque. We see what is there on the screen and nothing more. On the screen are images selected to influence our choices in ways we find it difficult to resist. Just follow the money. Commercial and political advertisers *could* reach mass audiences in much less expensive ways. But none of them, from print advertising, radio, direct mail, personal appearances, or telephone solicitations approach the persuasive power of television.

Before discussing studies that reveal the irresistible power of advertising, let me reiterate that I do not expect any immediate political reform that would, say, ban political ads in favor of "free" air time for candidates; however, I believe such a step would be constitutional, especially if the courts can be persuaded that televised advertising communicates in a fashion quite different from post-Enlightenment assumptions about rational speech. Nor do I expect any candidate or party to unilaterally disarm and avoid using television while the opposing party or candidate takes full advantage of the medium. I am making these arguments to

- indicate that the politics of deceit is not just a consequence of lying politicians, but, rather, is present in the very structure of our political practices
- to demonstrate the dissociation of voters from political practices and the deterioration of the public sphere
- to suggest that while we must seek to reform our campaign practices through legislation and through the courts, we must first reenter the public sphere as free individuals

If freedom and democracy are to survive, they will survive because we turned off our televisions and reengaged in a real public discussion. This is why the new internet-based activism can reach an historical importance that might otherwise seem unrealistic to suggest. For the first time since the dawn of contemporary campaigns—the last half of the nineteenth century—people from different walks of life in different parts of the country are having their voices and their arguments heard in a web-driven reconstitution of the public sphere.

The Power of Advertising

That said, we should look again at the study by Noggle and Kaid regarding the power of images in political advertising. The study tested concerns that "television advertising in political campaigns revolves around the possibility that as a form of persuasion, television's visual imagery may pollute the information needed by voters to make rational decisions." Particularly, the authors are concerned with new technologies that allow the manipulation of sound and images to alter, distort, or enhance reality. The concept is not a new one. In the early days of motion pictures, film theorists understood that the simple juxtaposition of images could create meanings which neither image originally possessed. The authors use the example of a Richard Nixon ad that "interspersed scenes of a laughing Hubert Humphrey with horrifying Vietnam War footage."

In the same study, research subjects were asked to evaluate ads with technological distortions and ones without distortions. In addition, levels of viewer sophistication were tested to see if those with so-called "visual literacy," those who understand how reality can be manipulated by the medium, were less influenced by the distortions. In a nutshell, technological distortions worked just as you might fear. Ads that used such techniques in negative attacks on a candidate resulted in that candidate receiving a poorer score. Ads that distorted reality on behalf of a candidate made that candidate more acceptable.

More profoundly, it appears that even those educated about the technological manipulations of televised advertising are unable to escape its influence. "The level of visual literacy did not have any impact on the voter's susceptibility to the effects of the technological distortion in the spots," the authors reported.

They concluded, "These results identify a measurable problem in modern political communication: the presence of technological manipulations in political television spots can affect voter judgments about political candidates. The presence of such distortions has the effect sought by their producers: the distortions significantly increase the evaluations and vote likelihood of the sponsoring candidate and decrease the evaluations and vote likelihood of the opponent."

Some of these distortions are used so frequently that they have become standard practices in politics. I know because I have used them myself. In an earlier study, Kaid and Noggle found that technological tricks could be found in more than 40 percent of the presidential campaign ads in 1992 and 1996. My personal experience indicates the percentage is much higher than that. What kinds of distortions are we talking about?

In the 2002 Texas gubernatorial race, incumbent Republican Governor Rick Perry ran an attack spot against his Democratic challenger, businessman Tony Sanchez of Laredo. The spot included two former Drug Enforcement Administration officials implying that money laundered through one of Sanchez's banks had benefited Mexican drug cartel leaders who subsequently murdered a DEA agent. Ignoring details—that the money in question was innocently accepted and properly reported to the federal government—the ad strongly implied that Sanchez was somehow personally involved in the murder. Playing upon racial stereotypes and twisting reality into almost unrecognizable form, the ad received extraordinary criticism from an outraged press. Nonetheless, the ad's message was powerful and irresistible to viewers. I was manager of the Sanchez campaign, and our pollsters and media consultants had been careful to test the possibility of this attack in advance. In focus groups throughout the state, we showed our own version of this expected attack. We expected it because the banking issues had received minor publicity 20 years ago. The facts made it clear that there was not even an allegation of wrongdoing either by Sanchez or by the bank, but we knew that this would not stop the manipulation of the facts in a campaign context. The spot initially had a powerful impact on the groups. However, when allowed to discuss the real facts of the case in some detail over the course of an hour and a half, many focus groups participants saw through the deception. The problem is that in the real world voters have no public sphere equivalent to a focus group setting in which they can sit down with friends, colleagues, or strangers to discuss such things.

While working for Lloyd Bentsen during the 1988 Dukakis/ Bentsen race against George H.W. Bush and Dan Quayle, we knew when we saw the infamous "Willie Horton" spot that it would be damaging, even though the facts behind it were insubstantial.

In brief, the ad showed pictures of dangerous-looking African-American men pouring through a revolving door. The revolving door symbolized what the Bush team hoped Americans would view as the Dukakis policy on crime. Once again, a racial stereotype was used to raise fears in the minds of voters, and no amount of explanation could compete with the distortions of that spot.

Former U.S. Senator Max Cleland, a Vietnam War veteran who lost three limbs in combat, was the victim of a reality-distorting spot at the hands of his Republican opponent, U.S. Representative Saxby Chambliss. The spot juxtaposed images of Cleland with pictures of Saddam Hussein and Osama bin Laden, and it criticized Cleland's commitment to "homeland security." Even fellow Republican John McCain was outraged by the ad. No reasonable voter in Georgia or anywhere else could consider Cleland a supporter of Hussein or bin Laden. The attack was patently ridiculous. Nonetheless, it worked; the visual association damaged Cleland severely. Voters could not resist the message that Cleland somehow stood for making the world safe for our enemies, even though he had been severely injured fighting for America in Vietnam.

While these are just some notable examples, there are many, many others. It is common practice in designing negative ads to use unflattering and even altered images of one's opponent. Soundtracks can be tweaked to make an opponent sound weak or silly and your candidate strong and forceful. All these things can be done without departing from facts, which can be checked. The overall impression that an ad makes on its viewers cannot be checked against facts. Such impressions are subjective, after all. So contemporary political professionals take refuge in the "truth" of the verifiable information in an ad, knowing all along that what the ad really communicates is something quite different from truth or reality.

Working with Bob Squier in Ann Richards' 1990 race, we closed the campaign with a negative attack on Clayton Williams. The ad contained a few of Williams' own statements, all of them well known, all of them accurately reported by the spot. But the visual was enhanced with a frightening green tone, and as the camera zoomed in on an ugly photo of Williams, his very visage seemed to dissolve in graininess, deconstructed, as it were, by his own outrageous statements (he had likened rape to bad weather and had wondered aloud whether Richards "had gone back to drinking again"). There was not one fact misrepresented by this spot. But it communicated much more than Williams' ill-chosen words. I mention this to note that the misrepresentation of reality is not just a Republican strategy, although Republicans often seem to be more at ease with it than many Democrats I know.

Bugs Bunny at Disneyland

Other recent studies highlight additional effects of advertising on its audience. A favorite is a 2002 study by Katherin A. Braun-LaTour, Rhiannon Ellis, and Elizabeth Loftus. Adult subjects were shown a print ad for Disneyland that asked them to recall their own youthful visits to the park and to remember how excited they were to shake the hand of Bugs Bunny. The results revealed that sixteen percent of those shown the ads insisted afterwards that they actually shook the darn rabbit's hand at the amusement park. But Bugs Bunny is a Warner Brothers character, which is why this ad was used in the study. There was no possibility that the researchers had called up actual memories; Bugs would not be caught live or animated at Disneyland.

"Is it all right for marketers to knowingly manipulate consumers' past?" the study asks. "On the one hand, the alteration will occur whether or not that was the intent of the marketer...On the other hand, there are ways in which the marketer can enhance the likelihood that consumer memories will be consistent with the advertising messages. At the very least, consumers ought to be aware of the power."

The problem is that awareness of the power of advertising does not seem to affect our ability to resist it, as the previous study showed and which our experience confirms. While this study involved a print ad, the authors and others say televised advertising is much, much more powerful because of the force of the medium and the usual repetition of the ads. (A rule of thumb in political advertising is that enough airtime should be purchased that the target audience of voters will see a given ad at least 10 times.)

Other recent findings in the marketing, advertising, and cognitive science fields also suggest that advertising works in ways earlier generations would have found frightening.

Harvard marketing guru Gerald Zaltman said, "When asked, many consumers insist that they rely primarily on their own first-hand experiences with products—not advertising—in making purchasing decisions. Yet, clearly, advertising can strongly alter what consumers remember about their past and thus influence their behaviors." In other words, even when we think we are making rational self-interested decisions, we are acting in part on false memories created by skilled media artists.

Chuck Young, an Albuquerque ad man, said in an important industry study that "[I]t could be argued that the purpose of showing scenes of a product or products being consumed or used in television commercials is to create a form of *virtual consumption experience*. When fed into the episodic memory system, these might become indistinguishable from real experiences of the individual—much like the phenomenon of 'false memories' of childhood that some psychologists have reportedly been able to create." Here is an advertising professional deadpanning about the benefits to marketing of a *virtual consumption experience*. Like Zaltman, Young appears to overlook the dark side of his observation, which is that while we are being fed virtual experiences that we cannot distinguish from reality, what is really being consumed is our sense of self. In a very real sense, when President Bush appeared in a flight suit on board an aircraft carrier, the image was irresistible. For some Americans, Bush is the conquering hero he appeared to be, and nothing will make them see him differently. We *remember* him as heroic, although this "memory" is at odds with the facts of Bush's past—he avoided Vietnam by joining the National Guard and then failed to report for duty for several months.

Memory is a notoriously vulnerable cognitive capacity. Psychologist Daniel L. Schacter has catalogued memory's soft spots. He points out that memory's weaknesses can also be strengths. The constant reediting of our lives, the imprecise nature of memory, can afford us additional opportunities to respond to unpredictable circumstances. In other words, we pay a price in the accuracy of memory for our ability to think creatively. "Memory's vices are also its virtues, elements of a bridge across time which allows us to link the mind with the world," Schacter wrote. This is another example of how evolution has produced a way to enhance our freedom, while at the same time opening us up to the possibility of manipulation. But is there a troll under the "bridge across time," a troll with the magic power to alter our pasts and thus somewhat determine our future? Current research indicates that there is.

An important part of our memory system is found in a recently discovered neurological "mirror system." Recent brain imaging studies of the so-called mirror neurons have found that the same neurons fire when we perform an action and *when we see that same action performed*. This contributes to Chuck Young's virtual consumption experience. I see someone shake Bugs Bunny's hand; I shake Bugs' hand. Bush rattles a saber; I draw my sword. Such is the stuff memories are made of. All of us are somewhat familiar with this phenomenon. Have you ever felt a smile appear on your face just as an actor smiled on television, or felt the muscles tense in your arms as the quarterback threw a pass? Do you get the urge to yawn when you see someone else yawn? Mirror neurons play a role in these common experiences.

During the 2000 election, there were a few days of controversy revolving around a Bush ad in which the word "rats" was found. It came and went faster than the eye could read and raised questions about the evil power of subliminal advertising. There has never been any proof that such subliminal messages work at all. But the urban legend persists, perhaps because some part of us recognizes a certain helplessness before the television screen. The above studies and observations have nothing to do with subliminal messaging in its usual sense. The authors of the studies are not crackpots, and, in fact, most of them extol the power of advertising because that is their business.

Of course, there are differences between artfully crafted thirty-second ads and television news and programming. Part of the power of television advertising comes from its use of repetition. As mentioned earlier, a typical viewer must see an ad a minimum of ten times before it has fully worked its way into his consciousness. Partly this is because of the way we watch television, even the way we try to ignore ads. In television news or programming, usually there is no such repetition. Typically, then, the actual information of a telecast news report is not completely overwhelmed by its images. However, there are substantial similarities that should not be overlooked. Sometimes news footage is repeated over and over again. Bush's appearance on the deck of the USS *Abraham Lincoln* is an example of how television imagery can be controlled and how those in control of the imagery can manipulate viewers. Former Vermont Governor Howard Dean, with his odd rant on the evening of the Iowa caucuses, broke two political rules at the same time. He let the imagery get out of control, and he displayed an ignorance of the power of the medium. The political press covering the campaign finds this unacceptable from a candidate. He paid a heavy price for the errors.

Wray tells us that "because of television's sense of being there, citizens are likely to miss the fact that the sense of the personal being conveyed is false—a political contrivance." As mentioned before, the intimacy we feel with those we see on television is an illusion. Here we can again see that deceit, intentional or not, sits at the center of what has become our dominant venue for political communication. Wray makes another observation relevant to our discussion of freedom: Television "washes over the viewer. It cannot wait for reflection; it must move on." Recall the recent discoveries of neuroscience, in which our conscious moments appear to be punctuated by an active desynchrony of the neural assemblies that make up our thoughts. This pause constrains, but does not determine, subsequent conscious acts. I am not aware of any studies to determine if television viewing inhibits this essential "letting go." However, we are all familiar with the feeling that the more we watch television, the more we tend to watch. It does not *feel* voluntary. Perhaps the effect Wray describes is a conscious macro-effect and not an effect at the subconscious, neural level. Either way, our ability to reason and reflect does appear to be inhibited by television viewing.

"Television's corruption of vibrant democratic politics is not the product of a demonic mastermind," Wray says. "If that were so, then change might be more easily accomplished. It is, rather, the result of a logical concatenation—of small and immediately rational decisions leading to epic irrationality." Epic it is. It cannot possibly make sense that we lean most heavily for our essential political information on a medium that seems to subvert the kind of free rationality long felt essential to a democracy.

Overcoming Political Advertising

There are important efforts under way to curb the power of advertising. The most sophisticated and well financed is the effort of the Alliance for Better Campaigns, run by former *Washington Post* reporter Paul Taylor. The Alliance is seeking to curb the demand for money to pay for advertisements by increasing the amount of free airtime broadcasters afford candidates. The Alliance also supports efforts to fund campaign advertising with federally issued vouchers paid for by a small fee on users of the broadcast spectrum. A valuable and thoughtful proposal backed by Senators John McCain and Russell Durbin, it has not fared well to date. But it is a beginning.

The main villain for the backers of the proposal, however, is not advertising. It is the money needed to buy the advertising. Regardless of where the funding comes from, the dependence on advertising in politics remains a threat. Advertising is rewriting our pasts as it determines our future. In George Orwell's *1984*, O'Brien, the character who ultimately breaks the will of protagonist Winston Smith, says, "Who controls the past controls the future. Who controls the present controls the past." Later in his interrogation and torture of Smith, O'Brien asks Winston if the past has "real existence," standing by to continue the torture if Winston answered incorrectly. "The feeling of helplessness descended upon Winston. His eyes flitted towards the dial. He not only did not know whether 'yes' or 'no' was the answer that would save him from pain; he did not even know which answer he believed to be the true one."

Winston's ambivalence is not unlike the reaction from many voters who are asked whether they would like to see fewer or more political ads on television. Despite complaints about negative advertising, many voters know they rely upon ads for political information. They also know, however, that there is a problem with their dependence on advertising.

The two most often heard arguments against any restrictions on political advertising are that it is essential to getting information about candidates and issues and that any restriction would be a violation of free speech as interpreted by the Supreme Court.

Stephen Bates, once a visiting scholar at the Libertarian Cato Institute, authored a lengthy policy analysis, "Political Advertising Regulation: An Unconstitutional Menace." Bates argued that a ban on political advertising would leave voters without the information they need to make informed choices. He mentions, in particular, Curtis Gans's proposal in 1979 to abolish political ads and Gans's less restrictive 1982 proposal that would allow ads but ban certain "production material," such as props and other techniques that add emotion. Instead, he recommended limiting candidates to "talking head" shots in neutral settings. "All of the criticisms of political television advertising fail under close scrutiny," Bates said. The ads are a cost-effective way for candidates and officeholders to communicate with their large and diverse constituencies. Without them, there might be an information void. Throughout his analysis, however, Bates holds that television advertising is technically no different from the spoken word or the written text. Speech is speech, and no accommodation is made for the profoundly different ways that humans process information from different sources.

Bates brushes aside ad critics who complain that the ads facilitate lies and demagoguery, which he notes have long been a part of the political scene. Television advertising does not generate billions and billions of dollars a year just because it reaches large numbers of people. Television is used, most advertising professionals will admit, because it is a powerful persuader. I may have a face-to-face encounter with you in which I try to change your memory of some event. Remember the joke, "Are you going to believe me or your lying eyes?" The humor hinges on the impossibility of my accomplishing my goal. But television has no such problems of credibility. Our memories are vulnerable to its seductions.

But Bates disagrees. "There is nothing magical about political advertising, positive or negative, with or without production material. It does not overwhelm the viewer's natural skepticism or subvert his rational faculties," he writes. As we have seen, however, it appears to subvert our rational faculties in profound ways. If this is so, even Bates admits the courts might look again at whether political television ads are fully protected by the First Amendment. "A narrow exception might exist for speech that demonstrably bypasses the rational faculties, such as subliminal advertising," he wrote.

In *U.S. et al v. Playboy Entertainment Group Inc.*, the Supreme Court overturned provisions of the 1996 Telecommunications Act that placed some restrictions on the content carried by cable television. "It is rare that a regulation restricting speech because of its content will ever be permissible," Justice Anthony Kennedy wrote for the 5-4 majority. "Indeed, were we to give the Government the benefit of the doubt when it attempted to restrict speech, we would risk leaving regulations in place that sought to shape our unique personalities."

But what happens when it is not the regulation but the advertising it regulates that shapes our unique personalities? Is it possible that our memories are not essential to our unique personalities?

Hardly. Memory is the core of personality. Without it we would have no sense of self in which to invest a personality. Admittedly, the neurological research was not available to Bates when he wrote his comprehensive account of the issue. The First Amendment has always enjoyed a privileged place in the opinions of the Supreme Court, and political speech is the most precious of all. Nonetheless, the above decision and others open the possibility of at least discussing the continued dominance of television advertising in politics.

In *Rowan v. U.S. Post Office Department*, the Court upheld restrictions on direct mail solicitation, finding constitutional a citizen's right to erect a wall "that no advertiser may penetrate without his acquiescence." In that case, the wall that could not be penetrated was the threshold of the home. How about our heads and hearts? And in *FCC v. Pacifica Foundation*, the Court upheld restrictions on the broadcast of George Carlin's infamous "dirty words" comedy routine in which, again and again, he repeated words that some people found offensive. Alluding to an earlier opinion, the Court said the routine was like a "pig [that] has entered the parlor." A pig in the barnyard is fine. A pig in the parlor is not. Recognizing that "the broadcast media have established a uniquely pervasive presence in the lives of all Americans"—in other words, that media find us in barnyards and parlors alike—the court said the First Amendment allows us some measure of privacy.

Advertising that reaches into the parlors of our past are clearly beyond any conception of free speech considered by the Founding Fathers or the Supreme Court. The Constitution does not guarantee me the right to alter your past. Since 1974, the Federal Communications Commission has had a regulation on the books that would prohibit "deceptive" manipulation of our private memories, whether the manipulation was intended or not.

4

DEAD POPE MUSIC

The Press and American Politics

Interested men who are not to be trusted; weak men who cannot see; prejudiced men who will not see; and a certain set of moderate men ... will be the cause of more calamities to this continent than all the other three.

Thomas Paine
Common Sense

Traveling with then vice president George H.W. Bush in the 1984 Reagan-Bush reelection campaign, a somewhat bored and restless press corps took out its frustrations on the hapless flight crew of a last-minute Pan American charter. A burly, boisterous television news cameraman donned a gorilla mask and slipped up behind an already impatient attendant. He tapped her on the shoulder. She turned around to find a hulking gorilla in her face. Her yelp brought laughs from the other rowdy passengers, and a stern warning from their victim that the press plane would be grounded if such behavior continued. Cooped up as they were, shuttled from one staged, un-newsworthy event to another, the press corps' antics were understandable. The predictability of the campaign would be countered with a little unpredictability from the Fourth Estate, in their play if not in their work.

The incident has stayed with me because it is symbolic of the way many political newsmakers and bystanders, as well as the more partisan-minded members of the general public, regard the press. They believe journalists are gorillas-in-our-faces bent on calling attention to themselves by ridiculing the more responsible and respectable among us who sacrifice for the sake of public service or who simply want to keep the passengers safe until the airplane is on the ground.

Almost everyone with a strong political opinion believes the press holds to the opposite opinion. Rupert Murdoch and Roger Ailes started the conservative Fox News channel because they believed, or said they believed, that American journalism—print, broadcast, and cable—was skewed to the left. It would be their strategy to turn the tables on the so-called liberal, establishment media. This time, Ailes donned the gorilla mask and surprised the reporters and executives of CNN, ABC, NBC, and CBS.

Liberals believe the press is captive of their conservative corporate owners. They point out that the same Washington, D.C., journalists who were tough on President Clinton became docile sycophants of President Bush. During my years as a daily political journalist I received my share of such complaints from both sides. Like most reporters, I figured that as long as I was making partisans of all stripes angry, I was probably doing a fair job. Still, the relationship of the press to the American public and to the political leaders and would-be leaders it covers is a complex one.

In this chapter I point out some of the deficiencies of the news media and examine how the current circumstance developed. Many of these deficiencies are structural. Some are the fault of greedy owners. But I do not want to underestimate the extraordinary amount of unbiased information that is made available by journalists. We never should rely exclusively on the news media for politically important news. Such information needs to be obtained in conversation, in dialogue, and not just from the prepackaged, one-way communications from the press. Citizens in a democracy have to reenter the public sphere, look for different sources of information, and let their own opinions be heard. This is already beginning to happen, and the politics of deceit will be diminished by our efforts. But a deeper understanding of contemporary political journalism may serve as an inducement for citizens to more fully live within the truth.

Bias in the Press

Generally speaking, the news media leans toward the status quo, toward conservative interests. Its commercial nature means it must seek the largest audience on behalf of the advertisers that support it. The effort to capture the largest audience means the press has to offend as few people as possible. Radical change is not good programming. The best formula for political coverage is: great conflict over minor differences. Even better, forget the policy differences and cover politics as a horserace. This formula, seen in the growth of process journalism and its emphasis on polls, campaign strategies, and personalities, gives the illusion that the public is doing the evaluating and the press is simply reporting what the public thinks and how the candidates are reacting to what the public thinks. Of course, this reverses the true sequence of persuasion.

Candidates tailor their messages to the findings of opinion research that has already considerably narrowed message possibilities. Candidates, too, look for ways to reach the largest possible audience, and this means they take the least offensive positions while trying to appear bold. Alternately, candidates disguise radical proposals in soft, comforting, and deceitful language. Bush's "compassionate conservative" message hides the radical domestic and international policies of his administration. Where is the compassion in Bush's insistence that, on his word, an American citizen can be declared an "enemy combatant" and held forever without access to the courts or even a lawyer? Where is the moderation in the military policy of preemption in which the United States can ignore international law and invade foreign countries when the president believes they may at some future time become an ill-defined or undefined threat to American interests? But well-crafted messages such as these are communicated through advertising, and the press then evaluates the effectiveness of the advertising. A skilled candidate's public appearances are as carefully constructed as his or her advertising, and the press is left to deliver candidate banalities, plus, of course, their own insights into the goings-on at the racetrack, including how the public is betting at the moment.

Nonetheless, a surprising amount of critical information is delivered to citizens via the news media. Exaggerating perceived press bias is a strategic decision of the Right, and, to some degree, a way of building solidarity on the Left. Raising doubts about what people think they know has allowed partisans on the Right to open doors for their own messages. "The press is biased," they say. "Listen to me, because I'm going to give you the real facts." As political and media analyst Eric Alterman points out, how could so many Americans believe there is a liberal bias (47 percent in a 2002 Gallup poll) in the mainstream media if they were not receiving an overwhelming amount of news about that alleged bias? In other words, attacks on the so-called liberal media are making their way into our consciousness. It is not likely to be coming from the liberal media themselves. "The right is working the refs," Alterman wrote. "And it's working. Much of the public believes a useful, but unsupportable, myth about the SCLM [So-Called Liberal Media] and the media itself have been cowed by conservatives into repeating their nonsensical nostrums virtually nonstop."

The commercial nature of the news media necessarily constrains what is reported. This is not likely to change, though. With regard to mainstream news media—the cable and broadcast networks, major daily newspapers, local broadcast news on radio and television—there is little possibility of structural change. We may succeed one day in busting up the global news and entertainment giants. But we are not, for instance, going to move to a system of public ownership. It is unrealistic of us even to try.

One famous failed experiment in public newspaper ownership was the short-lived Los Angeles Municipal News. Created by city ordinance, the Municipal News began publication on April 17, 1912.

It was closed by city ordinance on April 9, 1913. The ordinance authorizing the newspaper required that political parties polling at least three percent be given free space in the newspaper. When socialists, communists, and other parties began taking advantage of the opportunity, LA town fathers fought back with everything they had. Led by the then-reactionary Los Angeles Times, the anti-public-ownership forces succeeded in having the newspaper shut down. It is impossible to imagine today's media barons allowing real competition to develop with their own tax dollars. The Public Broadcasting Network, National Public Radio, and Pacifica Radio qualify as publicly owned or nonprofit outlets. As should be expected, their political coverage is less constrained by conservative interests. Without the commercial demands of corporate news, they are free to explore issues and ideas in more depth. Their service is invaluable, and deserves to be strengthened financially (through private donations and public money). People involved in alternative media should do what they can to keep public TV and radio vital.

While insiders debate press bias, however, critical issues go unresolved. A poor child in inner-city Detroit does not care about the credibility of journalists. He wants to eat. He needs access to quality health care. He needs to share in the possibility of freedom his country has promised is its primary mission. For him, the debate over press bias is just another deception, a diversion intended to erode confidence in our sources of news, allowing the attackers to posture as the only sources who can be believed.

I worked as a daily journalist for fifteen years. Many of those years I reported on politics and government. Certainly I had my biases. I am human, after all. However, I must say a word here about the nation's working journalists. Most are skilled professionals devoted to finding and reporting the truth. They have a deep and abiding respect for democracy and the critical role they play in keeping democracy healthy by informing their readers or viewers with truthful, important information. Sometimes they fail.

There is little doubt that the biases of their outlets' owners creep into their presentations. Why would we expect it to be otherwise? For instance, some of the same people who serve on a newspaper's editorial board (the group who decides the paper's editorial page opinions) often play a role in determining what stories are reported and where those stories are placed in the paper. This is done directly, in daily "budget" meetings in which decisions about the following day's paper are made, or indirectly, through more general editorial leadership. Why would we expect them to toss their opinions aside when these decisions are made? To their credit, many try and many succeed. "News value" is often thought of as a kind of transcendental metaphysical quality that is not mired in the sloppy world of value, opinion, and emotion. That news professionals even attempt to hold to this unrealistic but beneficial posture says something about their commitment to eliminating their own biases from their coverage.

Nonetheless, if relied on exclusively for political news by the citizenry, the mainstream news media present difficulties for a democracy of informed citizens. And despite the efforts of so many hardworking and honest journalists, these structural qualities contribute to the politics of deceit. The media make it difficult for a wide variety of political views to be heard and understood by the general public. Certainly the corporate consolidation of media sources exacerbates the problem. A vital democracy needs a healthy variety of opinions and a tolerance for the opinions of others. We see evidence of an imperiled democracy when one or two national radio networks are so dominant that they can incite national "spontaneous" right-wing protests of the country-rock band the Dixie Chicks simply because one of its band members was critical of Bush. There are individuals who hold diversity and democracy in such contempt that they consciously manipulate the news. Rubert Murdoch and Roger Ailes are two such individuals. Fox News is a right-wing network. Its slogan, "Fair and Balanced," is intended as a poke in the eye to the other networks rather than a standard aimed at by Fox News.

President Bush complains of a "filter" on the news that interferes with his message and prevents him from determining in advance what the American people know and do not know. A filter that weighs the evidence and that presents opposition views to the president's pronouncements is one role that the media in a democracy is supposed to play. Bush, like other great complainers such as Richard Nixon's disgraced vice president Spiro Agnew, betrays his own contempt for real democracy. In effect, he is saying, "I should be able to tell the American people anything I want without interference from reporters and those who disagree with me." What is ironic is that this complaint comes from arguably the most skilled manipulator of the press in modern history. Few presidents have so boldly argued that their administration can keep secret what it wants to keep secret. The public's right to know is limited to what the president and his handlers think will reinforce the policies of the administration. With the exception of national security information—advance knowledge of troop movements, for example—in a democracy, there should be no policy limiting access to government actions.

Evolution of the News Media

Our access to information is already limited by the nature of contemporary news media. As media critics Todd Gitlin and Jeffrey Scheuer have argued, the media—especially broadcast media—are more amenable to the style of the Right. It is like this despite the efforts of journalists and even some owners who work hard at presenting truly balanced views. For instance, television news keeps our attention by breaking down large topics into smaller, emotional pieces that are easier to digest. The technical evolution of the television medium—and the competition for ratings and advertising dollars—has made it necessary for the news to move at a faster pace, to simplify complex stories and issues. Otherwise it cannot hold its audience's attention. This simplification makes it easier to view the world and its many vagaries and confusions in black-and-white or good-and-evil terms. Gitlin wrote, "Since conservatives tend to be more Manichaean than liberals, and more zealous about their politics, conservatives play better on the air, and so, for commercial reasons, television and radio talk will be disproportionately right-wing."

This partly explains why we have seen an explosive growth in right-wing radio and—-with Fox News—right-wing television, with no equivalent growth in liberal radio or television. There is also more start-up capital available for politically conservative enterprises and a much more sophisticated infrastructure of conservative think tanks and third-party organizations to support them with research and guest "experts." We should question, however, whether a transformation of the news media into clearly partisan newspapers, broadcast radio, television, and cable channels would be an improvement over the imperfect independent media we now have. In the early decades of our country, newspapers were partisan. They were little more than public relations organs of different parties and candidates. This began to change toward the end of the nineteenth century. The transformation was, at least initially, driven by business reasons rather than noble dreams of an independent press. Newspaper owners found they could appeal to a larger audience by appearing to rise above obvious partisan connections. The Associated Press (AP) was launched in the mid-nineteenth century by a group of New York City newspapers looking for ways to cut the costs of news gathering. The AP had to deliver its stories in a more neutral-appearing style because very different newspapers with different editorial positions would carry those stories.

Of course, in the late nineteenth and early twentieth centuries, the neutrality and independence of the news media were relative concepts. The reaction of the establishment press in Los Angeles against the publicly owned *Municipal News* is good evidence of the limits that owners and their friends in business and government placed on the so-called free press. Upton Sinclair, in 1919, published *The Brass Check*, the first thoroughgoing critique of the media published in this country. Sinclair was a socialist, and he was regularly persecuted and his views misrepresented by the hard-bitten news types of his time. He wrote, "Not hyperbolically and contemptuously, but literally and with scientific precision, we define Journalism in America as the business and practice of presenting the news of the day in the interest of economic privilege."

Sinclair argued that publicly owned papers like the defunct *Municipal News* were part of the solution to corporate domination of the news. He viewed that paper's one-year life as proof that such a public enterprise could be so effective that the powerful California interests moved quickly to shut it down. Of course, his analysis overlooks the fact that the *Municipal News* was unable to avoid execution. Sinclair was, however, a galvanizing writer who backed up his critique with engaging, if alarming, fact. The title, *The Brass Check*, refers to the chit that patrons used in houses of prostitution at the time. Such was his opinion of the press. But he correctly identified the barriers that corporate-dominated journalism erected against the free and open exchange of ideas in a democratic public sphere.

In an introduction to a new edition of *The Brass Check*, media analyst Robert W. McChesney pointed out that Sinclair offered a radical critique that rejected all possible solutions but those that attacked the problem at its root. He advocated public ownership and strict laws prohibiting misrepresentations by the press, for instance. Sinclair rejected an idea that is central to my argument, that what is needed is a reemergence of the citizenry into the public sphere, a multiplication of voices and sources of news. He did so in typically colorful prose: "Is it not obvious that society cannot continue indefinitely to get its news by this wasteful method? One large section of the community organized to circulate lies, and another large section of the community organized to refute the lies! We might as well send a million men out into the desert to dig holes, and then send another million to fill up the holes."

McChesney also pointed out that Sinclair's contemporary apologists for journalism felt that the recent move to professionalism would resolve the difficulties presented by reporters captured by their corporate bosses. This was the second transformation of American journalism. The first, of course, was the rise of independent newspapers, free of direct partisan ties to a candidate or political party. The second was the professionalization of journalism. Schools of journalism opened, standards were set, and unbiased, objective coverage was encouraged. "The editorial decisions would be made by trained professionals who would not reflect the biases of the owners and advertisers and would learn to sublimate their own biases as well,"

McChesney said. No doubt news quality was enhanced as better-trained reporters and editors entered the business. But the overall impact was to let the steam out of the reform effort. "Professionalism lowered the menace of commercial journalism just below the threshold of public outrage and held it there with a combination of mild internal reform and stunningly comprehensive public relations to compensate for the ever-present reality of business as usual," wrote McChesney.

In the 1920s, radio began to capture the imagination of Americans. Newsreels, filmed news reports that played before feature movies in theaters, became more and more popular. Printed news was now accompanied by the sights and sounds of national and world events. It is difficult to overestimate the impact of these new communication technologies. With them came the development of a mass audience. Film and radio were unifying society and fragmenting it at the same time. Audience members were brought together as never before. Radio listeners knew the rest of the nation was listening to the same program at the same time. Moviegoers knew the newsreels and films that mesmerized them were having the same effect on audiences throughout the country. Truly national news media were born. At the same time, however, the new media seemed to isolate citizens from one another. People retreated to their homes to listen to radio. Neighborhood gatherings diminished. Civic life came into the home, privately. Movie patrons sat in darkened theaters. The films seemed intended for the single consciousness, even in full venues.

Another paradox emerged with radio and newsreels. The stories carried in the new media seemed at once more real and more ephemeral. There was much greater immediacy, but less interpersonal engagement. The creation of a mass audience seemed to unite Americans, but in truth it divided them. And with it came the turn to a more private, personal self: people became concerned less for the welfare of others and more focused on individual freedom-to-will. Radio and film also added credibility to the existing print press. Pictures and sounds added an air of realism to the news. The camera does not lie, many believe. When a newspaper story, radio news-cast, and newsreel gave more or less similar accounts of events, con-sumers believed they were receiving a more realistic portrait of the world than was possible for previous generations.

Sinclair, who had railed against the press in 1919, would in 1934 see and feel firsthand the power of the emerging new media. In that year Sinclair, having quit the Socialist party, won the Democratic nomination for governor of California. Hollywood moguls, bankers, real estate tycoons, and the heads of utility companies reacted with shock, anger, and action. Working together for a common purpose—and joined by the seven hundred California newspapers that opposed Sinclair—they launched what in effect became a political lynching.

As historian Greg Mitchell details in his account of that cam-paign, the 1934 California race became the first big campaign to uti-lize what was then the new media in an overwhelmingly successful propaganda campaign. Fake newsreels attacking Sinclair were pro-duced and run in movie theaters by Irving Thalberg, the beloved producer known for his gentleness, and other studio executives. Radio serials produced by the country's first great commercial adver-tising firm, Lord & Thomas, attacked Sinclair. In this campaign we can see the emergence of contemporary politics. "Media experts, making unprecedented use of film, radio, direct mail, opinion polls, and national fund-raising, devised the most astonishing (and visually clever) smear campaign ever directed against a major candidate," wrote Mitchell.

Clem Whitaker had in 1933 established Campaigns Inc., a full-service agency that provided candidates with advertising, public relations, polling and opposition research. Whitaker had noticed the transformation already occurring in politics as the power of political parties, local bosses, and grass roots organizations began to wane with the rise of radio, "independent" newspapers, newsreels, and sophisticated polling and voter targeting techniques. Whitaker did not work directly for Sinclair's opponent, incumbent Republican Governor Frank Merriam. Instead, he established a front group out of San Francisco, the California League Against Sinclairism. Another front group, United for California, was established by the anti-Sinclair movement in Los Angeles. It hired the Lord & Thomas firm. Joined by Hollywood studios, these groups became a true contemporary campaign juggernaut.

Lord & Thomas produced four, fifteen-minute, anti-Sinclair radio serials of the type they had previously produced for commercial clients. "One of the shows, *The Political Observer*, was a straightforward current-events program, albeit with an anti-Sinclair twist," wrote Mitchell. "The other three series displayed a good deal more flair. In Turn of Events, based on the March of Time concept, actors impersonated famous people. Weary and Willie followed the adventures of two hoboes from the Midwest who hop a train for California, answering Sinclair's call." Because Sinclair promised an end to poverty, his opponents claimed half a million hoboes would descend on California if he was elected.

But the most startling innovation arrived in California movie theaters in the weeks before the election. Political short films made to resemble newsreels and called *California Election News* used on-the-street interviews with actors and non-actors to skewer Sinclair. Narrated by a voice describing himself as the "Inquiring Cameraman," the shorts showed less-than-appealing characters endorsing Sinclair, lovable and respectable types endorsing the Republican Merriam, and the homeless and out-of-work coming to California for Sinclair's free ride. As Mitchell points out, "The unselling of Upton Sinclair increasingly relied on visual images...the visual propaganda appealed to the emotions and proved even more persuasive than brilliantly executed appeals to reason. Words on a page suggesting that Upton Sinclair was an atheist or a Red simply did not pack the emotional wallop of watching a middle-class family fleeing from an alien horde."

Sinclair lost, of course, though post-election Hollywood was packed with irony. According to Mitchell, one report had Louis Mayer, one of the most virulent opponents of Sinclair's, trying to hire him as a screenwriter. Twentieth Century Pictures wanted to film a play Sinclair had authored. Zeppo Marx, one of the original Marx

Brothers, predicted a movie about Sinclair's unsuccessful campaign for social justice would become "a four-star hit." Governor Frank Merriam, reelected with the help of Hollywood, promptly tried to tax movie admissions and raw film stock. Democrats, with the help of Hollywood producers, outraged by Merriam's betrayal of their interests, beat the governor in the next election using fake newsreels and other techniques pioneered in 1934.

The supposed realism and credibility offered by radio, newsreels, and the new professionalism in journalism seduced audiences. The media age of politics was born as voters were crassly manipulated in ways they could not possibly resist. Merriam even complained that he felt left out of his own campaign, Mitchell wrote. It seemed with all the propaganda aimed at Sinclair there was no room for newsreels, planted newspaper stories, billboards, or radio serials about Merriam. And the California newspapers hardly comported themselves as unbiased observers of the election. Virtually all of the state's 700 papers endorsed Merriam and attacked Sinclair. The *Los Angeles Times* carried a daily box on its front page containing twisted, out-of-context quotes from Sinclair (many from characters in his writings that were represented as Sinclair's own utterances). Mitchell tells the story of a conversation that *New York Times* reporter Turner Catledge had with *Los Angeles Times* political editor Kyle Palmer. Catledge, dispatched to California to write about the race, asked what Sinclair was really like. "Turner, forget it," Palmer replied. "We don't go in for that kind of crap that you have back in New York—of being obliged to print both sides. We're going to beat this son of a bitch Sinclair any way we can."

Mediated Reality

In 1934, the power of the politics of deceit reached levels unheard of in earlier days, and political journalism at the time was part of that power. Few railed against the deceptions. It was politics, after all. But few understood the beginnings of a true dissociation of democratic citizens from the public sphere. A new reality was created. Direct knowledge of our political realities was now mediated, structured through a system of one-way communications that earned our trust through their verisimilitude. These new powers did not have the same terrifying consequences as they had in Germany and Italy at the time. For one thing, political divisions dating from earlier years remained strong. Sinclair had received 900,000 votes to Merriam's 1.2 million votes. But the power of the politics of deceit had grown tremendously.

With the coming of television, that power once again rose exponentially. Television combined the force of radio, film, and newspapers into one medium. If radio had seemed magical in the 1920s, television seemed other-wordly, the stuff of science fiction (which, not coincidentally, enjoyed an explosion in popularity during these same years, much as the birth of radio was accompanied by a popular interest in the occult). In 1949 there was a television set in one out of ten American homes. A decade later nine out of ten American homes had a television. Much has been made of the historical coincidence of the Cold War, McCarthyism, and the Age of Television. American Studies professor Thomas Doherty argued that much of the popular and academic criticism of television accepts a conventional account that McCarthy's skillful use of the new medium caused widespread fear and panic that opened the way for witch-hunts and intolerance. What is often left out of this account, Doherty argued, is the role television played in McCarthy's undoing. In fact, he said that we too often overlook television's great benefits. "Of the incalculable ways that television transformed American life—in family and friendships, leisure and literacy, consumer habits and common memories—the expansion of freedom of expression and the embrace of human difference must be counted among its most salutary legacies. During the Cold War, through television, America became a more open and tolerant place," Doherty said.

I do not share Doherty's unequivocal conclusion. He points out the contested nature of much television programming. It was, after all, news broadcaster Edward R. Murrow who is credited with deflating McCarthy's popularity. He also believes that racial and sexual stereotypes and prejudices have been loosened by television. He made his point simply in an interview with the *Boston Globe*. "On TV variety shows and live TV dramas [of the 1950s], you're seeing images of African-Americans coming into your living room . . . You're seeing these images of integration in the South that would have never been in local papers or movie screens. TV is a much more progressive influence on American culture in the 1950s that [it is] usually given credit for," he said. In the book, Doherty says there are "two central truths about American culture in the age of television . . . First, television gave reporters a rough parity with politicians . . . Second, television depended upon the very freedoms of expression and access that McCarthy sought to shut down. Ultimately, the insatiable demand for material—more thought, more talk, more tales, more personalities—override the timidity of the medium in the presence of power."

But Doherty misses the bigger issue. By relying on the virtual reality of television, especially television news, the line blurs between the real and the unreal. Deception under these circumstances is much easier to get away with. Our lives are encapsulated by a virtual environment. There is no doubt that contemporary media can and do have important benefits. While helping Joe McCarthy's rise to fame, television also played a key role in bringing him down. Doherty mentions other televised moments in which average Americans were shown standing up to McCarthy, even facing him down. This is why it is so important to understand the weaknesses of the media while taking advantage of its benefits. Only to the extent that we engage with other sources of information can we begin to overcome the power of televised imagery. Knowledge of the manipulative effects of the media is not enough. If we remain passive consumers of one-way communications, even communications from responsible sources, we risk permanent exile from the public sphere.

Among the first nationally televised live events were atomic bomb explosions conducted by the American military at Yucca Flat, Nevada. As Doherty tells the story, on April 22, 1952, anxious viewers watched as a voice called, "Bomb away," before seeing their screens light up in a flash. The blinding light of the blast, however, caused the camera's orthicon tube to fail. Viewers complained "about poor audio quality and erratic reception distorted by geometric swirls and diagonal bars." What was the entertainment magazine *Variety*'s headline? "A-Bomb in TV Fluff Fizzles Fission Vision."

In March 1953, another atomic bomb demonstration was televised nationwide. A two-household homestead was fabricated at the test site, complete with mannequins in each home. It was called "Doom Town." This time the camera worked. Doom Town disappeared. Soon thereafter hydrogen bomb tests were televised, the images telecast repeatedly. It was an auspicious beginning for the youthful medium. The images still bounce around our collective consciousness. They reemerge, transformed into different visions: the shooting of Lee Harvey Oswald, Neil Armstrong on the moon, the *Challenger* explosion. Who could doubt our access to an unmediated glimpse of these history-shaping events? But the images are mediated.

Some part of us recognizes the distance between reality and image. We know there are gaps between the images presented in the media and the reality outside our doors. But often we fill in these gaps with flights of fancy or even conspiracy theories. We watch Jack Ruby shoot Lee Harvey Oswald and we have to provide our own "why." We conjecture that Ruby was in on a conspiracy to kill President Kennedy and simply needed to silence an untrustworthy Oswald. The moon shot was staged in a remote Earth-bound desert. Kent State was not the error of frightened young troopers; it was a calculated and deadly signal from the government that street protests were no longer acceptable. Only the *Challenger* accident escaped being labeled the result of a conspiracy, in part because a brilliant physicist, the late Richard Feynman demonstrated—on television—that the explosion was caused by a mundane, easy-to-understand rubber O-ring.

Musical News

The tension generated by our attempts to cope with this torrent of sounds and images surfaces in the stresses and tensions in the relationships among the media, the government, and the people. A topic

that receives very little attention, the use of music in news broadcasts, can provide some insight. In a remarkable recent essay, film
composer Carter Burwell explores the use of music by network and
cable news shows. Music, commissioned from composers and agen-
cies, is used to brand the news shows, call viewers' attention back to
their televisions (much like the bells of old town criers), and set a
background mood for the topics under discussion.

In tracing the history of music in news media, Burwell begins
with the live music used to accompany newsreels in movie theaters.
To make it easier for conductors to find the appropriate music, publishers distributed music digests listed by dramatic need. One such
book offered three variations of war music and four variations for
"hurry" music for faster-paced imagery, for instance. Newsreels
became talking pictures in the 1930s and were delivered with prere-
corded sound. When television replaced newsreels in the 1950s, there
was, at first, much less music used in the news shows—probably
because television was much more regulated than films and was supposed to avoid editorializing. "If music was present at all, it was only
at the very start and end of the newscast, and it served primarily the
same branding function as theme songs did on serials and sitcoms;
unlike its role in newsreels, it didn't score the news," Burwell said.
"As studies of viewing patterns revealed that televisions often
remained on when Americans weren't watching, music was asked
once again to serve the function of the town crier's bell: to gather the
audience."

Music is put to much greater use in television news today. Burwell
said composers deliver it to their TV clients in "packages" consisting
of many different pieces for different purposes—in other words, to
create different moods depending on the stories the music will
accompany. He quotes Peter Fish, composer for *CBS Evening News*,
on the process: "The package for the [first] Gulf War was maybe 14
or 16 cuts, because basically there's tragedy and there's blood-and-
guts. But if you do something for *The Early Show* you have to do
tragedy, blood-and-guts, general news, sports, Christmas, Easter,
Thanksgiving, Election Day, and what I call 'dead Pope music,' for
when the Pope finally dies."

Dead Pope music? Here we see one of the great dilemmas of contemporary news media. They have a responsibility to their viewers to make the news understandable, and setting a mood makes that job easier by relaxing viewers into the spirit of the particular story. They also have a responsibility to the owners and to the advertisers who pay the freight. And so they enter a "mood enhancement" competition of sorts with their rivals. Furthermore, news programming must remain entertaining to keep pace with non-news programming. What would happen to news viewership if news broadcasts failed to match in sophistication and emotional impact the regular programming of sitcoms and dramas? The audience for news would certainly decline. In meeting these responsibilities, newscast managers do their best to keep their shows interesting and involving. It is not a conspiracy, and, in context, it is not irresponsible.

Burwell noted that for the 2003 Iraqi War, the network news shows ordered packages that were "serious and uplifting." While the networks did not ask for martial music or overtly hawkish melodies, it "is hard to avoid the impression that much of the music for the coverage of this Gulf War strove to make one 'feel good' about the war. This is particularly true for CBS and Fox, which invoked contemporary rhythm tracks to give an undeniable air of excitement to the proceedings. Clearly the networks had come to the conclusion that this was what the public wanted."

As Elvis sang, we are caught in a trap. Musical accompaniment to the news is supposed to simply reinforce its message. It is inevitable, though, that it colors the news. Music that did not match the news report it accompanied—say, Simon and Garfunkel's "Feelin' Groovy" behind the assault on Baghdad—would not work. (However, music is often used this way in film. Two examples: Donovan's "Atlantis," was heard in Martin Scorcese's *Goodfellas* while a man was beaten to death; in Stanley Kubrick's *Full Metal Jacket*, soldiers sing the Mickey Mouse Club theme song while marching through an eerie, war-torn landscape.) The mood set by music intended to help get and keep our attention necessarily communicates how we feel about the information it accompanies. News shows do not want to make us feel bad about the war. So they cannot help but make us feel good.

Said Burwell: "We want to feel good about ourselves, the advertisers want us to feel good about their products, the producers want the advertisers to feel good about the news shows, the state wants the producers to feel good about its government. Someone has to compose the music for all this good feeling." Burwell suggested that we reverse the common recommendation that the media stand in an adversarial relationship to government, "because the government lies to us." Instead, "the media should stand in a quasi-adversarial relationship to us, the viewers, because we lie to ourselves." I agree with him that there is very little chance of this adversarial posture being chosen, not because there is a secret government calling the manipulative shots, but because the demands placed upon the media are in conflict.

What Is To Be Done

It is easy to see that our free choices are somewhat circumscribed by the media. Leaving out those who opposed the war on principle, a great number of viewers are going to feel better about the war by watching—and listening—to network news broadcasts. This war-boosterism was also enhanced when competition led most of the major press into another trap, accepting the military's offer to "embed" reporters with our soldiers in Iraq. I was opposed to the invasion of Iraq. But if I had been a journalist entering that frightening and unpredictable conflict with a band of brothers and sisters, even as an independent observer, I could not help but sink into a subjectivity that put the interests of the military ahead of the interests of my readers. This is not to say that I would, if un-embedded, have put our soldiers in harm's way. But, out of bed, I may have found stories that removed the troops from danger faster.

What, then, is to be done? How do we avoid the seemingly unavoidable reduction in human choices brought about by a ubiquitous media that manipulates as it informs, despite the intentions of its responsible practitioners? Knowledge of the manipulative power of the media is not enough. The media-savvy are just as susceptible to deception as those with no knowledge of the media's technical grammar. Deep structural changes are not likely. Public ownership would relieve the commercial pressures from the media and theoretically make the news more accountable, but this is an impractical, utopian pipe dream. Competition among various media provides accountability and drives journalists to pursue stories important to citizens of a democracy. More rigorous government regulation of the media fails for similar reasons, with one important exception. In the United States we have the laws necessary to inhibit the growth of media conglomerates that threaten to consolidate our sources of news in the hands of a very few corporations and individuals. We should enforce these laws. No one has been more eloquent on this topic than journalist Bill Moyers. The consolidation of media and the platforms provided the religious, partisan, and corporate interests of the right wing have led to "a democracy that is so polarized it is in danger of being paralyzed and pulverized," Moyers said to the National Conference on Media Reform in November 2003. But Moyers has faith that the trend can be reversed.

He points to the passage of the Federal Communications Act of 1934, which was aimed directly at preventing the kind of media monopolies we see emerging today. "The clear intent was to prevent a monopoly of commercial values from overwhelming democratic values—to assure that the official view of reality—corporate or government—was not the only view of reality that reached the people," Moyers said. The passage of the Telecommunications Act of 1996 ended this antipathy toward the consolidation of communications companies. Limits on the number of media outlets a company could own in a single market were relaxed. It is instructive to look at how one company, Clear Channel Communications, took advantage of the new rules.

In 1996, Clear Channel owned 43 radio stations. According to a Cornell University study for the American Federation of Labor and Congress of Industrial Organizations (AFL-CIO), the company now owns 1,239 stations—four times the number owned by next largest radio company—that reach 100 million listeners. It is the number one concert promoter and the largest owner of live-entertainment venues and outdoor advertising displays in the United States. In 2002, it sold 30 million concert tickets. Then came the controversial Federal Communications Commission rules, passed on June 2, 2003, which was, as Moyers put it, "a relaxation of the rules governing ownership of media outlets that would allow still more diversity-killing mergers among media giants." A change in the definition of radio markets, however, might force Clear Channel to sell a few of its stations. It will be worth the loss, though, as other radio groups point out the change in market definition will stop them from growing large enough to offer Clear Channel any competition.

During the FCC deliberations, groups such as MoveOn.org helped generate 750,000 comments to the Commission from citizens, 99 percent of them opposed to the new rules. Nonetheless, the FCC moved ahead with its plans. Whether or not Congress will reverse the FCC's legislation is unclear, although there is substantial alarm in Congress and around the country about the consolidation of media into the hands of a few giant companies.

Clear Channel's growth allows us to see the dangers of media consolidation. It strongly impacts public opinion. Until recently, Clear Channel's Washington, D.C. operation did not even have a news department. But during the debate over the 2003 Iraqi War it managed to sponsor 18 pro-war rallies around the country. Its cozy relationship with President Bush and other Republican elected officials is well known. Partner Tom Hicks bought the Texas Rangers baseball team from Bush, and Clear Channel, its owners, and employees have together donated significant money to their friends in elected office. Clear Channel says its many acquisitions since 1996 offer "synergies," which allow it to make more for less. But the real synergy appears to be the near-merger of the company and its friends in high places.

The radio giant's impact on recording artists—creators of the music—is significant and symbolizes the dangers that media consolidation presents to voters—the creators of democracy. Because Clear Channel owns so many radio stations, performance venues, and the nation's largest concert promotional company, it can and does force artists to play by its rules. Recording artists who must rely on Clear Channel stations to play their songs are forced to play at Clear Channel performance venues or deal with its concert promotions company. This is a company that has automated many of its stations, using sophisticated techniques to make a radio personality seem to be local when, in fact, the personality's voice is being edited and used in several different locations. The local feel is pure deception.

Voters' choices are limited in advance by the power of major media. Their ability to negotiate "better terms" with their elected officials is diminished by the one-way nature of communications in our virtual public sphere. Access to the public sphere is expensive, and the voices of too many citizens are simply denied airtime. But many recording artists have remained independent of major labels, ignoring companies like Clear Channel, booking their own tours, using the Internet to distribute their music. Voters, too, are turning more and more to independent news sources, many of them just beginning to emerge through the power of the Internet. "The web has enabled many new voices in our democracy—and globally—to be heard: advocacy groups, artists, individuals, non-profit organizations. Just about anyone can speak online, and often with an impact greater than in the days when orators had to climb on a soap box in a park," Moyers says.

The proliferation of alternative news sources has been profound and holds great promise for the future. Excellently edited sites like Common Dreams, Truthout, Alternet, and many others make accessible a great diversity of progressive voices from around the country and the world. Web logs, or blogs, have provided a refreshing spontaneity to coverage of the 2004 presidential campaign and other national and global news events and issues. The Independent Media Movement represents a radical new development that has attracted a worldwide audience of millions and hundreds of new online venues for budding journalists and concerned citizens to let their voices be heard. According to *Columbia Journalism Review*'s Gal Beckerman, the movement was born in the late 1990s with World Trade Organization protests. Activist organizers in Seattle established an independent media center where journalists could bring their stories and get them online. An Australian computer programmer developed a technological solution that allowed the journalists to post their stories to the site from their own computers. The indie movement involves local collectives that gather and report the news independently through radio, print, the Internet and other venues. There are now 120 local independent collectives around the world, sharing information with one another and distributing news to their audiences.

Beckerman says the indie móvement's open publishing ethos "has allowed activists from Brazil to Italy to Israel to Los Angeles to answer the revolutionary demand that inspired this grass-roots movement: Don't hate the media. Be the media." This could be a better answer to the question asked earlier, "What is to be done?" Citizens in contemporary democracies have to reemerge into the public sphere to be seen and heard, to see and hear others. The fledgling indie media movement is one way that this can happen. According to Beckerman, the inspiration for such a movement came from Mexico's Zapatista movement, when Subcommandante Marcos released a videotaped message that said, "The world of contemporary news is a world that exists for the VIPs—the very important people. Their everyday lives are what is important: if they get married, if they divorce, if they eat, what clothes they wear and what clothes they take off—these major movie stars and big politicians. But common people only appear for a moment—when they kill someone, or when they die," Marcos said. He correctly diagnosed our retreat into personal pleasures and the media's role in that retreat.

Writes Beckerman, "Instead of simply conforming to this reality or becoming paralyzed with cynicism, Marcos proposed a third option. "To construct a different way—to show the world what is really happening—to have a critical world view and to become interested in the truth of what happens to the people who inhabit every corner of the world." That is the role the indie movement has chosen for itself.

Beckerman points out an example of successful independent press advocacy that happened last year in Illinois. The Independent Media Center (IMC) in Urbana took up the cause of Ahmed Bensouda, a pro-Palestinian activist who had been detained by the United States Immigration and Naturalization Service (INS) after 9/11 for a minor violation. Here is how Danielle Chynoweth, one of the founders of the Urbana-Champaign IMC, described the effort: "... the IMC followed the story hourly online and kept its doors open 24 hours for supporters to walk in, get updates, and organize. Under the Patriot Act, the federal government was going to bring evidence against him that neither he nor his lawyer would ever hear. We tracked the situation carefully, there was an outpouring of public pressure, and they called off the secret evidence." Relentlessly advancing the story day after day, the IMC eventually forced the INS and federal prosecutors to back down. Bensouda was released. The intrepid new journalists had raised the visibility of a case that, under the post-9/11 circumstances, would probably not have been vigorously pursued by local or national mainstream media.

Chynoweth, asked to tell a gathering of indie news types how to put an IMC together, said, "Just start. Our local IMC had its humble beginning as a group of 15 meeting weekly in my living room starting September 24 in the year 2000. We collectivized our equipment and began reporting two days after our first meeting. Our first project was to cover local solidarity protests with the Anti-International Monetary Fund and World Bank protests in Prague." Prague is the city where Vaclev Havel and others began their practice of "writing to the desk," of speaking out and living with the truth. No matter whether the speaking out takes place in a small living room or simply to a friend, there is power in the communication. The indie press movement is a more technologically sophisticated way of writing to the desk.

Robert McChesney, after attending an indie media summit at the Urbana-Champaign IMC early in 2002 said, "The issues that led to this first summit were simple: How can we get more progressive voices in our media? How can we improve the quality of community radio broadcasting? How can we take advantage of under-utilized resources like public access TV channels? How can we get all of these institutions working together with each other and with independent media centers, in order to obtain maximum return on our resources and maximum impact for our labors?" McChesney here is talking about synergy, but in a way quite different from the owners of Clear Channel. Clear Channel's alleged synergies are aimed only at the bottom line. The uniformity of their broadcast product and their political involvement is a byproduct of their devotion to profit. McChesney is talking about independent voices working together across many different communication venues to bring diverse opinions into the public sphere.

The indie media movement has begun to take on a coherent identity. It is a specific, quasi-organized experiment in media reform. The movement is still young, and the obstacles it faces are serious. As Beckerman notes, the very technologies that allowed it to blossom have already forced the movement to make difficult choices. The New York City IMC, for instance, found it was simply impractical to continue a wide-open publishing format. The group's web site was inundated with postings that simply were too off-the-wall. Meaning was being stripped from the site by an avalanche of postings that took time to sift through. So editorial guidelines had to be put in place. McChesney pointed out that the indie movement "is not obliged to be a movement for every viewpoint under the sun. They need to make tough editorial decisions, and that's not something to be despondent about. The problem is not that you have to make decisions. The important thing is that you make them based on principles that are transparent."

The indie movement seems poised to make the transition early American pamphleteers made as partisan newspapers organized around political parties, candidates, and causes in the early nineteenth century. To survive, as Beckerman notes, it will have to become more organized and efficient. But most of all, ways must be found to raise the profile of the new alternative media. There is a danger of the movement becoming fragmented. But independent-thinking individuals and groups are right to "just start," to let their voices be heard, to let the energy gather. The movement should not be confused with the much talked about "public journalism," or civic journalism advocated by communitarian-leaning professors of journalism and some news professionals. This approach would have reporters and editors shed their pretense to neutrality and become more involved in public affairs. The in-it-but-not-of-it pose struck by professional journalists does contribute to the dissociation of citizens from the public sphere. An editor of mine once confessed that he had never voted because voting would violate his pledge to neutrality. Never mind the secret ballot, he said. He would know he held secret political leanings. Many professional journalists have reacted strongly against the idea of public journalism. To them it feels like an academically driven theoretical approach recommended by those who teach because they cannot do. Don Corrigan, a communications professor at Webster University, wrote in the *St. Louis Journalism Review* last year that public journalism "sent traditionalists into fits." Most trained professionals in journalism felt objectivity was key to finding and reporting the truth; detachment let the public know their commitment to objectivity and independence; balance lent credibility to the enterprise.

Perhaps the argument would not be so intense if we quit searching for a new dominant model for the news. Corrigan is certainly right when he points out that the right wing has taken full advantage of the public's willingness to accept a partisan press. "The politicization of the news media is the triumph of American talk radio, conservative weeklies and the rise of Rupert Murdoch and Roger Ailes' Fox News," he wrote. He reported that Matt LaBash, a senior writer for Murdoch's *Weekly Standard*, was positively gleeful with the turn to partisan reporting. "It's a great way to have your cake and eat it, too," said LaBash. "Criticize other people for not being objective. Be as subjective as you want. It's a great little racket." Corrigan believes the right-wing press may cause a backlash they will regret. "They may not have an inkling of the food fight and the backlash their politicization of the news media could trigger." I am for the backlash, and for all new approaches to reporting the news. The proliferation of new voices and opinions and a more engaged journalism has a place in a democracy. The successes of science have led us all to believe that there is a single path to the truth, that eventually a perfect model for professional practice will emerge. I think this is nonsense. What is needed are openings for new ideas and observations. Advocates for public journalism should not seek to replace mainstream, objective reporting. They should seek to supplement it. And traditional journalists should not be threatened by civic journalism. There is a place for that kind of reporting. Uniformity is the enemy of freedom and democracy.

We should not forget that there is already a healthy tradition of partisan reporting on the left. The *Nation* comes to mind. In Texas, the *Texas Observer* has been representing progressive journalism since 1954. Its alumni include Ronnie Dugger, Molly Ivins, Jim Hightower, Geoffrey Ripps, and dozens of other skilled writers and editors. Independent newspapers are thriving. Project Censored, a media research group out of the University of Sonoma, lists more than 400 independent newspapers, journals, and magazines in its guide to independent media. Journalists in this milieu work hard for less pay than can be found in mainstream journalism. But the standards of their reporting are just as rigorous. Remember I.F. Stone and his weekly? Who could argue that his reporting, while representative of progressive journalism, did not place the truth above pure partisanship? The point here is that America is not without the resources to break through into a revitalized public sphere.

One of the most remarkable developments in the last two decades is the emergence of street papers: publications written, edited, and distributed by the homeless in cities across America and around the world. According to one published estimate, there are approximately 50 street papers in the United States and another 60 around the globe. Typically, they are sold on street corners for a dollar or so. The first such paper, *Street News*, emerged in New York City in 1989. In

Chicago, the homeless publish *Street Wise*. It has captured 60,000 readers, making it the third-largest newspaper in Chicago. The papers, perhaps modeled after the *Hobo News* of the early 1900s, allow those at the bottom of the economic ladder to give us their perspective on the news. Kevin Hawley tells of the pieces written by Peter McGuigan in *Street Feet*, the street paper of Halifax, Nova Scotia. McGuigan "evaluates policy changes from the perspective of a social assistance recipient," Hawley said. "Rather than deal in abstractions based on economic forecasts, budget projections and other 'official' pronouncements, McGuigan's analysis is grounded in his experience as a social assistance recipient and school crossing guard."

Hawley sees a clear distinction between public journalism and street papers. "Whereas public journalism tends to frame policy deliberations in terms of competing economic and political philosophies, street papers reveal the human cost of social policy based on political expediency and accounting columns and ledgers," he wrote. The writers and editors of America's street papers, in other words, have decided to become the media rather than hate the media.

Because we receive an overwhelming amount of information every day, it is easy to believe the quality and the quantity of news we receive is acceptable. We should not be misled. Much of the news we see is of a high quality. But it is not enough. Most people now get most of their political information from paid advertising, not from the news. (An exception is during national elections, when the press corps rises to the one race in which their reporting can shape a contest—at least in the early stages before the advertising is placed, or during the primaries where the advertising is placed in only in primary states.)

Bill Moyers got it right when he said those involved in alternative media need to expand their reach. "We have to raise an even bigger tent than you have here. Those of us in this place speak a common language about the 'media.' We must reach the audience that's not here—carry the fight to radio talk shows, local television, and the letters columns of our newspapers . . . We must fight to expand a noncommercial media system—something made possible in part by the new digital spectrum awarded to PBS stations—and fight off attempts to privatize what's left of public broadcasting. Commercial speech must not be the only free speech in America," he said.

Today's journalism does not present a transparent window onto the world. Reality is bent as it is mediated, like sunlight through water. When you reach for the truth it turns out to be somewhere else. Skilled marketers, advertisers, and public relations professionals know how to take advantage of this parallax view. They fill our ears and eyes with apparently corroborative testimony. When President Bush told Americans that Saddam Hussein and Osama Bin Laden were connected, a majority of Americans believed it. But, research shows, Fox News viewers tended to believe it in greater numbers than those who turned elsewhere for their news. This is because the corroborative testimony—slanted as it might be—was so much more powerful on Fox, which, of course, is what Fox News wanted. The point here is not to slam Fox once again. Rather, the point is that it is a perfect example of how deception rides at the center of our political practices.

Rupert Murdoch and Roger Ailes will not change their ways. But we can change ours.

5

THE THREATENED HABITATS
OF DEMOCRACY

*Men who look upon themselves born to reign, and others to obey,
soon grow insolent; selected from the rest of mankind their minds
are early poisoned by importance; and the world they act in dif-
fers so materially from the world at large, that they have but little
opportunity of knowing its true interests, and when they succeed
to the government are frequently the most ignorant and unfit of
any throughout the dominions.*

Thomas Paine
Common Sense

T
he most underreported political scandal in America today is
the systematic effort of some in the Republican party to suppress the vote of those whom they believe—with probable
cause—will vote against them. Their efforts are aimed primarily at
minorities and the poor. The perpetrators betray the spirit of democracy and the intentions of the Founding Fathers. By their actions
they make it plain that their own interests, the interests of the privileged class, take precedence over the health of the Republic. Tactics
are employed every election cycle (and even between election cycles)
that are aimed at scaring the poor away from the polls, illegally strip-

ping them from voting rolls, or just denying them the opportunity to cast ballots by turning them away once they reach the polls. Those in charge deny their complicity and condemn the practices. But the damage is always already done before the condemnations come.

Back in 1993, Webster Todd, brother and former campaign manager of then governor-elect Christine Todd Whitman (President Bush's first Environmental Protection Agency director), described the campaign's strategy this way: "That is where a lot of our effort went and a lot of our planning, getting out the vote on one side and voter sup—and keeping the vote light in other areas." *Time* magazine printed the quote, noting that he spoke "almost using the term voter suppression." Following this same New Jersey gubernatorial election, Christine Todd Whitman's top strategist, GOP consultant Ed Rollins, created quite a controversy when he told a group of reporters that he had bribed the ministers of African-American churches to stay home and "sit and watch television" rather than urge their parishioners to vote, according to *U.S. News & World Report* (now simply *U.S. News*). Most of the preachers' followers, of course, were expected to vote for incumbent Democratic Governor Jim Florio. Later, under investigation by the United States Department of Justice at the urging of outraged Democrats, Rollins said he had made up the tale.

Nobody made up the stories involving Florida in the 2000 election. Thousands of African-American voters were effectively disenfranchised. Many innocent citizens were incorrectly purged from voter rolls by a contractor hired by then Secretary of State Katherine Harris to purge convicted felons. Other irregularities were well noted: Would-be voters were intimidated and threatened with arrest.

As we will see, there are less overt ways in which votes can be suppressed, and Democrats are not completely guiltless. Negative campaigns can and do have an effect on an opposing candidate's base voters. It is a commonplace political strategy to try to confuse and demoralize an opponent's most likely supporters. Such citizens are less likely to go to the polls. But Democrats (at least since so many Southern conservatives became Republicans) do not commonly engage in voter intimidation. It is generally true that the higher the turnout in an election, the better a Democratic candidate will do. So Democrats typically spend more time and money trying to coax their supporters to the polls than they do trying to keep Republican voters at home. Later we will catalog some well-known incidents of voter suppression, measure their impact on our already beleaguered civil society, and look at intriguing new studies that illuminate ways voter participation can be greatly enhanced. Among these are the recognition that citizens tend to participate in politics when they can engage in meaningful political conversations with friends, family, or neighbors. To some degree, nonvoters have been "ghetto-ized." They live and work in areas where political information is not readily available, especially in important face-to-face encounters with others in the community.

Given the short-term tactical needs of contemporary political campaigns, it is not likely that long-term solutions will be financed or undertaken by political candidates. They have too much to get done in too short a time. As we have sadly seen, even the health of our democracy is sacrificed by some who put winning political power above the interests of voters. There is no other explanation for voter-intimidation campaigns. When so many people demonstrate by their actions nothing but contempt for the very habitats of democracy— what we might call the pathways of proximity that assist us in the sharing of political information that ultimately determine our voting behavior—what hope can we have that these same people will do anything to protect those habitats from destruction?

Democracies depend upon free and open elections in which all eligible voters are granted unfettered access to the ballot box. In fact, it can be argued that a system of government that allows parties or individuals to illegally block others from voting is not a democracy at all. Here, the politics of deceit are unambiguous.

Why the GOP Suppresses the Vote

But first, let us explore the question of why Republicans would engage in voter-suppression tactics. Yes, they do so in part because they want to win. If their Democratic opponent's supporters do not go to the polls, their chances of success are much greater. In fact, Republican pollster Bill McInturff sums it up nicely in a John Nichols piece in *The Progressive*. "Politics is about two things: Mobilizing your voters, and not mobilizing the other side. Both are valid goals," he said. Valid perhaps, but antidemocratic and disgraceful as well. Maybe, however, the motivation is not so simple. A study published in 2003 by the *Journal of Public Economics* provides a deeper and more disturbing answer. The study, by Dennis C. Mueller and Thomas Stratmann, found in a worldwide study of 38 democracies (classified as weak or strong democracies) that increased voter turnout is associated with more equal distributions of income. "Citizen participation has a direct negative impact on income inequality," the study said bluntly. When turnout climbs, income is distributed more fairly. When it falls, the rich get richer and the poor get poorer, as the saying goes. This is a strong incentive for the party of privilege to strategically suppress voter turnout.

The study also found a relationship between the size of government and voter participation. The more people vote, the more equitable individual income, the larger the government. The study does not speculate on the reasons for this, although one reason is that it takes effort to build a nation on the principles of social justice. I do not believe this is due to a law of economics. I think it is instead due to historical inequities that cost more to eliminate than to create or maintain. The study also found, however, that "increasing participation by the poor and uneducated actually improved the outcomes of the political process as measured by economic growth." In other words, national economies performed better when more citizens participated in the process. This would appear to alleviate the concerns of nineteenth-century philosopher John Stuart Mill, among others, who worried that poor decisions would result from the participation of unlanded, poorly educated citizens. Slower economic growth was a factor of the size of government, not greater voter participation.

And before conservatives shout, "I told you so," we should examine another disturbing trend that the study uncovered when the same 38 countries were divided into subgroups of strong democracies (where direct links between voter preferences and government policies were demonstrable) and weak democracies (where such links were not as clear). In the weak democracies of Latin America, as measured by the reduced sensitivity of government policy to voter decisions, leaders found ways of growing the size of government without reducing income inequality. "This result supports the prediction that government serves the interests of the upper classes in countries with weak democratic institutions, at least in Latin and Central America," the study said.

It should be the case that in places where voter participation is high and governments have grown, income inequality was reduced. But this is not always true. "In the weak democratic, Latin American countries, however, the indirect impact [of increased voter participation on income inequality] is positive." This means that economic disparity increases as government grows. "Participation increases government size and (weakly) government transfers, but both of these lead to greater income inequality," the study said. The authors say the results support the arguments of earlier studies that show how the privileged classes are able to capture the government "and bend its policies to advance their interests at the expense of the larger electorate. The privileged classes govern both the private sector and the public sector, and use the latter to maintain and enhance their economic status," wrote Mueller and Stratmann. Bush's huge increases in government spending, combined with tax cuts for the wealthy, begin to look suspiciously like the economic model of the weak democracies of Latin America.

Remember that a weak democracy is defined as one with a reduced correlation between government policies and voter preferences. In the United States, much public opinion polling shows widespread support for the economic policies of Democrats, with substantially less support for those of Republicans. As pollster Stanley Greenberg said, even after the Republican sweep of 1994, most Americans preferred Clinton's economic policies to Reagan's, and President Bush is receiving generally low marks for his handling of the economy. In this instance, we do resemble the weak democracies Mueller and Stratmann studied. Such democracies are vulnerable to looting by the privileged classes. After such a capture is complete—and it is far from complete here—it might no longer matter to the privileged whether or not the less-privileged go to the polls. Typically, such a circumstance evolves when a single party dominates to the extent that opposition party or parties are reduced to token status. Because the choices of voters are effectively eliminated in such a scenario, it does not matter whether citizens vote or not. The privileged can even call for mandatory voting and grant the franchise to everyone. Voter suppression is no longer necessary.

1934: Voter Intimidation Matures

In the United States, when the privileged believe voter suppression is necessary, they do not hesitate to take up arms (sometimes literally) and get it done. In the 1934 California campaign of Upton Sinclair against incumbent Republic Governor Frank Merriam, we find the Republicans hatching one of the most sophisticated voter intimidation schemes undertaken up to that time. Albert Parker, a member of one of Los Angeles's most prestigious law firms, had been made secretary of United for California, a front group formed to undo Sinclair. As told by Greg Mitchell in his history of that year's California election, Parker believed Sinclair's supporters had secured some illegal voter registrants to support his insurgent effort. Parker remembered a successful voter purge scheme that had happened some years before in New York. He wired a friend and asked him to get in touch with the former U.S. prosecutor who pulled it off.

The friend, Eli Whitney Debevoise, went right to work. But the former prosecutor, George Medalie, reported that while voting illegally might be a federal crime, fraudulent registration was not. However, Debevoise relayed the message that the accusation of fraudulent registration could be used in a public relations campaign that would intimidate voters, even legally registered voters. The plan included drawing up two lists of allegedly illegal registrants. One would be made public. The other would be sealed and given to a cooperative district attorney. No one would know whose name was on that list, and any Democrats might worry that if they showed up to vote they would be hauled off to jail. Medalie's successor, Thomas E. Dewey, future Republican presidential candidate, also weighed in with the advice to make sure the FBI cooperated and the Justice Department appointed deputy U.S. marshals to appear at the polls.

On October 15, United for California announced that it had turned over the names of 20,000 illegal registrants to authorities and had evidence that another 200,000 Democrats—15 percent of the party's registration—were illegally registered. The *Los Angeles Times* cooperated with Parker's intimidation scheme, writing on the front page that "it would be far better for a few honest persons to lose their votes than for a hundred thousand rogues to defeat by fraud the majority will of the people." But on the first day of court in the lawsuit challenging the supposedly illegal registrants, only seven of the named "illegal registrants" showed up. All were legal voters. Undeterred, United for California filed a second lawsuit, accusing an additional 33,000 of illegally registering.

Before long the intimidation campaign ran into a little trouble, though not before successfully informing would-be voters to beware. Two assistant court administrators resigned in protest. Sinclair supporters challenged the scheme at the state's highest court. The court brought the would-be voter purge to a halt on October 31. But publicity is all Parker and his fellow schemers wanted—and they got it. There is no telling how many Californians refrained from going to the polls out of fear they would wind up in legal trouble. The presence of so many policemen and marshals on election day did not help matters. But this is the way of well-orchestrated voter-intimidation efforts. However ham-fisted and ill-conceived they may seem, the message gets through to unsuspecting citizens who are unsure of their rights. Publicity is not what New Yorker Eli Whitney Debevoise, who delivered strategic advice on the plan to his friend in California, wanted—at least publicity about voter intimidation and suppression. He was shamed by news coverage of his involvement, and he replied swiftly to newspaper accounts of his culpability. He said only voters who know their registrations are illegal "could be intimidated by secret indictments."

So it was with some sense of familial symmetry that in 1982 another Debevoise, U.S. District Judge Dickinson R. Debevoise, signed an order prohibiting the Republican National Committee (RNC) from engaging in voter intimidation or voter suppression campaigns. Judge Debevoise, a distant cousin of Eli's, was cofounder of the prestigious international law firm Debevoise & Plimpton. The firm, according to Hoover's directory, now represents the Democratic National Committee (DNC), which obtained the order against the RNC from Judge Debevoise in 1982. This is just to point out that prominent players are involved in voter-suppression campaigns as advocates or opponents. Efforts to intimidate voters are not limited to fringe elements.

Judge Debevoise's ruling came in a lawsuit filed in 1981 against the Republican National Committee by the Democratic National Committee. The suit sought to end Republican "ballot security" initiatives that were really designed to scare citizens from the polls. The issue was raised in the 1981 New Jersey gubernatorial race between Democrat James Florio and Republican Thomas Kean. Florio lost, and Democrats charged that the GOP had conducted a well-orchestrated campaign to intimidate minority voters. The GOP "Ballot Security Task Force" sent letters to minority citizens. When the letters were returned for bad addresses, the task force claimed the citizens' voting privileges should be challenged because they no longer lived at the address listed on the voter rolls. The group sent the election supervisors a list of 45,000 suspect names.

On election day, the group posted large signs in polling places. Printed in red ink, they said: "Warning. This area is being patrolled by the National Ballot Security Task Force. It is a crime to falsify a ballot or to violate election laws." Off-duty deputy sheriffs and police officers—wearing pistols on their hips—were hired to patrol targeted African-American and Hispanic polling places. Debevoise's order blocked the RNC from conducting such campaigns of intimidation on a national level. The Republicans signed the order saying they would refrain in the future. But once again, the damage had been done. As in California in 1934, the publicity surrounding controversial intimidation efforts is essential to their effectiveness. Promising not to do it again only generates another story in the press that tells vulnerable minority voters that they had better watch out. And the promises are never kept.

The year that Debevoise ruled, Republicans in Texas launched a similar effort that echoed past outrages and eerily foreshadowed the Florida election controversies of 2002. In 1982, the Texas secretary of state, David Dean, acting as the state's chief election officer, distributed to local officials a list of 29,000 alleged convicted felons who should be struck from voter registration rolls. Unfortunately for Dean, the list contained the name of a Democrat running for the state legislature at the time. He was forced to recall this list, but not until after the signal was sent to would-be voters that law enforcement was breathing down their necks. The strategy behind such a list is not just to keep guilty felons from voting. It is to tell minority citizens that law enforcement is carefully monitoring their behavior. Showing up at the polls, in other words, could put them at risk, whether they are law-abiding citizens or not.

Texas Republicans did not stop there. Signs were posted at minority voting places that read, "YOU CAN BE IMPRISONED." The signs said they had been posted on the orders of local law enforcement, but they were actually posted by Republican election workers. So much for keeping their promise to Debevoise. The list of felons and the intimidating signs resulted in legal actions in which everybody promised to stop their bad behavior. The interesting thing about the 1982 contest was the name of the incumbent Republican's consultant: Karl Rove, the same Karl Rove who led President Bush's 2000 campaign, the same campaign that resulted in the notorious Florida voter purge involving alleged felons.

Rove's history of dirty political tricks has been well documented elsewhere. But the Florida 2000 controversy raised awareness of voter intimidation efforts. All the classic intimidation tactics were employed: The inaccurate list of felons purged at least 1,000 law-abiding African-American citizens from voter registration rolls, costing them their right to vote. Minority citizens were stopped and questioned at police checkpoints established near polling places, and citizens were challenged at the polls and not allowed to vote.

The contempt for democracy demonstrated by partisans who think nothing of violating their fellow-citizens' right to vote is staggering. Not only are election outcomes potentially altered, the health of civil society itself is threatened. It betrays a lack of trust in democratic outcomes. "We know best," backers of these illicit and illegal campaigns say to themselves. "And so to the end that our judgment will prevail, we must silence the voices of those who disagree with us." But democracies are viable only to the extent that citizens' voices are not silenced. And there is every sign that Republicans will continue to employ minority voter-suppression tactics. In 2002, John Ashcroft's Justice Department announced a "Voting Integrity Initiative" to deal with voter fraud. Peddled as a program to reduce fraud, the initiative immediately undertook an investigation targeting Native Americans in South Dakota. Similar suppression techniques were discovered in Arkansas, South Carolina, and elsewhere. To make matters worse, a section of the Help America Vote Act passed by Congress in 2002 contains a section requiring citizens to produce a picture identification card at the polling places if they registered to vote by mail and had not voted at their current location before. A 1994 Louisiana study showed that African-Americans were five times less likely to have a photo ID than whites.

Voter suppression is both a cause and a symptom of our collapsing public sphere. Many recent studies have shown declines in civic involvement, from participation in elections to membership in voluntary clubs. "The great civic transformation of our time has diminished America's democracy, leaving gaping holes in the fabric of our social and political life," wrote Theda Skocpol, director of the Center for American Political Studies at Harvard University. She added, "The civic past cannot be revived, of course... Nevertheless, critical aspects of the classic civic America we have lost need to be reinvented—including shared democratic values, a measure of fellowship across class lines, and opportunities for the many to participate in organized endeavors alongside the elite few."

The Marginalized Electorate

Authors Matthew A. Crenson and Benjamin Ginsberg believe the public has been all but eliminated from meaningful collective participation in our nation's political life. According to them, "... contemporary political elites have substantially marginalized the American mass electorate and have come to rely more and more on the courts and the bureaucracy to get what they want. We call this pattern 'personal democracy' to distinguish it from popular democracy, a way of doing business that required elites to mobilize nonelites in order to prevail in the political arena. It is personal because the new techniques of governing disaggregate the public into a collection of private citizens. Their experience of democracy is increasingly personal rather than collective." Having lost healthy avenues of communication among our fellow citizens, we become individual consumers of political goods rather than social producers of political outcomes.

This is even reflected in the way we talk about government and politics. Crenson and Ginsberg point to the Report of the National Performance Review of government overseen in the early 1990s by then Vice President Al Gore. Gore described the review as an effort "to make the federal government customer friendly." That sounds like Walt Disney, who wanted Disneyland to be known as the "happiest place on earth." This may be a worthy goal for an amusement park. It might also be nice if the government treated its citizens with respect. But the government does not have customers. It has constituents. We are not supposed to consume political products. Citizens are supposed to be producers in the public sphere. Stripped of avenues for discussing political, social, or economic concerns with one another, we are left to satisfy private desires without regard to the greater social and political context from which we expect those satisfactions to emerge. Political practices intended to drive people from the public sphere, practices like voter-intimidation campaigns, are just the egregious examples of the many ways in which citizens are driven to retreat from civic participation.

There has been considerable discussion in recent years about the diminished quality of our shared life. There are many specific culprits: the availability of television in the home, the widening gap between rich and poor, the decline in voluntary civic associations at the local and national levels. Confining our gaze for the moment to political engagement, we can see in the decline of national political parties a symptom of a broader and deeper pathology. National political parties served as voluntary associations in which millions of Americans could participate in negotiating approaches to public policy. Often they became dominated by one privileged interest or another. Political bosses created factions within parties in which they could advance their own goals while continuing to participate in larger national debates. Two waves of reform—1900 to 1920 and 1960 to 1980—combined with other cultural forces to greatly diminish the participatory nature of political parties, the opposite of their purported intent. The reforms, especially Democratic Party reforms, were intended to open the back rooms to underrepresented constituents, breaking the hold of political bosses. Well intended, the reforms contributed to the rise of media politics. Political convention halls were transformed into television studios. Delegates became extras, well-coached and scripted to present a party's message to the national media audience.

Like so much in contemporary politics, the conventions are made to look like the political conventions of old. Delegates still wear funny hats. The halls erupt into raucous demonstrations from time to time. But the unexpected seldom happens. Since 1968, when coverage of the Democratic National Convention in Chicago was dominated by violent confrontations between Mayor Richard Daley's police and antiwar demonstrators, political parties have worked hard to protect their televised celebrations from untidy conflicts that will weaken the carefully planned convention imagery. Parties have become professional organizations rather than voluntary associations. In most elections today, parties are irrelevant except as labels for candidates and funnels for money.

Television pressured candidates to put their money into advertising rather than the organization. The primary selection process for candidates relied more on media and less on associations by and among party members. So primaries now are like elimination tournaments in sports. Citizens around the country sit at home and watch the performances of candidates in faraway states. Color commentators explain the proceedings, pointing out the strengths and weaknesses of the performers. It happens at a distance. Of course, citizens in each primary state do participate. There is an air of old-time politics surrounding the Iowa caucuses, for example. They are designed to create conversations and negotiations among citizens who attend the caucuses, which are organized around small voting precincts. For instance, if a candidate fails to receive the minimum 15 percent support at a caucus, supporters can decide to compromise with supporters of another candidate. The negotiations do not involve real give-and-take about policy or campaign platform, however. In Iowa in 2004, Dick Gephardt's supporters joined John Kerry's supporters when it became obvious that Gephardt would do poorly. But no concessions from Kerry supporters on behalf of their candidate could be negotiated. The caucus attendees are not empowered to do so. Nonetheless, the Iowa caucuses do give us a glimpse of old-style political engagement.

Voting participation in American elections has declined as the opportunities for citizens to engage in political conversations with one another have declined. "The nineteenth-century pattern of mass mobilization has little in common with the conduct of American politics today," wrote Crensen and Ginsberg. "For the last generation, voter turnout in the United States has averaged slightly more than 50 percent in presidential contests." But, the authors point out, that average disguises a more disturbing trend: The affluent continue to vote at nineteenth-century levels, with about 80 percent of eligible affluent voters participating. But among the poor and those who are not as highly educated, turnout has sunk to about 30 percent. Sixty million Americans entitled to vote fail to do so, Crensen and Ginsberg reported. And the authors wonder why candidates and parties continue to ignore this vast pool of potential supporters. "The vast sums spent on holding the loyalties of current voters have failed to give either party a decisive political edge," they wrote. "Divided government and political stalemate seem more acceptable to party elites than an effort to shift the political balance by activating the politically inert."

Disappearing Voters

Matthew Dowd, now a Republican strategist for President Bush, used to work for Democrats. Each election he would present convincing evidence to Democratic candidates that money spent on bringing new voters to the polls would be wasted. He was not the only political consultant to offer this advice. In fact, most professionals shared the belief that no matter the resources devoted to the effort, turnout was determined by historical patterns that followed cultural trends so complex that short-term efforts at engaging new voters in a particular election were bound to fail. Money is usually spent communicating with voters who have previously participated. Those who have not participated fall through the cracks. It is a vicious cycle. They need information to become involved, but they are denied the information because they have not been involved. Recently there have been some modest successes in increasing the turnout among reluctant voters.

In Texas, however, the midterm elections of 2002 proved that the conventional wisdom held, but not because of historical forces that are impossible to overcome. It held because of the difficulty in engaging a substantial number of voters in meaningful and beneficial political conversations, person-to-person. That year, Laredo businessman Tony Sanchez was the Democratic gubernatorial nominee. Demographic changes in Texas made it clear that even modest increases in turnout among Hispanics—who traditionally vote Democratic—could return a Democrat to the governor's mansion. In fact, part of Sanchez's motivation for entering the race—he had never before been a candidate—was to try to get new people involved in elections. To do so would bring benefits to Texas that would last beyond the life of his possible administration. And even if he failed to win, the recruitment of hundreds of thousands of Texans into the state's political life would be an accomplishment. So significant resources were devoted to the effort. Young people were employed to knock on doors in less affluent neighborhoods throughout the state. Sophisticated technology was used to track these contacts with voters. Millions of phone calls and pieces of direct mail were directed to registered voters who had not previously taken advantage of their eligibility. In the end, turnout ticked up slightly, but not enough.

But I do not believe that forces beyond our control make it impossible to involve new voters in elections. I think we are going about the effort the wrong way. Additionally, some of our political practices actually discourage participation, as we saw with the discussion of voter-suppression campaigns. We should remember that in most elections, incumbent elected officials play significant roles in a campaign cycle, even a cycle in which they may not be on the ballot. It is estimated that several decades of gerrymandering have left only a handful of congressional districts—no more than 25!—open to competitive challenges. Now, incumbents have obviously already garnered enough supporters to win elections. What motivation do they really have to spend time and money getting new, unpredictable voters to the polls? Yet, in many jurisdictions these same incumbents—or their supporters or consultants—will play a significant part in get-out-the-vote campaigns. Consequently, most of the resources are devoted to citizens with proven voting histories.

"Democratic mobilization becomes the norm when would-be leaders can achieve power and influence only by drawing others into movements, associations, and political battles," wrote Theda Skocpol. "Elites must have incentives to organize others, if democratic mobilization is to happen regularly. Such incentives were certainly in place in earlier eras of U.S. history—when party politicians could win elected office only in close-fought, high-turnout elections and when association builders could attain national influence only by spreading networks of chapters of dues-paying members all across America." There are few incentives for politicians to organize the currently uninvolved. And often, when there are incentives, essential elements of successful movement-building are missing.

The lesson of the 2002 campaign of Tony Sanchez in Texas—a campaign that I managed and one in which we had incentive to reach out to new voters—was that many eligible voters who had not participated in past elections seemed immune to traditional political communications. Advertising, direct mail, telephone calls, and canvasses were not enough to change their voting behavior. Certainly, other elements played a part in suppressing this vote. The incumbent governor, Republican Rick Perry, spent substantial sums attacking Sanchez in advertising. Negative advertising has long been known to depress voter turnout, even among citizens committed to supporting the candidate under attack. This happened in Texas, and many who may have been tempted to cast their ballot for the first time were left unsure about their candidate. That uncertainty was enough to keep them home.

One reason for this can be found in an analysis by political scientist Gani Aldashev, who asks why citizens acquire political information instead of why voters participate in elections. It turns out that voting is a function of information acquisition by citizens. The higher the quality of information they possess, the more they are inclined to participate. So how do we enhance their ability to receive relevant information? Aldashev's answer: Citizens get their most important information in conversation with people they know, person-to-person, in social exchanges in which both participants recognize the benefits of exchange. In other words, while some critical information is obtained from the one-way communications of political campaigns, this information is less important to [previously unregistered voters in] a decision to vote than meaningful exchanges of information with one's neighbors, coworkers, friends, or peers.

Aldashev tested five predictions: "Citizens acquire more political information when the elections appear salient to them; they acquire more information if they get higher benefit from social exchange, or political conversations; they acquire less information if the cost of getting informed is higher; citizens from the same social neighborhood acquire similar amounts of political information; informed citizens vote more readily." Most campaigns try to make the stakes of the upcoming election important to voters. But insufficient attention is given to Aldashev's other predictions. Voter participation will increase if and when citizens are able to acquire valuable political information from friends, family, coworkers, or others in their communities. Preparing the ground for such increases in information exchange could be costly in time and money. On the other hand, the returns increase exponentially.

All of these predictions were confirmed by a study of 3,000 individuals over several weeks following the general elections in the United Kingdom on June 7, 2001. Aldashev said his main empirical finding was that people living in a neighborhood of politically informed citizens were more inclined to participate in an election than those who were not.

Social exchanges are simply conversations between two people. Political conversations take place more frequently when new or confirming information is given or obtained and when the psychological risks and commitment of time is low. According to Aldashev, acquisition of political information depends upon mutually reinforcing behavior. That is, we risk political conversation with those whom we believe are better informed, and they are more likely to reciprocate when they believe we are informed.

To sum up, citizens participate more readily in democratic elections when they are able to give and receive information from their friends and neighbors. One can imagine a kind of tipping point where social relations reach such a level that the benefits of political conversation are apparent to all. The more information is obtained, the more people vote. But contemporary political campaigns (especially Democratic campaigns) ignore the critical nature of social exchange. It is odd that professionals in the political community make this error, because they themselves live in a "neighborhood" that perfectly exemplifies Aldashev's analysis. They call their own social exchanges with colleagues and neighbors "buzz." It is easy for them to receive social benefit from conversational encounters because they are certain in advance that their interlocutors also have relevant information.

Increasing Political Participation

Campaigns and candidates would greatly increase their chances of getting new or infrequent voters to the polls if they would pay attention to the importance of person-to-person communications. It is much easier to follow Adam Smith's advice and make our communications maximally usable to our listeners in face-to-face encounters. One reason personal conversations are so effective for delivering information is that listeners, to different degrees, can resist messages from conversational partners. In fact, many who study the evolution of language believe that the spoken word itself evolved in relation to our capacity to distinguish true or false representations. So we can see a significant qualitative difference between one-way communications such as television advertising and conversations with our neighbors.

Looking again at some of Aldashev's findings, we discover that people who trust others are better informed on political issues. Citizens involved in voluntary organizations and citizens who own their own homes are also better informed. We see this reflected in the dramatically different voting patterns of the affluent, who tend to vote much more regularly, and the poor, whose participation in elections is on a steady decline. One of Aldashev's most interesting findings is that religious people are much more likely to vote than nonreligious people.

If we glance at Aldashev's predictions we begin to see that Republicans have had a much more fertile field of potential voters than Democrats. The findings virtually describe the suburban Republican voter, a voter who owns her own home, is more economically secure and so can afford to trust those that surround her, has available leisure time for volunteer activities, and is religious. In contrast, the middle class and the poor are less secure in their jobs and are likely to move more often, making lines of trust with neighbors difficult to establish. They have little time for volunteer activity since, typically, both spouses work. One common thread, however, is religion. By recognizing the importance of religious belief to voting behavior, Republicans have been able to reach middle and lower class voters who might otherwise not be available to them. (This is greatly simplified. Republicans' more skillful use of the language of values is also key in this regard, as is the emotionally charged issue of race.) But in spite of Republican economic policies directed to benefiting the wealthy, substantial numbers of less affluent Americans set their own economic interests aside and support Republican candidates. By recognizing that churches are among the remaining few places where people gather in voluntary association and where the benefits of social exchange are high, Republicans have paid special attention to cultivating political conversations within places of worship.

Before anyone jumps to the conclusion that the more affluent are simply better citizens because they vote more often, we should recall the dramatic steps taken by many politically involved and affluent Republicans to frighten their opponents from the polls. And we should remember how Republicans generally oppose policies that would promote trust among citizens (Attorney General John Ashcroft talks of new law enforcement programs that would have us all informing on each other), increase job security, provide more leisure time for the less wealthy, increase educational opportunity for all, and renew our older neighborhoods. Republicans benefit from the status quo.

There is also evidence here about why negative advertising seems generally more effective when used by Republicans against Democrats than when used by Democrats against Republicans.

Economic, social, and cultural conditions are such that Republican supporters are able to establish more resilient networks of social exchange. Aldashev makes the point that a speaker's certainty about a political view contributes to her decision about whether to risk political conversations with others. Negative attacks, like those mounted against Tony Sanchez in Texas, raise doubts among would-be supporters, and so they are less likely to risk voicing their opinions in conversation. This lowers the information content available to the neighborhood, and in a kind of downward spiral, large segments of a population can become disinclined to vote. On the other hand, Republicans have invested time and resources in developing avenues for ongoing social exchange among supporters. Therefore, when a negative attack is launched on a Republican candidate there is an available network of support to bolster the certainty and self-confidence of those who otherwise may have felt doubt about their opinion due to the negative information of the attack.

Why, then, was former president Bill Clinton able to maintain his popularity while under constant character attacks from his opponents? First, the observation that negative advertising is of greater benefit to Republicans is a generalization that has many exceptions. But in the case of Clinton, it might be suggested that the personal attacks on Clinton were of such a nature that few people were discouraged from speaking to their friends and neighbors about them. In a sense, the attacks generated more conversation, not less. Most people were certain that Clinton had engaged in sex with Monica Lewinski. There was no uncertainty about it. Furthermore, there was no obvious connection between this behavior and Clinton's job performance. (It helped him immeasurably that the economy was strong. The situation would have been much worse for Clinton if the gossip was, "He's playing around while we don't even have jobs.") Despite the attacks, doubt and uncertainty were at a minimum; people were not afraid to risk social exchanges with regard to Clinton. What uncertainty there was tended to revolve around the extreme partisan reaction of Republicans in Congress. Liberals wondered, "Why impeachment over this?"

We have already seen how many cultural and political trends of the last century have been socially fragmenting, isolating us from one another, facilitating a retreat into more private, personal concerns. Understanding that our immediate social bonds play a significant role in our voting behavior, it is understandable that voter turnout has declined. The less we talk politics with one another, the less likely we are to vote. Our political practices, however, contribute to the social isolation that diminishes political participation. In a typical campaign, most resources will be targeted to "likely voters." Most advertising is aimed at a broad audience, and so the unique concerns of different socioeconomic groups, different neighborhoods, and different ethnic and racial backgrounds are smothered by more general messaging. Communication venues that can address more local concerns—radio, direct mail, telephone calls, and canvasses—take a back seat to television advertising. In addition, they are targeted to likely voters as well. Pollsters concentrate on collecting and measuring the opinions of people who have voted previously.

It will be up to political parties and other organizations to find ways of promoting neighbor-to-neighbor political discussion. The question is: Can such endeavors catch up to and overcome the continuing deterioration of our civic life? For just as we are looking for ways to revitalize the public sphere, there are forces at work that are difficult to overcome. For instance, the flurry of mergers and acquisitions of media companies that followed the passage of the U.S. Telecommunications Act of 1996 is having just such an impact. A recent study demonstrates the consequences of media consolidation on African-American communities throughout the United States, consequences that tend to drive down voter participation.

New Obstacles to Participation

In comments filed with the Federal Communications Commission on January 2, 2003, the National Association of Black Owned Broadcasters, Inc. (NABOB) and the Rainbow/Push Coalition, Inc., said that the number of minority-owned broadcast facilities declined

14 percent since passage of the Telecommunications Act seven years earlier. According to NABOB's director, Jim Winston, by the end of 2003 that number had grown to 20 percent. The Act relaxed limits on the number of media outlets that could be owned by a single company. The minority broadcasters group cited the FCC's own "Diversity of Programming Study" that revealed "empirical evidence of a link between race or ethnicity of broadcast station owners and contribution to diversity of news and public affairs programming across the broadcast spectrum."

This conclusion is supported by a recent study, "The Effect of Minority Population on Minority Voter Turnout," written for the National Bureau of Economic Research by Felix Oberholzer-Gee and Joel Waldfogel. They found that African-American–owned stations targeted to African-American audiences had a significant positive impact on turnout. But when stations targeted to African-American audiences were owned by whites, there was no such impact. The authors also confirm their theory of electoral acceleration, a term they use to describe cascading increases in political participation. As more like-minded individuals move into a neighborhood, for instance, voter turnout increases. This also squares with research showing the positive impact of person-to-person social exchanges on voter turnout.

But the structure of media markets also has an effect on electoral acceleration. Using data collected from before and after passage of the Telecommunications Act, the researchers found that as the number of African-American–owned stations decreased, voter participation decreased. "As the size of a group increases, members of this group can enjoy a larger number of media products that are specifically tailored to their tastes," the authors wrote. "The existence of these channels of communication make it easier for candidates to target campaign efforts at the group, thereby lowering the costs of learning about the candidates' positions and thus increasing the likelihood of participation."

NABOB's Jim Winston said that Clear Channel Communications, far and away the largest owner of radio stations (it owns 1,200; its closet competitor, 300) now brags that it is the largest broadcaster to an African-American audience. He said the effects of Clear Channel's buying spree depend on the market. In some markets Clear Channel switched an acquired station's format from African-American–oriented programming to country music. In other markets, Clear Channel might buy a country station and convert it to African-American programming. The new Clear Channel station would then drive African-American owners of the competing stations out of business, replacing community-oriented programming with Clear Channel's canned approach.These findings make it clear that campaign communications delivered through the media do make a difference in the amount of information that is available to voters. However, this information becomes much more valuable—as proven by increases in voter turnout—when there are closer ties among members of a community. These ties are easier to achieve as the numbers of a minority increase in any particular neighborhood. In such a circumstance trust increases among neighbors, the cost of information acquisition goes down; as more neighbors become informed voter participation increases exponentially. When less information is delivered to these communities (because of shrinking minority ownership of local radio, for instance), voter participation is diminished.

Complex socioeconomic forces play a significant role in determining levels of voter interest and participation. Media moguls are not buying up African-American radio stations in order to suppress voter turnout in those markets. They buy them because it allows them to control a greater share of the media marketplace. In other words, it has to do with their bottom line. The pursuit of their own financial interests does impact voter turnout.

In many ways we are engaged in class conflict. If only half of all registered voters continue to participate (one third of eligible voters) in presidential elections, as has been the case in recent decades, there will be more economic disparity in our future. The rich will continue to get richer and the poor will get poorer. Sweeping economic and cultural developments continue to erode our bonds with one another. We spend less time talking with neighbors. We spend more time watching television or engaging in other private pursuits. We work longer hours to make ends meet. As these bonds disappear, so does our ability to collect relevant information about candidates and issues. When we discuss these issues with one another less frequently, we slowly disengage from the political process. The process is self-reinforcing. The more that control over policy is limited to the very wealthy, the less likely the less fortunate among us are to raise our voices in protest at the ballot box. Of course, economic catastrophe could change this dynamic, as it did during the Great Depression. A decade of Republican dominance came to an abrupt end when the economic crisis became so acute that the self-reinforcing broke down. No progressive would wish for a return of the Great Depression. Instead, we must find ways of interrupting the cycle, realizing that in some sense we are playing catch-up.

When political professionals point to historical voting patterns and argue against campaign initiatives aimed at significantly increasing turnout, they are recognizing the huge economic, socio-logical, and psychological forces that are in play. Voter-suppression efforts help reinforce the uncertainty and self-doubt that can plague poorer communities. Such campaigns are antidemocratic, but they are also cruel class put-downs. They are a message from those who believe themselves to be more important than those who learn from their culture that their role in a democracy is insignificant. Voter intimidation of the kind we have surveyed does draw indignant chal-lenges from many. But to the members of a working family trying to make ends meet with little time to analyze the psychological damage done by such discrimination, all that is heard is their relative unim-portance. They are demoralized.

Such forces cannot be overcome with a campaign phone call, a voter registration drive, a piece of direct mail, or a radio ad. Instead, the evidence is that progressives should work to develop intra-community networks in which nonvoting citizens feel comfortable exchanging political opinions. In the Texas gubernatorial race of 2002, great effort was made at communicating with registered but nonvoting citizens. Every traditional form of campaign communication was tried. We discovered that these citizens were so alienated from political culture that traditional communication techniques simply were not enough. Now we know why. Many of these voters are young. In a turbulent economy they move frequently, following available jobs. While many are churchgoing, their transient existence interrupts their ability to form tight community bonds. Political discussion among them is rare. In addition, just the effort to stay afloat economically leaves little time for civic involvement. They work two and three jobs at a time. They are committed to their families. There is simply little time left for politics, especially when the culture seems to tell them that it really does not matter what they think or how they will vote.

Add to this bleak picture Republican efforts aimed at discouraging turnout—signs at polling places that threaten arrest, the presence of rent-a-cops wearing pistols on their hips—and it is easy to see why turnout among the poor and middle class remains low. In light of all this it is probably better to ask why turnout reaches even moderate levels rather than continue wondering why it so low. Mass media, while providing information to the electorate, also serve to distance and alienate many voters from the decision-making process. The very structure of marketing-driven political campaigns lends itself to deception, further alienating voters who begin to believe no action on their part can affect what is taking place in the new, virtual world of politics. It is also well known that gaps between election days serve to dampen enthusiasm for turnout. This is known as electoral periodicity. But the solution is not necessarily more frequent elections. The solution is year-round political engagement.

New Deal Unity and Great Society Division

The last significant increase in presidential election turnout happened during the mid- to late-1930s. "Presidential election turnout outside the South rose from less than 57 percent of eligible voters in 1928 to more than 73 percent by 1940. A large percentage of new voters were unemployed and had received some form of relief under the auspices of New Deal programs," wrote Crenson and Ginsberg. The reason? The administration of Franklin Roosevelt made it a priority to consolidate its gains by reaching out to voters—especially those who had suffered the most during the Depression. Unfortunately, the South was not included in the ambitious plans. Roosevelt and his strategists were afraid of alienating Southern white Democrats by moving aggressively to get more African-Americans to the polls. Roosevelt's efforts in the North were made much more effective by his administration's strategic organization of various New Deal initiatives. Local Democratic leaders played significant roles in delivering New Deal benefits to citizens. In other words, while citizens' economic status was improved by such programs as the Civil Works Administration and the Federal Emergency Relief Administration, they were also engaged by Democratic activists in the process. Almost overnight people found others in their community with whom they could discuss politics. As their day-to-day fight against Depression-era poverty found allies among Democrats, many of the forces that discourage political involvement were overcome. The gains, however, were short-lived.

"Though the New Deal mobilization effort was impressive, it was incomplete and temporary," wrote Crenson and Ginsberg. "The two forces upon which Roosevelt had relied, organized labor and urban political machines, both lost political potency after World War II. Labor was internally divided by struggles between radical and moderate unionists. New technologies challenged the machine's domination of the electoral process. The use of the new broadcast media permitted political candidates to run successfully for office without organization support." We lost not only the infrastructure for successful voter outreach, we lost the motivation as candidates began relying more on communicating to mass audiences rather than negotiating personally for the support of local voters through the quickly eroding local patronage systems.

The 1960s presented another opportunity for rebuilding community-centered voter education efforts, but internal squabbles among Democrats inhibited the potential electoral impact of the Voting

Rights Act of 1965, the War on Poverty, and the Civil Rights Act of 1966. To begin with, expanding the voting rights of minorities antagonized Southern Dixiecrats, the conservative white Democrats who had proved so essential to the Roosevelt coalition. Our current "Red State/Blue State" divide evolved from the antagonism of Southern whites, an antagonism strategically nurtured by two generations of Republican officeholders and strategists. The late Lee Atwater's famous "Southern Strategy," developed for Richard Nixon, successfully drove a wedge among Southern whites and minorities, including African-Americans and Hispanics. Atwater was Karl Rove's mentor, and Rove inherited the political skills of exploiting race subtly, frightening whites about rising minority voting strength while pretending, as President Bush did, to be "a uniter, not a divider."

But President Johnson's Great Society programs also divided where the New Deal had united, as Crenson and Ginsberg describe. The growing political strength of minority voters antagonized many Democratic northern bosses. Labor feared competition for jobs. Minorities and Vietnam War protesters found themselves battling traditional Democratic stalwarts like Chicago Mayor Richard Daley as much as they had to fight against conservative Republican opposition. This increased the pressure on Democrats to broaden their message to a wider audience through the mass media. Democratic coalitions fragmented, and Democrats turned more and more to competing with Republicans for that valuable species of citizen, the "swing voter." Texas can provide an illuminating portrait of the rising power of the suburban independent voter.

In 1978, the Lone Star State elected its first Republican governor since the Reconstruction era, when Bill Clements beat a popular Democratic state attorney general, John Hill. Considered a long shot when he launched his campaign, Clements used his resources wisely and successfully mobilized the rising suburban class in Texas. It was a trend not lost on Democrats, who recaptured every statewide office in 1982 with a brilliantly conceived swing voter program financed by U.S. Senator Lloyd Bentsen and Lieutenant Governor Bill Hobby; the program was designed and executed by former Bentsen aide Jack

Martin and political operative Dan McClung. Temporarily, Democrats successfully captured the imagination of the all-important swing voter. There were efforts to mobilize the traditional Democratic base as well, of course. But strategies to win among voters who might vote Democratic one year and Republican the next (hence the swing in the demographic's moniker) was paramount. It was a war the Democrats could not win in the long run.

In 1986 Clements, beaten by Democrat Mark White in the 1982 sweep, returned with a vengeance. He won his grudge match against White. Ann Richards captured the governor's mansion for Democrats in 1990. This came to pass in large part because of her appeal to both the traditional Democratic base (she had been active in the Civil Rights movement) and because her Republican opponent, political neophyte Clayton Williams, alienated more sophisticated suburban voters with his clownish, insulting behavior on the campaign trail. These were the years in which contemporary media politics triumphed in Texas, as happened throughout the nation. The result? Democratic candidates spent more and more of their resources on winning support among suburbanites, while the less fortunate, who seemed resistant to even small efforts to increase their turnout, were increasingly ignored. Also, Republicans were simply smarter about the importance of grassroots politics. While Democrats concentrated their meager efforts to build turnout among traditional Democrats, Republicans were carefully building their church-based grassroots network which afforded citizens energizing, year-round engagement in political issues.

George W. Bush defeated Ann Richards in the 1994 governor's race. Martin was the first to recognize that the younger Bush would benefit from his father's defeat at the hands of Bill Clinton in 1992. Texas voters, Martin said, felt the first president Bush had been wronged. They wanted to set it right. And by their lights they did. Campaigning as a moderate in suburban areas, Bush successfully eliminated Richards' strength among white suburban women. Voter turnout among minorities and other traditional Democrats remained poor.

The next significant challenge to Republican supremacy in Texas came in 2002, when Democrats nominated the popular Dallas mayor, Ron Kirk, for the United States Senate, and wealthy Hispanic businessman Tony Sanchez for governor. Significant resources were devoted to turning out the Democratic base. But many of these voters had been ignored for so long, turnout in their communities was just slightly better than average. Meanwhile, Republican turnout—no doubt assisted by white anxiety at the prospects of people of color representing them at the highest level—blossomed. In other words, the presence of successful, credible minorities at the top of the Democratic ticket was more effective at turning out Republican voters than it was at turning out Democratic voters.

Endangered Citizens

Today, Republicans hold every statewide office in Texas. They control the Texas House of Representatives and the Texas Senate. Such is their power that they were able to pass a new congressional redistricting plan that threatens to oust the remaining moderate Democrats—who largely represent rural Texas in the United States Congress. The Republicans have all but admitted to this long-term strategy: They want to reduce the Democratic party to the party of have-nots and become the exclusive party of the haves. Given the fact that in Texas, as throughout the country, the have-nots greatly outnumber the haves, this would appear to be a shortsighted strategy. But history has taught them that poverty and alienation from culture and politics inhibits voter participation. They are not worried about a popular revolt against economic policies that further exacerbate poverty and destroy opportunities for advancement among the state's less advantaged. In a sense, those policies are simply extensions of their notorious voter-intimidation campaigns.

The Republican assault on the habitats of democracy may have gained them a temporary advantage at the polls. But it has had devastating consequences on the health of our democracy. When a significant segment of the population is absent at the polls, political interests will be reduced to squabbling over the support of those who are voting. This explains the emergence of the Democratic Leadership Council, the moderate Democratic organization that persists in fighting for middle-of-the-road positions that will appeal primarily to white, suburban citizens. When the privileged have adopted political practices that guarantee disproportionate representation of economic and social interests at the polls, and when those practices are accepted with a shrug from journalists, we have reduced democracy to a shadow game. The great masses of America are reduced to second-class status.

Our contemporary political practices have turned America into a company store. Deceptively, the store appears like it is there to help. But small wages force workers to buy on credit. Debt keeps them bound to the coal mine. Bound to the poor wages of the coal mine, workers are forced to return to the company store and fall further into debt. "I load sixteen tons, and what do I get? Another day older and deeper in debt," sang Tennessee Ernie Ford, concluding, "I owe my soul to the company store."

In just such a vicious cycle, poverty and alienation demoralize citizens and dissociate them from their political leaders. Unable to effect political change that could help them escape their servitude, they remain effectively disenfranchised, which, in turn perpetuates the economic circumstances which political participation would help them escape. In order to get hired by the company store, even fair-minded Democrats cannot afford to alienate the store's stockholders. So they try to develop moderate policies that might give the underprivileged some hope but that the owners do not find threatening. It is an impossible task. The owners decided long ago that they were in a win-win situation. Every once in while, when it looks like some of the indebted might cause trouble, they can be reminded with signs posted in the neighborhood reading, "You could be imprisoned."

What the economically privileged forget is that all this effort at maintaining a social, economic, and political divide costs them more than it saves them, especially with regard to their own freedom. Because, as we have seen, freedom is a social concept in which the freedom of one is intimately related to the freedom of all. Sociologists and criminologists have known for decades that early childhood intervention—on health care, education, and early identification of physical or mental difficulties—can prevent future crime. The cost of this intervention is a fraction of the cost of juvenile or adult incarceration, not including the broader social, economic, and psychological costs of crime. Why, then, do we not pursue this course? Many suggest that it is because the benefits of such an approach are not immediate. In other words, gratification is delayed.

But I suggest the reason that the privileged are willing to spend more money after it is already too late to solve the problem is because they really do not view it as a problem at all. Instead, it is just another way to enforce the political order. Republican strategists are very fond of their lists of felons. And those not on the lists when they are released get the clear message that if they oppose the company line of the company store they may one day find themselves on such a list. Now, both felons and their privileged, would-be victims are forced to live in gated communities.

For those who believe this case is overstated, I submit a simple policy suggestion. If we truly do believe that all voices should be heard in a democracy, we should make it easier for everyone to vote. Election Day should be a full holiday, so employers cannot intimidate their workers into staying home. Same-day registration would also make it easier to vote. There will not be many Republican supporters of these simple ideas. But there are no good arguments against them. Economic costs would be minimal, while the benefit to democracy would be great. The only result would be an increase in voter turnout. Oppose these reforms, and you oppose that consequence.

Before this will happen, though, enough new voters will have to go the polls to elect leaders who will commit themselves to restoring democracy and revitalizing the public sphere. The next two chapters discuss strategies that might help make that happen. We will look more deeply at ways we can broaden the opportunity for political participation, including the recent rise in internet activism that made such an impact on political life in 2004.

6

LANTERN BEARING AND THE AMERICAN COVENANT TRADITION

Four or five united would be able to raise a tolerable dwelling in the midst of a wilderness, but one man might labour out the common period of life without accomplishing any thing; when he had felled his timber he could not remove it, nor erect it after it was removed; hunger in the mean time would urge him from his work, and every different want call him a different way.

Thomas Paine
Common Sense

In 1879, British novelist and poet Robert Louis Stevenson set out for San Francisco from New York. Along his journey through the American heartland, he composed essays and journal entries, subsequently published in the slender volume *Across the Plains*. Among them was "The Lantern Bearers," a reminiscence about a simple childhood custom that bound the energetic egos of adolescence into a secret society, of sorts. American psychologist and philosopher William James said the essay "deserves to become immortal, both for the truth of its matter and the excellence of its form." James included a long meditation on the "Lantern Bearers" in one of his famous lectures to educators, published as *Talks to Teachers*. It was entitled "On a Certain Blindness in Human Beings." James said his popular essay was his most cherished work, containing the essential perceptions upon which his whole philosophy was based. This is saying a good bit, as James' work has had tremendous influence on American and continental sociology, psychology, philosophy, and politics. James was moved by the story because it pointed to the way humans establish social relationships with one another.

Stevenson talks of growing up in Edinburgh, Scotland, where he and his friends would, toward the end of September, "...begin to sally from our respective villas, each equipped with a tin bull's-eye lantern." The oil-burning lanterns, common on the belts of police officers and fishermen, were worn by the boys underneath their buttoned-up topcoats. Chancing upon one another in the night, Stevenson and his friends would quietly reassure one another that they did, indeed, sport their bull's-eye lanterns beneath their coats. Theirs was a covenant of kinship, in which each was allowed the satisfaction of bearing a lantern, and all were bound by their mutual pursuit. Stevenson shows that the strength of social relationships grows from our awareness that the bonds are based on the mystery we remain to one another. The poignancy derives not from the hiding of the lanterns, but from the youths' understanding that what bound them together was concealed. And it was this covenantal bond that James celebrated.

James saw that Stevenson's childhood game revealed an essential mystery of human life. Though bound together as humans, the innermost thoughts of others remain unavailable to us. Each of us is unique, and each of us is bound to others by this unknowable uniqueness. We cannot see into the private thoughts and feelings of others. But to acknowledge this impenetrable otherness is the first step toward a future experienced together. Presuming to know the private hopes, fears, joys, and pains that lie behind the eyes of our neighbors, we are apt to project our own private universe onto their lives. Said James: Understanding the mystery "absolutely forbids us to be forward in pronouncing on the meaningless of forms of existence other than our own; and it commands us to tolerate, respect, and indulge those whom we see harmlessly interested and happy in their own ways, however unintelligible these may be to us. Hands off: Neither the whole of truth nor the whole of good is revealed to any single observer, although each observer gains a partial superiority of insight from the peculiar position in which he stands."

Jan Patočka believed this to be one of the mysteries that thrust humanity into history. Faced with the unanswerable and the problematic, evolving beyond a simple grappling with material conditions of existence, philosophy and history were born. Politics became the name for our effort to overcome this certain blindness, to find ways to negotiate our differences and discover common solutions to the difficulties faced by all. The dissolution of social mechanisms for working out our differences—and celebrating our similarities and common purposes—has contributed to the deterioration of the public sphere and made possible the ascendancy of the politics of deceit.

Here, then, is the foundation of covenants, of mutual agreements among a people living or working together, covenants that facilitate freedom, our freedom, and the freedom of those with whom we live. This is another way of explaining an essential component of freedom-to-experience. Our choices are our own, but they are carried out in the context of our responsibility to others. When that responsibility is acknowledged, our own freedom is enhanced. James's description of the brief glimpses we may be granted into the consciousness of others also points toward awakening in ourselves new possibilities: "Only in some pitiful dreamer, some philosopher, poet, or romancer, or when the common practical man becomes a lover, does the hard externality give way, and a gleam of insight into the ejective world, as Clifford called it, the vast world of inner life beyond us, so different from that of outer seeming, illuminate our mind. Then the whole scheme of our customary values gets confounded, then our self is riven and its narrow interests fly to pieces, then a new centre and a new perspective must be found." Without these moments of illumination and insight, we sink into overdetermined futures dependent solely on the past; freedom slips away, like a Scottish kid with his lantern in the night.

Alone Together

In today's world, with our social lives fragmented as we retreat more and more into private pursuits, we have few ways of participating in covenants with others. Without them, freedom-to-will triumphs, but it is a hollow victory. The fragmentation is exacerbated by our political practices, which drive us further and further apart by eliminating avenues for public discussion of our common problems and possibilities. Here is a telling statistic from Robert D. Putnam, author of *Bowling Alone*, the definitive work on our deteriorating civic life: "The last three decades of the twentieth century witnessed an accelerating trend toward more and more voter contacts but fewer and fewer party workers. By 1996 this ratio was 2.5 times greater than the equivalent figure in 1968." Instead of inviting people into political groups, we are communicating at a distance. At the same time volunteers were leaving political life, the parties experienced a boom in budgets and paid staff. Imagine the difference between hearing about Stevenson's bull's-eye lantern sport and living it. The experience, needless to say, is quite different, even though we learn something significant from reading or listening to it. But now there are no lanterns under our coats. I am sure that if a group of children today were found running around a neighborhood with flashlights hidden under their jackets they would be picked up on suspicion of burglary. Putnam's book explored the fate of social capital in America. Social capital "refers to connections among individuals—social networks and the norms of reciprocity and trustworthiness that arise from them." Social capital has value, but it is not, as Putnam said, always a "kumbaya" positive value. Strongly bonded groups can become exclusionary. Nonetheless, in recent decades we have suffered from a deep depression in terms of social capital. With regard to political participation, Putnam put it in raw numbers: "... [W]e now have sixteen million fewer participants in public meetings about local affairs, eight million fewer committee members, eight million fewer local organizational leaders, and three million fewer men and women organized to work for better government than we would have had if Americans had stayed as involved in community affairs as we were in the mid-1970s."

The fabric of our social and political life has been torn, putting freedom and democracy at risk. Evidence of this transformation is everywhere. How many gatherings descend into embarrassing silence when political differences of opinion enter the conversations? It is as though we are not supposed to talk about public matters, but only relate accounts of our private lives. Sociologists can ask, seriously, whether citizens are still necessary to politics. It is another symptom of our porphyria, a condition of information dysfunction in which citizens become so distant from one another that collective negotiation is all but impossible. To solve our political difficulties we must seek a cure for this condition, but it is exceedingly hard when our political practices themselves contribute to the social illness.

The roots of the difficulty can be found at the very birth of politics, as Jan Patočka has shown us. When the complexity of natural and community life confronted humans with the possibility of living for something beyond life itself, beyond mere surviving, and our gazes turned outward to the mysteries of one another and the natural world, human consciousness itself was altered. Something of the "self-enclosed" private universe of daily survival remains with us, even after the possibility of freedom is upon us. In fact, the economic uncertainty faced by the poor and the middle class, the illusion of redemption through private consumption, and the dominance of private entertainments available in the home have, as we have seen, caused a retreat to this private universe. Still, with humanities' move into freedom, the certainty of the private life lived only for itself is undone. "Nothing of the earlier life of acceptance remains in peace;

all the pillars of the community traditions, and myths, are equally shaken, as are all the answers that once preceded the questions, the modest yet secure and soothing meaning, though not lost, is transformed," Patočka said.

Humans, it could be said, have never recovered from our movement into history and politics. We are in good—or at least old—company with our struggle to negotiate our mutual future in this immense and pluralistic universe. Most of ancient religion and literature, in fact, is a record of the struggle. So while we attempt to come to terms with what appear as brief, temporally insignificant, parochial difficulties of a democracy that has been around for only 200 years, we should keep in mind that the terms are different, but the struggle for human freedom is the same.

The Covenant Tradition

Before we can examine even modest proposals for restoring the vitality of the public sphere, we should outline a theoretical framework for recommended action. As it happens, that framework can be discovered in what is known as the covenant tradition of political and civic life. This tradition is usually linked to Old Testament traditions in which covenants among the people of Israel and between humans and God are made explicit. It was revitalized by Puritan settlers in America, who pursued morally based, voluntary agreements among citizens as the foundation for mutually beneficial community rules, guidelines, or laws. The Latin word for covenant, foedus, is the root of the English word federal, pointing to the importance of the covenant tradition to the design of our federal Constitution and the organization of our political and civic institutions.

Daniel Elazar, author of the monumental four-volume work *The Covenant Tradition in Politics*, has more than any other contemporary political scientist urged our reawakening to this powerful tradition. Much of the discussion that follows is based upon his insights. What is this tradition? "A covenant is a morally-informed agreement or pact based upon voluntary consent and mutual oaths or promises," Elazar wrote. This voluntary consent "provides for joint action or obligation to achieve defined ends (limited or comprehensive) under conditions of mutual respect which protect the individual integrities of all the parties to it."

Covenant emerged as human beings awakened to the possibility of freedom, to a life beyond the concerns for mere survival. In this regard it had to account for the bonds of kinship, but also for the freedom to consent, to voluntarily enter into agreements with other members of one's community. Kinship, of course, is not voluntary. We cannot choose the families into which we are born. But the integration of the family into the public sphere required a framework for cooperation. The covenant tradition provides this framework.

We can see immediately that the tradition relies upon freedom-to-experience, to an understanding that one's freedom is linked to the freedom of others. Responsibility to oneself and to one's community becomes central to its possibility. Elazar explicitly links the covenant tradition to the work of William James, referring to our world as a "federal universe." James, Elazar said, "argued persuasively that the universe is a federal universe, that is to say, built on diversity, but a diversity that is systematic, i.e., that its parts relate to each other. Such a universe is grounded in covenant, but it includes not just the commitment but the operative parts as well." In James's mind, acknowledging the pluralistic nature of the universe does not mean reducing human lives to atomistic, isolated existence. Nor does it demand the submergence of individual personality into oneness. Instead, "every part, tho it may not be in actual or immediate connexion, is nevertheless in some possible or mediated connexion, with every other part however remote, through the fact that each part hangs together with its very next neighbors in inextricable interfusion," James wrote. So while the joys of secretly concealing a bull's-eye lantern are privately felt, they depend upon a covenant with one's compatriots.

Elazer identifies three forms of political organization: hierarchical, organic, and covenantal. These three forms correspond to the choices Alexander Hamilton recommended in *The Federalist 1*. "It has been frequently remarked that it seems to have been reserved to the people of this country, by their conduct and example, to decide the important question, whether societies of men are really capable or not of establishing good government from reflection and choice, or whether they are forever destined to depend for their political constitutions on accident and force," Hamilton wrote in 1787. Reflection and choice correspond to the covenant tradition. Force corresponds to the hierarchical; accident corresponds to the organic. Political arrangements in the hierarchical model are usually founded by conquest and are organized like the military on a pyramidal model. In the organic model, political organization seems to grow naturally, with a powerful or talented political elite controlling the organization from the center, as in the innermost of a series of concentric circles. Parliamentary democracies can take this form, with those in control forming a kind of self-perpetuating club, even if they are occasionally chosen by those outside the inner circle.

The covenant model, however, is characterized by a matrix, "a group of equal cells framed by common institutions. Its founding comes about because equal individuals or individual entities join together through a covenant or political compact as equals to unite and establish common governing institutions without sacrificing their respective integrities," Elazar said. A constitution becomes pre-eminent in the covenant tradition, as the voluntary agreement among citizens is given legal form in a living document. "Normally, a covenant precedes a constitution and establishes the people or polity which then proceeds to adopt a constitution of government for itself," Elazar said. "Thus, a constitution involves the implementation of a prior covenant—an effectuation or translation of a prior covenant into an actual frame or structure of government." The precedent of the covenant, however, is vulnerable to an evolving legalism that may devolve into endless disputes of constitutional interpretation. Mutual agreements can become arguments over individual rights, an emphasis on the personal and private, and a diminution of the interpersonal nature of the covenant.

Said Elazar, "The politics that flows from that constitution is a politics designed for people of equal status based on negotiation and bargaining among them which is designed to be as open as possible." Our contemporary political practices have diminished our common ability to negotiate and bargain with one another, closed the public space in which the negotiation could take place, and, while delivering ever more information through the mass media, left most of us ignorant of critical national interests and decision-making.

The covenant traditions arose from biblical history, as William Johnson Everett notes in his essay on Elazar, "Recovering the Covenant." "The Bible can be seen as a series of case studies in Israel's struggle to be a Holy Commonwealth. The political wisdom we find in the Bible seeks to hold together the dynamics of power with the requirements of justice. Both are necessary ingredients in the struggle for proper relationships under the human conditions of frailty and aspiration." The political wisdom of the Bible is demonstrated by its portrait of the constant struggle to balance the possibilities of freedom "with the fundamental need for trustworthy relationships."

Elazar probably overstates a unique genealogy for the covenant tradition. Such exaggerations can lead to dangerous conclusions, as groups elevate their status above outsiders or consider themselves a privileged or chosen people. As he himself points out, the early American settlers found a similar political arrangement already existing among Native Americans, especially the League of the Iroquois in the Northeast. Influenced somewhat by their contact with Europeans, the Iroquois political order evolved into a covenant-based confederacy in the seventeenth century. The Iroquois Confederacy subsequently influenced the thinking of Benjamin Franklin. Looking for unique sources of our political and cultural traditions is always a problematic enterprise. Religious covenants do not necessarily lead to democratic institutions. In fact, they may lead in the opposite direction. The point is that they serve as the forebears of civic covenants.

In the nineteenth century, beginning in Germany, an obsession with Ancient Greece had populations squabbling over the rightful inheritors of the Greek tradition. The obsession culminated with the Nazis, who believed they were a privileged race, the second coming of the Golden Age of Greece. Recent scholarship has uncovered much more trade and influence among ancient peoples than was previously known. Finding unique sources of cultural traditions in the past is no longer possible, although much contemporary ethnic and racial conflict is based on such misguided theories of national or ethnic identity. Productive, democratic covenants cannot be based upon an exclusivist view of one's own people. Covenant politics and democracy are not descendants of one tradition or two. They emerged from cross-cultural influences in humanity's confrontation with the possibilities of freedom. As globalization of the American experience accelerates, we would be wise to remember the multiple influences on contemporary politics and culture at home and in other lands.

In Greece, Plato and Aristotle estimated the appropriate size for democracies based upon mutual agreement. Plato believed the ideal size to be about 4,000, if governance was to be achieved through face-to-face encounters. Aristotle believed it was possible for a democracy to grow as large as 250,000. Plato and Aristotle were right to question the viability of a covenant among populations so large that people knew few of their leaders and only a small number of their fellow citizens. The size—and potential growth—of America's population played a significant role in the design of our civic republicanism, in which representative government and a balance of powers sought, among other goals, to bridge the distance among citizens and protect mutual agreements from the overweening power of the few. American democracy was born of the confrontation between covenantal Reformed Protestantism and Enlightenment ideas about civil society. Said Elazar, "In many respects the modern epoch brought with it a secularization of the covenant tradition as the aspirations to achieve a covenantal commonwealth gave way to the aspiration to achieve a civil society."

The Puritans called their covenant-based social and political organization "federal theology." It was transformed into civic republicanism by the authors of the Constitution, who were schooled in classical thought and Enlightenment philosophy. Excesses of the Church and the Enlightenment belief in the power of reason over superstition led to an emphasis on secular covenants rather than on religious-based, moral ones. Nonetheless, the principle of a voluntary agreement among people preceding the development of a formal constitution remained central to the vision of the Founding Fathers. We see the American Covenant reflected in the language of the Declaration of Independence, asserting that "all men are created equal, that they are endowed by their Creator with certain unalienable Rights, that among these are Life, Liberty and the pursuit of Happiness." The nation, however, oscillated between covenantal and organic theories of political organization. Two-time vice president John C. Calhoun expressly advocated an organic approach, arguing for naturally emergent rule by a virtuous elite. All humans are not created equal, he said, and only those favored by fortune deserved liberty. This view persists to this day, as those who ascend to privilege sometimes assume that the trappings of power prove their virtue, while those remaining outside the sphere of economic or political influence come to believe their station in life is limited by their lack of such virtue.

"The most intransigent constitutional problems arose from the incompatibility of two schemes of authority; the federal union joined a theory of consent-based government with notions of naturally emergent rule," wrote Barbara Allen in her essay, "Martin Luther King's Civil Disobedience and the American Covenant Tradition." Allen pointed out that "the organic ideal was also premised on theories of biological determinism and racial superiority that directly opposed the principles of covenant." The conflict led to radically different constitutional theories. In one—let us call it the states' rights theory—the union represented a compact among the states, and "the source of authority within a state was of no interest to the whole." In the covenantal view, the rights of individuals within the states were of paramount importance to the union.

Hierarchy versus a Covenant Among Equals

Further complicating the picture, a hierarchical approach to governance also has its place in the American ethos. Although contrary to all notions of government that require consent of the people, the hierarchical, pyramidal approach remains undisguised in:

- our recurrent imperial attitude with regard to international affairs
- our valorizing the president as commander-in-chief
- our obedience to authority
- our mythologizing of individuals involved in the "Conquest of the West"

This psychological tendency has been with us since families were confronted with the need to cooperate with other families and humans moved into history. Indeed, obedience to strict and powerful figures of authority still asserts a strong influence on our political dialogue.

But the real submergence of our covenant tradition occurred in the early nineteenth century, when "the shared assumptions about natural rights and community had given way to an increasingly text-based construction of constitutional rights," as Allen put it. "As a result, constitutional law might be more easily detached from any sense of its antecedent or transcendent foundations." Perhaps the most significant period of this transformation occurred during the period in which John Marshall served as chief justice of the United States Supreme Court. The Marshall Court rejected the concept of an antecedent covenant to the Constitution. Instead, the judiciary's responsibility lay in interpreting the textual issues that arise in legal disputes. The Marshall Court, said Allen, "approached the Constitution as a text of 'expoundable law,' less dependent on jurists' perceptions of natural justice and more securely tethered to laws adopted in formal acts of consent."

It was Abraham Lincoln who managed to revive the covenant tradition, arguing that the history of the emergence of the Union and binding agreements that preceded the Constitution prohibited unilateral separation of a state. "In Lincoln's view, neither the will of the people nor that of the states could be exercised lawfully or morally for a purpose inconsistent with securing those unalienable, original rights," Allen wrote. "On the theory that the presidential oath to 'preserve, protect, and defend the Constitution' by executing the laws faithfully imparted a duty that might exceed the letter of the law, he asserted that an otherwise unlawful action of the president might become lawful by becoming indispensable." Still, only through the use of force in the Civil War were Lincoln's views triumphant.

The Civil Rights Movement and Covenant

In the 1950s, however, a powerful voice emerged advocating a return to the covenant tradition: Dr. Martin Luther King, Jr. "Our preference for the letter rather than the spirit of the laws seems to follow logically from our desire for constitutionally limited government," said Allen. "King's political thought and action draw this logic into question, however, challenging Americans to assume a covenantal orientation in reassessing their constitutional faith." King recognized that the Civil Rights movement could not succeed without appealing to the moral vision that informed our laws and our Constitution. Disappointment with the promises of Reconstruction and the "whites only" sign on the doorways to the public sphere required a revolutionary stance. "King joined a vision of community drawn explicitly from his Christian ministry with the secular ideals of liberty and justice articulated in the Declaration of Independence, The Federalist, and the United States Constitution," said Allen, agreeing with Elazar's judgment that the Civil Rights movement became one of the most "comprehensive expressions of the covenant tradition."

King explicitly invoked premises of the covenant tradition in American history in a speech given in Nashville in 1962. "Deeply rooted in our political and religious heritage is the conviction that every man is an heir to a legacy of dignity and worth. Our Hebraic-Christian tradition refers to this inherent dignity of man in the Biblical term the image of God. This innate worth referred to in the phrase the image of God is universally shared in equal portions by all men," King said. The same idea was expressed in the Declaration of Independence. "All men," it says, "are created equal. They are endowed by their Creator with certain unalienable rights, among these are life, liberty and the pursuit of happiness." In the same speech, King delivered an impassioned plea for an understanding of human freedom that went beyond freedom of will. "The very phrase, freedom of the will, abstracts freedom from the person to make it an object; and an object almost by definition is not free. But freedom cannot thus be abstracted from the person, who is always subject as well as object and who himself still does the abstracting. So I am speaking of the freedom of man, the whole man, and not one faculty called the will."

By reaching back to the voluntary understandings that preceded the Constitution, King transcended legal arguments. At the same time, he recognized that more conservative avenues of political action could not be effective within the context of a diminished, segregated public sphere. Nonviolent civil disobedience would raise the visibility of the movement while demonstrating the transcendent moral character of the movement and refocusing the nation's attention on the covenant tradition. King's stature within the community of African-American churches, and the engagement of other church leaders and their members in the cause, lent the movement strength and numbers. In addition, the churches provided a community forum in which political participation was encouraged, hope was rekindled, and temporary setbacks in morale overcome. The churches became precisely the kind of public political space missing from so much of our civic life today.

King's approach also avoided the shortcomings of much contemporary communitarian thinking with regard to improving civic participation. Many of those who decry our lack of civic engagement focus upon renewed participation in local, usually apolitical, clubs and causes. Putnam titled his book *Bowling Alone*, the implication being that renewed interest in bowling leagues would help revive the American civic spirit. Theda Skocpal complained that such recommendations fell far short of the mark. Classic civic America included "shared democratic values, a measure of fellowship across class lines, and opportunities for the many to participate in organized endeavors alongside the elite few," she said. But King linked local face-to-face encounters to broader national goals and strategies. The Civil Rights movement embodied the strengths that Skocpal identified in American civic participation in the nineteenth century. Academics, lawyers, and white upper-middle-class students joined the efforts of African-American activists. By reinventing the covenant tradition, King invoked transcendent moral principles that applied to all Americans. The Civil Rights movement drew its strength and power from the courage and commitment of participants at the local level; however, they understood the global implications of their struggle.

Communication within a Covenant-Based Democracy

Another way of analyzing the covenant tradition and developing insights useful to a reinvigoration of our public life involves a look at modes of human interaction. Communications theorist James W. Carey identified two categories of communication. The first he identified as the transmission theory, in which communication imparts human knowledge across space. Subject A sends information across some distance to Subject B. The second Carey called the ritual theory of communication, which "is directed not toward the extension of messages in space but toward the maintenance of society in time; not the act of imparting information but the representation of shared beliefs." Both types remain alive in American culture, although the ritual approach is seldom pursued or studied. Both derive from religious origins. In fact, as we will see, the transmission view was integral to the culture of the Puritans, and their overemphasis of this mode of communication contradicted and undermined their covenantal social organization.

The transmission theory seeks "the transmission of signals or messages over distance for the purpose of control," Carey said. Its cultural power derives from the profound human endeavor to extend our dominion to new worlds. "The desire to escape the boundaries of Europe, to create a new life, to found new communities, to carve a New Jerusalem out of the woods of Massachusetts, were primary motives behind the unprecedented movement of white European civilization over virtually the whole globe," Carey wrote. This migration "represented the profound belief that movement in space could be in itself a redemptive act. It is a belief Americans have never quite escaped."

Ritual communication, however, is linked to such terms as "sharing," "participation," and "association," Carey tells us, adding that "the archetypal case under a ritual view is the sacred ceremony that draws persons together in fellowship and commonality." In ritual it is not information but confirmation that is communicated. A ritual communication is performative. Prayer, chant, ceremony, and celebration take precedence over the sermon or the admonition, the latter being key components of Puritan practice. The Puritans' emphasis on the practical—on work—and their belief in the redemptive qualities of their expanding domain combined to elevate the transmission theory. But this is somewhat at odds with their own covenant tradition, which involves the voluntary sharing of common values and beliefs. The transmission theory is dominant in most industrial cultures; its exaggerated dominance over ritual communication is better suited to hierarchical organization and conquest, or to an organic organization in which an inner circle of leaders exchanges information with others outside the leadership circle. All cultures transmit information across space, but in many—especially archaic cultures—the power of ritual communication is retained.

However, as history has shown us, sometimes ritual is staged by political leaders—Hitler's rallies at Nuremberg come to mind—to bond their subjects to them. But the coercive use of ritual is simply a disguised form of information transfer across space. It is no coincidence that Leni Riefenstahl's famous propaganda film about the 1936 Nuremberg rally was titled *Triumph of the Will*. The participants—or better, the targets—of such faux rituals may not understand the difference at the time. As the philosopher of freedom Isaiah Berlin noted, the exclusive pursuit of freedom-to-will or positive freedom can lead to the confusion of liberty with desire for recognition or belonging. In such a circumstance, we relinquish our freedom to an authority we expect to "will" on our behalf. Staged propaganda rituals can facilitate the brutal sacrifice of the self to an authoritarian presence.

True ritual communication cannot operate in such a way because a prior covenant among participants has already established their equality. Rather than relinquish freedom, choices for action are multiplied and freedom-to-experience is enhanced through participation in celebrations of covenantal solidarity. In our own covenant tradition, the Fourth of July, which marks the day in 1776 that Congress approved the Declaration of Independence, could serve as a covenantal celebration of its famous phrase that "all men are created equal." Instead, it has become a somewhat hollow faux ritual celebrating a kind of nationalistic pride.

It was part of King's genius that he recognized the importance of ritual communications to the Civil Rights movement. The participatory nature of his speeches to African-American congregations, frequently interrupted by "Amens" and expressions of approval, are perfect examples of the ritual form. What is key is the absolute opposition to faux ritual we see in King's approach. King was urging his listeners to seek broadened freedom-to-experience on their own behalf. He was not asking that they relinquish their liberty to him so that he might will on their behalf.

King also understood that modern mass media was ill suited to such ritual communication. Carey noted that one who examines the news under a ritual theory will find many similarities with traditional religious ritual. "We recognize, as with religious rituals, that news changes little and yet is intrinsically satisfying; it performs few functions yet is habitually consumed," he wrote. The news is drama, not information, Carey said, and it invites our "participation on the basis of our assuming, often vicariously, social roles within it." But the participation in the rituals enacted by the news is an illusion. News, delivered by television or newspaper, is a one-way transmission of information. There is no effective means for viewers to participate in the events shown or discussed, although transitory emotional engagement in, say, the *Challenger* explosion or the attack on the World Trade Center seem to bring us together in some kind of communal event.

The marches and demonstrations of the Civil Rights movement were intended to capture media attention. But they were not staged to invoke illusions of participation on the part of the television audience. In fact, they were meant to disrupt habitual ways of thinking about race in America. While the leaders were conscious the marches would be viewed from a distance, they were intended to provoke thoughtful Americans into rethinking our covenant tradition and our oft-expressed belief that we are a nation of equals. The Civil Rights marches were intended to communicate something of the ritual flavor that accompanied the participants in the streets. But they were the very opposite of a propaganda rally.

Barbara Allen's description of the structural qualities of King's efforts provides an excellent picture of political practices that can operate at the local level to establish strong community relations while reaching out to the larger national audience necessary for meaningful political change. "King's early emphasis on local, face-to-face negotiations and on the empowerment of local African-American communities, coupled with his simultaneous insistence that sectional differences in fundamental civil rights give way to a common moral and constitutional standard, also evince a federal [covenantal] standard," Allen wrote. King provided us a framework for overcoming the politics of deceit by repopulating the public sphere. We should not seek to replicate the Civil Rights movement. We could not do so even if we wanted to. Many of its features were products of the different era in which it emerged, and it grew out of a strong religious community grounded in spiritual covenant. But in its simplest structural outline—recalling us to the American Covenant Tradition through local face-to-face organizing while demonstrating by example the best of that tradition to the broader national audience—the Civil Rights movement can light the way.

The Industrial Areas Foundation: Revolution from the Ground Up

One organization (perhaps more accurately described as a network of linked organizations) that follows a similar structure is the Industrial Areas Foundation, or IAF. The name is something of a misnomer, as few of its participants work or live near heavy industry. Rather, the name refers to its founding, in 1940, in industrial sections of Chicago. It is now the oldest and largest community-organizing institution in the country. Based on principles developed by the late Saul Alinsky, the group's practice is called relational organizing. Its iron rule: "Never, never do for others what they can do for themselves." They absolutely refuse to "will on behalf of others." Activists and leaders emerge from among the populations in which IAF groups function. Responsibility for oneself and others is key to freedom-to-experience, and IAF activists learn early that there is no freedom without personal responsibility and commitment to the freedom of others.

Ernesto Cortes, whom we in the Texas press and government knew as Ernie, is perhaps the organization's best-known personality, though he and others are careful to keep the spotlight on local members and the work they accomplish. Cortes explains the IAF (in Skocpol's book) as "the center of a national network of broad based, multiethnic, interfaith organizations in primarily poor and moderate-income communities... The central role of IAF organizations is to build the competence and confidence of ordinary citizens and tax-payers so that they can reorganize relationships of power and politics

in their communities." The IAF receives support from church congregations, and it recalls the covenant tradition in its expression of
shared moral concerns as revealed in biblical and other religious stories. At the same time, the organization is never confused about the
separation of church and state. That is part of its understanding of
the civic covenant. Typically, the group will organize around a local
or state issue, and members are encouraged to assume leadership
responsibilities for their campaigns for economic justice, health care
reform, broadened educational opportunity, or smaller-scale (but
just as important) community projects like getting roads paved in
poor neighborhoods.

All action begins with a formal process of conversation, called the
"one-on-one." This is a conversation between two people about public life. The conversation is driven by questions each participant asks
of the other. The questions include, "Why are you here engaged in
building a political relationship? What is important to you? What in
your experience is at the core of what drives you to want change?"
From these individual conversations, the organizations identify concerns of many people in the group. They then create larger conversations around these core issues. These conversations take the form
of "house meetings" of no more than ten people, held in living rooms,
church basements, and so on. People there are asked to share their
personal stories as they relate to the larger concerns. At the end of the
house meeting, the group decides on further action—whether to
study an issue, to meet with an official to get more information, or
to meet in a larger group with others from similar house meetings.
At the same time, all members are asked to hold a certain number of
individual conversations with others to enlarge the circle of political
conversation. In this way the interested participants build an organization and an agenda.

The IAF does not seek the kind of publicity that many contemporary advocacy groups spend considerable resources courting.
Rather, like the adherents of the Civil Rights movement, they try to
communicate to the broader national audience by setting an example. However, IAF members are not shy. They are known for their

candidate forums in which political figures are grilled by the diverse and informed citizens of a local or state IAF group. Another key quality is an unassailable commitment to truthfulness. As a state-house journalist in Texas many years ago, I followed Ernie Cortes and other IAF members and leaders as they pressed their concerns with legislators, governors, lieutenant governors, and House speakers. They could not then and they cannot now match the financial resources of the business lobby. Instead, their effectiveness derives from their honesty. In a very real sense, their authentic voices draw an honesty from elected officials that might otherwise not emerge. They do not always win, but there is never any mystery about what they seek, who supported them, and who stood in the way of their goals.

In his book *Who Will Tell The People?*, William Greider said, "IAF gives up short-term celebrity on 'hot issues' in order to develop the long-term power of a collective action that is real." They avoid the kind of large-scale events that could attract national media attention. While living in the covenant tradition, they rely on the power of their actions, not news about the power of their actions. This is somewhat different from the Civil Rights movement: Its exponents leveraged national celebrity into increased attention on local causes, and this in turn demonstrated the need for national civil rights reform. The movement paid a price for this strategy, however. The pressures of the national media stage caused more than one rift in its ranks. Leaders of the IAF simply believe no concrete human problem is ever solved in or by the media. Still, their actions receive considerable attention, enough that their integrity and shared moral vision is communicated to a larger audience. They earn mentions in many books and articles that explore efforts to revitalize the public sphere.

In *What Next: A Memoir Toward World Peace*, a book "written specifically as an address to African America," as the author put it, Walter Mosley lays out four rules of fair treatment. They are elaborations or extrapolations from the core principle of the American Covenant that all are created equal: "First, I cannot be free while my neighbor is wearing chains. Second, I cannot know happiness while others are forced to live in despair. Third, I cannot know health if plague and famine thrive outside my door. And last, but not least, I cannot expect to know peace if war rides forward under my flag and with my consent." Mosley is laying out possible terms of moral agreement with his readers. It is a covenantal enterprise. Writing of the special perspective that African-Americans can bring to public debate, Mosley urges them, even in small ways, to let their voices enter the public sphere. Because citizens are swamped with information, held at bay by the media, he recommends that small groups of seven or so gather to discuss news events. "Alone, there are few who can follow the news in its entirety. But if there was a small group that met together in a den, a restaurant, or even on the phone or online once every two weeks or so, they would be able to share information that they'd gathered," Mosley wrote. This is a modest, human-sized suggestion. But it is precisely the kind of small, interpersonal exchange that can help citizens carry through on their commitment to a shared moral outlook. People need to gather to discuss political issues, to test their own viewpoints, to hear the opinions of others. It is the beginning of political action.

Mosley includes models for action. He believes citizens should start small, working for change in their communities. Like the leaders of IAF, he believes these and even larger activist efforts should be self-funded. "Most Americans have a jelly jar or coffee can somewhere that's about halfway filled with pennies, nickels, dimes and quarters . . . Change for change. It means many things. It might be a catchphrase for an entire movement," he says. Mosley understands the power of interpersonal communications. His books revolve around the successes and failures of human interaction.

Theda Skocpol recommends forming new voluntary organizations on small and large scales. She points out that among the benefits of nineteenth-century civic engagement—in political parties, clubs, and so on—was the bringing together of people from different classes into a common purpose. In recent years the AFL-CIO has opened itself to new kinds of political action at the local level. Skocpol applauds the move. In short, we can be very inventive in creating new avenues for citizen participation in public life. One of her suggestions has been mentioned above—make national Election Day a holiday. Voting has a reciprocal relationship to the depth of citizens' political engagement. While involved citizens tend to vote in greater numbers than the uninvolved, voting itself spurs other kinds of political involvement, as many behavioral studies have shown. There is no good argument against creating a voting holiday. It will make it much easier for citizens to vote. More people will vote, and so an Election Day holiday would broaden the viewpoints upon which our nation must draw to answer the challenges facing democracy and freedom in the twenty-first century. The only possible objections will come from officeholders and entrenched interests who will wonder at the effects on their careers and futures if significant numbers of new voters arrive at the polls. To them, I say the following: "Your terms of office, or the longevity of your parties or professional groups, will be over no matter what in a relative blink of an eye. With any luck, democracy will outlast your tenures."

Returning to the American Covenant Tradition, easily recognizable in the words of the Declaration of Independence, could serve to reintegrate disparate interests. We have more in common than we suppose. Without any sense of a shared moral vision, however, it is all too easy to cling stubbornly to habitual ways of thinking. Because terms like "moral vision" are often used by the right wing as code words for "do what we say," it must be stressed that covenants involve voluntary agreement. It is not a question of developing some rigid code and mandating that our fellow citizens follow its terms. The magic is in the act of covenanting.

Remember Barbara Allen's description of the framework of the Martin Luther King's movement politics: She spoke of King's "early emphasis on local, face-to-face negotiations and on the empowerment of local African-American communities, coupled with his simultaneous insistence that sectional differences in fundamental civil rights give way to a common moral and constitutional standard." A self-organizing and self-reinforcing political action will build interest and courage locally, rely upon its integrity, discipline, and sense of responsibility to capture the attention of citizens not yet participating in the movement, and be nourished by the imaginative involvement of others in its cause.

The seven neighbors who gather at Walter Mosley's suggestion to discuss contemporary political news and issues may one day find that they are making the news and changing the world. I would like to suggest a name for such groups to Mr. Mosley and to those who act on his advice.

Call yourselves the Lantern Bearers.

7

THE OTHER SUPERPOWER

The Internet's New "Interactivists" and the Public Sphere

It is not in numbers but in unity, that our great strength lies; yet our present numbers are sufficient to repel the force of all the world.

Thomas Paine
Common Sense

On February 15, 2003, 10.5 million people gathered around the globe to demonstrate their opposition to the American invasion of Iraq. It has been called the single largest day of protest in history. On March 16, a second wave of one million people in 130 countries took part in quiet, candlelight vigils that followed the setting sun around the world.

The sunset gatherings took place along what astronomers know as a terminator, a longitudinal marker that separates day from night. We cannot see the earth's terminator (unless we are talking about the ridiculous alias of the current governor of California). None of us can step from day into night or night into day. But just as we see the moon's terminator from earth, if we were to look back on the earth from the moon, we would see the border between day and night. The spring antiwar vigils took place just on the nightside. Gathering at a place called the terminator might imply an ending, but that evening marked a beginning. A new global activism was coming of age. In biology, events at the genetic terminator, where transcription of a DNA sequence stops, define the information a gene communicates to the future. And it was the future that was in the hearts of the million people gathered along the earth's westward-racing terminator that night.

"Never before in the history of the world has there been a global, visible, public, viable, open dialogue and conversation about the very legitimacy of war," Dr. Robert Muller said of the peace marches and protests after accepting a 2003 award for his lifelong service to the United Nations. Jonathan Schell relayed Muller's comments in an essay celebrating the global antiwar phenomenon as "the other super-power." The new superpower did not have borders, and it did not have a government. It did, however, have the Internet. By using the Net's miraculous dialogue-at-a-distance possibilities, organizers and participants—we might call them "interactivists"—were able to revitalize, at least temporarily, an international public sphere. The Net greatly enhanced activists' efforts to replicate the model for political engagement we found in the Civil Rights movement. They built a self-organizing and self-reinforcing political movement at the local level through existing networks of trust in which citizens felt confident expressing their moral outrage at the war. Demonstrators' courage and moral conviction were then made visible to the wider world in coordinated protests.

The Internet, of course, has been expected to transform the world since its inception in the 1970s. A review of the breathy books and articles about the Internet written in the 1980s and 1990s gives the impression that there was widespread belief that humanity had taken a profound evolutionary leap forward. Margaret Wertheim, reviewing the Internet's reception in a 1999 book, makes a compelling case that many cyberspace citizens felt it represented a kind of New Jerusalem, an immaterial but infinite space into which we are destined to migrate as a species. "The perfect realm awaits us, we are told, not behind the pearly gates, but beyond the network gateways, behind the electronic doors labeled '.com,' '.net,' and '.edu,'" Wertheim wrote. Some of this dreaming, she said, may be due to the loneliness and isolation that is a consequence of modern cultural trends and technological innovations. We are lonely, and the Internet, unlike some other technologies that have challenged human relationships on a fundamental level, is above all else a relational technology. Yes, users are still sitting isolated in their homes or offices, but they are interacting with others.

In medieval representations of the New Jerusalem, "one thing is certain, citizens will not be lonely" in the heavenly Empyrean, Wertheim said, detailing iconography of the era in which heaven is teeming with people. In just such a transcendent vision, Internet prophets believed the new communications tool would rebuild the lost bonds of community. "The Net, supposedly, will fill the social vacuum in our lives, spinning silicon threads of connection across the globe," Wertheim said. She points out that new technologies are not always immediately adopted. The technological basis of fax machines has been around since 1843, before the telephone, yet the technology was not fully developed until the 1970s. Likewise, the Chinese invented the steam engine more than 900 years ago, but failed to adopt its use. And videotext—a pre-Internet, telephone-based technology made available in the United Kingdom in the 1980s—flopped. But the Internet was barely established before its popularity was ensured. "The sheer scale of interest in cyberspace suggests there is not only an intense desire at work here, but also a profound psychosocial vacuum that many people are hoping the Internet might fill," Wertheim said.

Of course, there were other forces at work. The Internet matured in tandem with the personal computer revolution. Both industries were mutually supportive. Throw in the telecommunications industry, and you have a powerful engine driving interest in the new media. The otherworldly claims for cyberspace no doubt contributed to the irrational investment atmosphere of the 1990s, in which Internet-based companies that were losing millions and billions of dollars nonetheless enjoyed ridiculously inflated stock prices. Advice to investors took the form of folk legend. "I don't know/but I been told/the streets of heaven/are paved with gold." Business projections came to resemble those medieval frescoes Wertheim mentioned; there would be billions of consumers in cyberspace, and all that mattered to investors was what part of that "space" a business planned to dominate when the Rapture came. But the Rapture turned to stock market rupture. The flights to economic heaven had been over-booked. In fact, they had all been canceled, and the tickets were worthless.

But those with a more realistic approach to the Internet perse-vered. They modestly moved forward with their cheaper tickets to more earthly enterprises while the ticket scalpers were left outside the gates of the game. And there was a game on. The Internet has become a viable pathway to establishing new kinds of communities. Entrepreneurs attract customers to their sites by creating a sense of belonging. For instance, Amazon.com provides places for customers to rank books, make recommendations, and offer book reviews to other visitors to the site. I am not claiming that this commercial application is creating the kinds of bonds among citizens that we have seen are critical to the reestablishment of the public sphere. But I do believe that enterprises like Amazon have recognized our desire for community. This desire became clearly visible as the Internet matured. "If cyberspace teaches us anything, it is that the worlds we conceive (the spaces we 'inhabit') are communal projects requiring ongoing communal responsibility," said Wertheim.

Internet Possibilities

What we are interested in gauging here is whether the Internet can help reestablish a public sphere in which citizens are able to bridge the distance that has grown between the rulers and the ruled as well as among the citizens themselves. As we have seen, contemporary political life is dominated by one-way communications that are designed more to manipulate than to inform. Jürgen Habermas helped us understand that we have regressed to something like the medieval relationship between a king and his docile subjects. We sit passively before our rulers, who enter our homes through a television screen to which we cannot respond. It is interesting to note the similarities between our aspirations and those of medieval folk. In both instances, as Wertheim noted, humans fantasized about faraway realms in which true human community and peaceful coexistence would be restored. The dreams were present in medieval art, and they were manifest in our expectations of the Internet. We noted earlier that a similar spiritualist longing marked the birth of radio.

But there are unmistakable signs that the Internet has opened new possibilities for citizen involvement in public life. Leaving aside the vast amounts of information available on the Internet and dealing only with the interactivist phenomenon, we find that Net organizers have been remarkably successful in their recent efforts to involve millions of people in national and international political debates. Innovative organizations like MoveOn.org—which has skillfully utilized electronic mail, online petitions, local meet-up opportunities, and small-donor fundraising drives to raise the volume of progressive voices—have made it easier and more rewarding for citizens to reenter the public sphere. Measuring these successes against the criteria for authentic political engagement outlined in earlier chapters, we can judge the value of the Internet in the political realm. Then a realistic assessment can be made of the Internet's practical possibilities.

Internet activism received new attention from boosters and critics in 2003 and 2004. Its very success in opening a new space for people to be heard—the global antiwar protests, the struggle against media consolidation in the United States, resistance to the Bush administration's assaults on the working poor, on civil rights—raised expectations that a new era in politics was dawning. Political analysts, however, pointed to the rise and fall of Democratic presidential hopeful Howard Dean as evidence that the importance of the Internet had once again been exaggerated. In fact, the evolution of the discussion of the Internet as a viable political tool in 2003 and 2004 was like a highly condensed version of the cyberspace boom and bust talk of the 1990s. Joe Trippi, Dean's campaign manager, found himself profiled in prestigious newspapers and magazines for his Internet savvy and the advantage it brought to Dean in the prepresidential primary months. When Dean faltered, Trippi's strategy was questioned. Many of the same analysts who extolled the wondrous powers of the new medium before Dean lost the Iowa caucuses and the New Hampshire primary retreated to a "we-knew-it-all-along" skepticism. There were many factors at play in these shifting attitudes, not the least of them that the more celebrated campaign professionals and pundits come from a pre-Internet era in which television had the stage to itself. Still, there is a need to measure in some way the potential of the Internet in restoring the health of the public sphere, recognizing from the start that the Net is nothing more than a new interactive medium. While it can affect the balance of power by giving voice to those once excluded from public conversation, it will not serve us to hype its potential. It is what people do with it that counts.

Measuring the Health of the Public Sphere

Summarizing the criteria for a reinvigorated public sphere, we can establish some benchmarks. Participation in public life is contingent upon the amount and the quality of information available to citizens. The best source of political information comes from close relationships—friends, neighbors, family members, and others who have earned our trust. A citizen living in a neighborhood in which others are informed is much more likely to become informed, and therefore more likely to risk entering the public conversation. Social exchanges pay off for two participants when both are informed, and so people are more likely to engage in such exchanges when they have confidence in their own knowledge and the knowledge of their partner. The ability to give and receive information is critical. Earlier, we imagined a tipping point where the social benefits of exchanges reach such a level that the benefits of political participation become apparent to all within that peer group.

Following Theda Skocpol, we found that successful avenues for participation will include "shared democratic values, a measure of fellowship across class lines, and opportunities for the many to participate in organized activities alongside the elite few." Also, information exchanges among citizens need to follow Adam Smith's suggestion that our words should be maximally usable to our listeners. Our efforts to inform others should be open and honest, recognizing that our potential audience will voluntarily decide whether to ignore us, resist us, or join us in the conversation. Language itself evolved in relation to our need to tell the true from the false. Political communications should take this into account. People who trust others tend to be better informed on political issues. It follows, then, that building trust among our audience is key to winning their involvement. Although this is a rather obvious point, it is critical to the success of Internet initiatives, which must gain trust from people who are at some remove.

There have already been many efforts at deception on the Internet, with domain names used to fool visitors into thinking that they are looking at a candidate's or organization's site when they have really come to an opposition site intended to embarrass the authentic candidate or organization. But these deceptions do not survive for long. Usually, they are transparently deceptive. Also, because the authentic sites can so easily and cheaply communicate to a wide audience, it is a simple matter to define the fakes from the originals.

Vaclav Havel pointed out that life moves toward diversity and independent self-constitution and self-organization, while authoritarian (or as he put it "post-totalitarian") regimes demand "conformity, uniformity, and discipline." To be successful, strategies aimed at inviting citizens back into the public sphere will have to leave room for diversity, for "bottom-up" organization. Havel and Jan Patočka recommended living within the truth as a strategy for challenging the dominant authority. One way to do that is to simply speak up. In such practices as "writing to the desk," those who oppose the dominant powers must take action, even if it means speaking to a single friend or neighbor, or—as in Patočka's case—continuing to write even when one knows the government will prohibit publication.

We also explored a return to something like the covenant tradition that played a significant role in political life of seventeenth- and eighteenth-century America, in the revolt against England, and in the framing of the American Constitution. Political scientist Daniel Elazar described covenant-based polities as characterized by a matrix, by "a group of equal cells framed by common institutions." In contrast to the matrix structure are pyramidal or hierarchical organizations, and the organic structure, in which leadership is taken by those with "natural virtue" and who rule from inside the innermost sphere of concentric circles. He added, "The politics that flows from [covenant-based organization] is a politics designed for people of equal status based on negotiation and bargaining among them which is designed to be as open as possible." Participants in a political covenant typically reach agreement on moral viewpoints and negotiate actions based on those shared assumptions. In many circumstances, a shared moral vision is assumed as people of like mind gather.

Finally, we described the transmission and ritual theories of communications. Communications theorist James W. Carey characterized ritual communications as involving such terms as "sharing," "participation," and "association." Of necessity, such communications cannot be one-way. The participatory talks of Martin Luther King are examples in which listeners are invited to become part of the performance. Such communication is not of the transmission kind, in which item X is sent across space from Person A to Person B. Instead, in ritual communication the discourse among participants is simultaneous or near-simultaneous. The Internet-based phenomenon that comes closest to embodying this approach is the now-famous meet-up. While important information is exchanged, the ritualized meet-up (a local gathering facilitated by online tools that allow people to identify and gather with the like-minded) communicates to all participants simultaneously that they are there together.

Woven together, these themes—theoretical criteria for the effectiveness of Internet activism in reinvigorating the public sphere—place an emphasis on freedom-to-experience over freedom-to-will. Freedom-to-experience carries with it a shared understanding that freedom is a social phenomenon, that one's freedom depends on the freedom of others, and that such freedom carries with it responsibility to others and to oneself. It is not the case, as it is with freedom-to-will or positive freedom in Isaiah Berlin's formulation, that freedom can be reduced to people's ability to have what they will or to impose their will on others. This kind of freedom forces us into isolated lives in which private satisfactions takes precedence over the public engagement.

How the Internet Can Restore the Public Sphere

Internet activism would appear well situated to work within this theoretical framework for restoring the public sphere. I have been involved with MoveOn and have adopted its model to a similar organization, DriveDemocracy.org—but it is MoveOn that will serve as a reference point. However, the emphasis on MoveOn is not meant to slight other online activist organizations, all of whom deserve credit as political pioneers of the new medium. MoveOn was begun during the impeachment of Bill Clinton. It derives its name from its initial goal: The country should move on to issues of relevance to people's lives and drop the crude and highly partisan impeachment effort. Since that time it has grown to include 2 million people, people who contribute their interest, their voices, their time, and their money to progressive causes. It was MoveOn that organized the global antiwar candlelight vigils we spoke of earlier. MoveOn mobilized its members against the Federal Communications Commission's relaxation of media ownership rules that has, for instance, allowed Clear Channel Communications to become the dominant radio broadcaster to African-Americans, and, for that matter, the rest of the nation.

I helped coordinate MoveOn's national campaign against U.S. House Majority Leader Tom DeLay's unprecedented, mid-decade effort to rid Congress of moderate Democrats from Texas by shoving his own Congressional redistricting plans through a compliant Texas legislature. Even though redistricting is usually done just once a decade, Texas jettisoned a court-approved Congressional plan already in place. Similar redistricting coups were underway in other states, including Colorado, and MoveOn believed the partisan power play deserved national attention. The organization also grabbed headlines when it sponsored a national contest in which citizens were invited to submit television ads about President Bush. But do MoveOn's efforts fit within the model we have been discussing throughout the book?

In an interview, cofounder Wes Boyd used one word over and over with regard to MoveOn's mission and practices: "trust". He spoke as if he had been schooled in the impact on political participation of beneficial social exchanges, of developing a feeling of fellowship across class lines, and, most importantly, of building trust among MoveOn activists. He said that from its beginning MoveOn approached its work as a service to the politically disenchanted. "Service is about establishing trust, of having a deep regard and respect for the person—we think of them as friends—completely different from [traditional political communications]," Boyd says. As we have seen, the traditional communications tools of politics are aimed at breaking down citizens' resistance to messages. In the standard model, voters are targeted just as they are in commercial marketing campaigns and treated as consumers of political products rather than producers of political outcomes.

"Our relationship [with MoveOn activists] is reciprocal, and that means trust," Boyd said. "You don't violate the relationship. We extend trust to them, and we express trust that they will step forward if given the opportunity. When people step forward and say something, the likelihood of their acting when asked is some huge multiple of what it would be otherwise. If people don't feel safe enough to say to themselves that they have an opinion, it goes nowhere."

His comments square perfectly with the insights of research presented earlier. Participation in political affairs increases substantially when citizens are able to exchange mutually beneficial information with one another. According to sociologist Gani Aldashev, in what he termed his central empirical finding, a person's likelihood of voting improved dramatically when the amount of information available in the voter's community was slightly higher than average. Aldeshev also found that "the strategic acquisition game exhibits a key strategic complementarity: a citizen getting informed increases her [conversational] partner's expected benefit from acquiring information." As explained by Boyd, the MoveOn model aims at reaching this information tipping point, when the benefits of political conversation are apparent to all within a community. Even casual participation—say, answering a MoveOn call to action and emailing a member of Congress—increases the chances a person will gain valuable political insight. Taking action increases the likelihood a voter will gain additional information. That, in turn, enhances the possibilities for future action from that voter and from friends, colleagues, and neighbors whom that voter may encounter offline, in person-to-person exchanges.

Writer Andrew Boyd (no relation to Wes), in his analysis of online activism, spoke of the cascading effect brought about by person-to-person encounters and the forwarding of emails. MoveOn provides tools on its Web site that make it easy to forward information to one's own contact list, as well as tools that allow people to find others in their locale who share their viewpoints. "This 'tell a friend' phenomenon is key to how organizing happens on the net. It gives people who feel alienated from politics something valuable to contribute: their unique credibility with their particular circle of acquaintances. A small gesture to these friends can contribute to a massive multiplier effect," Andrew Boyd wrote. The New York Times reached a similar conclusion: "Some political scientists say that MoveOn.org may foreshadow the next evolutionary change in American politics, a move away from one-way tools of influence like television commercials and talk radio to interactive dialog, offering everyday people a voice in a process that once seemed beyond their reach," wrote Michael Janofsky and Jennifer 8. Lee.

The MoveOn model also embodies, to some extent, the recommendations of Vaclav Havel and Jan Patočka, who spoke of living within the truth by expressing opposition to dominant powers. Havel drew a distinction between the "aims of life" and the aims of post-totalitarian systems. The implication is that open, democratic organizations leave room for the expression of diverse points of views through self-organized, bottom-up mobilization. Dissident viewpoints no longer have to be written to the desk, or shared privately in a living room or den, out of sight of the authorities. A person's voice can be heard by millions through the power of the Internet, and just the potential of such an audience can boost the confidence of citizens who once felt shut out of the public sphere. Through small-dollar contributions to MoveOn, their views can also be embodied in mainstream media advertising and public relations.

It is important to note that MoveOn has not abandoned traditional communications in its campaigns. Rather, it adds the voices of its members to the national debate through ads made possible by their creative energy and small-dollar contributions, and through more traditional public relations efforts carried out by a skilled, professional team at Fenton Communications, a progressive public affairs organization. Wes Boyd is particularly proud of the creativity that has emerged from MoveOn's constituency. Soliciting creative ideas from its members—including produced television spots—has allowed MoveOn to anticipate trends in public opinion, he said. "We were weeks or months ahead on the deficit message," Boyd said, referring to the growing concern over the Bush administration's tax cuts for the wealthy and increased government spending. He refers to the phenomenon as "an emergent public mind." MoveOn activists "are out there with their neighbors. They may be more on the progressive side, but they understand what people care about."

Eli Pariser, the young campaign director for MoveOn, said, "Creative power is the power to build. It's based on the idea that collaboration and community build stronger societies—that if we strengthen the bonds between each other, if we trust, respect, and empathize with each other, we will be more creative, more resilient, more fair, and ultimately more collectively powerful. Positive social change, creative power, only happens when many people participate. I believe it can't manifest in small groups, it can't be isolated."

Some questions emerge when promoters of dialogue-based, inter-activist models take up the tools of traditional political communications. But as was noted earlier, unilateral disarmament—simply relying on the Internet and grassroots activism and refusing to use other traditional communications venues, such as television advertising—would be folly in our current circumstance. It is an unfortunate fact that most of us get our information from television, and if a message is to be heard by a wide audience, to television it must go. The good news is that by raising substantial sums from its base of small donors—supplemented with major contributions from philanthropists like George Soros—MoveOn is able to get progressive messages on the air. However, in one notorious case, the organization is not always successful: CBS refused to air a MoveOn ad critical of President Bush during the Super Bowl.

In addition, MoveOn is committed to responsible advocacy on behalf of its constituents. Traditional ads produced by experienced political consultants tend to focus on provoking conflict, Boyd said. Turning to its constituents for creative ideas allows MoveOn to focus its advertising "on messages with the most meaning, rather than messages which are the most outrageous."

When Pariser talks of enhancing MoveOn's creative energy, resilience, and power by promoting trust, empathy, and respect among participants, he is describing a kind of covenant-based polity organized as "a group of equal cells framed by common institutions." Daniel Elazar described a covenantal organization as "a morally-informed agreement or pact based upon voluntary consent and mutual oaths or promises." The voluntary agreement "provides for joint action or obligation to achieve defined ends (limited or comprehensive) under conditions of mutual respect which protect the individual integrities of all the parties to it." It sounds very much like the way Boyd, Pariser, and others of the MoveOn team describe their effort. We can also see parallels with Martin Luther King's model, in which a moral theme serves to unify local and national efforts. In fact, it is much the same theme: a renewed emphasis on the original American covenant expressed in the Declaration of Independence. All are created equal, and practices that promote inequality violate the spirit of the covenant.

Arriving at our last criterion, which recognizes a distinction between ritual and transmission modes of communication, Net-based activism appears to offer a hybrid version in which the transmission mode—concerned as it is with extending one's influence through space—is subordinated to the ritual mode, which is focused upon unifying community through time. Put another way, there is important meaning simply in joining with other members of MoveOn in a collaborative action of equals. The need to transmit new information to members across space is not done for the purpose of control, but for the purposes of building effective—and equal—participation. As mentioned before, Net-based activist organizations have developed ritualized terms and activities in a common language that also serves to unify participants: Meet-ups, refer-a-friend, take action, sign the petition—all are shorthand terms that link ritualized individual action to the larger collective enterprise.

This point leads me to disagree slightly with the *Nation*'s Andrew Boyd, who wrote that the Net is more or less a neutral technology, that it "does not favor the left or right." Because the Internet seems more congenial to matrix-like, covenantal organizations, it may not prove as useful for authoritarian or hierarchical schemes, which tend to be organizational patterns favored by the Right. We might think of the disadvantages the disciplined, hierarchical British Army faced when it encountered the more autonomous guerrilla warriors of the American Revolution. If the right wing is about anything, it is about control. This means that certain advantages afforded by the nature of the Internet may be lost on those who persist in authoritarian approaches to leadership. By the same token, interactivists cannot do without some structure. I do not believe it is accurate to claim that Howard Dean's Internet strategy failed him. I think it succeeded in involving hundreds of thousands of new voters in the political process. His decline had to do with more tradition variables in the political equation. But it was also obvious that his organization grew so large and so fast that it was difficult to mobilize. Internet organizations must have leaders. But because their mission involves inclusiveness and respect for democratic processes, this leadership is more likely to be open to actions that originate from its constituents.

Wes Boyd and the MoveOn team were smart to follow their instincts and make the building of trust among their constituents central to their mission and practices. As it turns out, trust appears to be a determinate of Internet use. People who tend to trust others are more comfortable with the medium, several recent studies have shown. "Without trust, it is conceivable that a robust, interactive on-line environment would not be possible, just as it would not be in the offline world," a 2003 study by Cynthia L. Corritore, Beverly Kracher, and Susan Wiedenbeck concluded. Just as we saw in our discussion of neighborhood-based, person-to-person social exchanges, the most valuable information—and the information most likely to motivate social or political engagement—is received in relationships of mutual trust. Such relationships in the offline world, however, are usually built over time after multiple encounters. We earn one another's trust gradually. How is that to be approached in the online world, where trust must be established among strangers, or among the newly acquainted?

The authors of the above study concluded that online trust is determined by external factors, such as a user's propensity to trust, and perceived factors, such as credibility, ease of use, and risk. The authors limited their study to website use, excluding other kinds of online activity, such as e-mail, open-post blogs, and instant messaging, which they think more closely parallels person-to-person communications. Nonetheless, their findings are useful. MoveOn, for example, could violate its relationships of trust by misinforming visitors to its site, asking them to take action based on the misinformation, spending contributions in a manner not consistent with requests for contributions, or complicating participation with a cluttered website or confusing instructions for action. On the positive side, MoveOn builds trust among its constituents when its organizers listen to their concerns and ideas for action.

Building Trust

What is interesting is that the need to build trust among activists tends to steer the Net-based organization in a direction that meets the criteria we have established for revitalizing the public sphere. On the flip side, our traditional political practices, based as they are on one-way communications intended to manipulate more than to inform, do not rely upon relationships of trust for their effectiveness. A television ad can be effective even when we do not know the sponsor. In many cases, especially with regard to negative attack spots used in political campaigns, the sponsors go to some lengths to hide their involvement in the knowledge that the ad is more credible when its author is anonymous. I am not speaking here about the importance of the trust in or credibility of a political candidate, which, of course, remains important—even if that trust is often misplaced.

Another study that examined the relationship between Internet use and social or political participation found that people who use the Internet primarily for information exchange tended to be more socially and political engaged than those who used it for entertainment. The study, published in 2001 by Dhavan V. Shah, Nojin Kwak, and R. Lance Holbert, said, "...information motives [as opposed to recreational motives, like game playing] for new media use related positively to social capital production...Indeed, with the panoply of mobilizing content available on-line, citizens who are armed with such information may be able to exert greater control over their environments, encouraging participation and enhancing trust and contentment." The authors suggest that Internet use may not be the sole cause of increased social engagement, but rather that Internet use and social engagement reinforce one another. They are mutually causal.

But the findings of this study and others also point to some of the practical difficulties facing the new interactivists. Social scientists have known for some time that socioeconomic factors help determine a person's propensity to trust others. As might be imagined, the ability to trust is diminished among people who suffer economic deprivation and live as minorities within an overly dominating majority. In other words, the very people who might benefit from online engagement are the least likely to so engage, for two reasons. One is the simple fact of cost. Computers and access to the Internet cost money, and many simply cannot afford to participate. But the second reason involves trust. Those who have been repeatedly punished by economic policies developed by distant strangers are not likely to overcome their skepticism of messengers they cannot see and do not know.

A study of Internet use in 17 countries by economists at IBM concluded that high expectations of economic expansion in less wealthy countries due to the global extension of the Internet were unrealistic. The reason? Because trust is so essential a determinant of Internet use, poorer countries in which citizens' ability to trust was diminished—along with their economic opportunities—were not likely to embrace the Internet. "Our results suggest that trust does, in fact, influence Internet adoption. Since low-trust countries tend to be low- or middle-income countries, this will result in a digital divide between these countries and higher-trust, higher-income ones." The study also suggested that government policies aimed at improving trust levels would tend to have a more dramatic impact on wealthy countries, meaning the digital and economic divides would grow all the wider.

We can extrapolate from this study to the American population, which Senator John Edwards has described as "the two Americas," one nation of wealth and privilege, another of poverty and alienation. Following the conclusions of the IBM study, it is not likely that Internet activism will be extended quickly to include less privileged citizens, even though it is on their behalf that many progressives battle. The IBM study's second finding is even more disheartening. Trust among citizens enhances economic growth by reducing what economists call "transaction costs." The study's authors examined the impact among rich and poor countries of proportionate investments in trust-building initiatives. The findings were discouraging. "High-trust countries will benefit proportionately much more from their investments in trust than will low-trust countries," they concluded. This buttressed their claim that since Internet adoption was keyed to trust, poorer countries were not likely to adapt quickly to the Internet.

An important conclusion to be drawn from this is that while the new interactivists may have opened the public sphere to new voices, without additional offline grassroots initiatives we may unintentionally exclude the very voices that have always had the most difficulty being heard. Wes Boyd recognizes this and believes the answer lies in the proliferation of different kinds of grassroots organizations, both on- and offline. "My personal vision of a healthy society is a diversity of institutions," Boyd said. Clearly, there is a need for all kinds of efforts to bring people back into public life. What makes solutions so hard to arrive at is that programmatic answers are so frequently off the mark. Remember the "Iron Rule" of the Industrial Areas Foundation: Never do for others what they can do for themselves. The problem with so many programmatic approaches is that they attempt to do just that. The trick is to understand the conditions under which political engagement takes place and then to provide those conditions in as many ways as we can.

I believe the argument is fraudulent that welfare initiatives lead to dependency. The New Deal suffered from no such setbacks. But there is a tendency for institutions of welfare to emphasize themselves and their programs over those they are attempting to assist. We should take this lesson to heart in our efforts to revitalize the public sphere. If we hold the freedom-to-experience above the freedom-to-will, if we take seriously its demands that we are responsible to ourselves and to others, we will find ways to reopen the doors to public life. When they are opened, when the structural barriers to political participation are removed, the people will return.

The new interactivism is one way to begin returning government to the people. Just as importantly, it demonstrates the powerful potential of the criteria we have suggested for developing a true public sphere. Internet activism works. It works by valuing the freedom of others to choose for themselves what course of action should be taken. It works because it promotes beneficial social exchanges among citizens. It works because political action is linked to a shared moral purpose. It works because it values diversity and democracy over control.

Some analysts believe the failure of Howard Dean to capture the Democratic presidential nomination is a sign of the Internet's limitations. Nobody ever believed that an organization intended to involve new voices in politics—even on behalf of a single candidate—was enough, on its own, to carry the day for Dean. Dean's problem was twofold. His Internet outreach was so successful that it became the campaign's main message, even when the campaign tried to address substantive issues. Nobody votes for a candidate because he has an innovative campaign manager, and Joe Trippi should be given credit for being innovative. Dean was also burdened by his early frontrunner status. He received such press notices for his campaign strategy that he could not help but be perceived as a frontrunner. But it is hard to be an insurgent frontrunner, and John Kerry's team should get credit for exploiting that weakness. None of these developments should be taken as some kind of field test of the power of the Internet in politics. If anything, the hundreds of thousands of new politically active young people is testimony to its success, not a benchmark for failure.

It is not a coincidence that the strengths of Internet organizing are the same as the strength's of Ernie Cortes's IAF. One takes place primarily on the Net. The other occurs in the streets, churches, and neighborhoods of America. One wonders what would happen if the these two armies were united. What if those accustomed to Internet activism partnered in a movement with those less accustomed to the virtual world? There are many ways this can happen, and it can be argued that unless it does, Internet-based initiatives will be limited in their reach. Close to 30 percent of Americans are not part of the Internet world, due to lack of access or interest. Among those 30 percent are the people we need most to find a place in the public sphere. None of us are smart enough to guess what is in the minds and hearts of the poor, the disenfranchised, and the truly alienated. We need to listen, and we will not hear them until they are by our side.

8

SHOOTING ELEPHANTS

The Language of Politics

He that would promote discord, under a government so equally formed as this, would join Lucifer in his revolt.

Thomas Paine
Common Sense

George Orwell did not have a good opinion of the language of politics. He believed it consisted solely of defending the indefensible. "Political language," he said, "is designed to make lies sound truthful and murder respectable, and to give an appearance of solidity to pure wind." Orwell's essay "Politics and the English Language" was written in 1946, but few of us today would disagree with his assessment of the language of politics of its merits. Even casual observers of the political scene recognize the banality of the political sound bite. Most of it is intended not to inform, but to confuse, deceive, or, as Orwell said, make nothing appear like something. Still, there is meaning in our political utterances, although it may not always be the meaning intended by the speakers. And that meaning is what brings us to the subject of elephants.

Ten years before penning his analysis of the emptiness of political language, Orwell, in his first great essay, told a story from his days as a subdivisional policeman in British-ruled Burma. Orwell hated imperialism, and so the insults, anger, and mocking laughter of the native peoples of Burma were doubly barbed, for he understood and sympathized with their resentment of their English overlords. One morning, word was sent to him that an elephant was on a rampage. It had broken free of its chains, killed a man, and ravaged a bazaar. Orwell grabbed a gun and soon found the elephant, now peacefully grazing at some distance from the crowd of 2,000 Burmese who had gathered to see what their white policeman would do. Orwell said he understood in that moment how it was that "when the white man turns tyrant it is his own freedom that he destroys." The elephant no longer presented a danger; to Orwell it seemed like murder to shoot it. But the Burmese left him no option. The imperialist policeman, haven taken upon himself the role of protector, would have to follow through and rid the village of the elephant or face the ridicule and laughter of those he ruled, who could see as clearly as he did that the great animal no longer presented a danger. He had no choice. He was trapped by the premises of his imperialist relationship with his audience. So he shot the elephant.

"Don't think of an elephant," advises linguist and cognitive scientist George Lakoff. "It can't be done, of course, and that's the point. In order not to think of an elephant, you have to think of an elephant." Lakoff, uses this exercise to illustrate for his introductory students in cognitive science the importance of "frames" in language. "If you negate the frame, you still activate the frame. Richard Nixon never took Cognitive Science 101. When he said, 'I am not a crook,' he made everyone think of him as a crook," said Lakoff. Language, it appears, can be as confining as Orwell's situation in Burma. We cannot not think of an elephant. Neither could the author of *1984*.

Our inability to not think of an elephant illustrates the way language frames work. They are mental structures we use in thinking that consist of images, words, or concepts that appear in our minds when we hear or speak a term. They appear as certainly as does the word "elephant" when you try not to think of it. Frames are like logical word associations, contexts that determine the meaning of a term. Frames are reference points in the communal imagination. Without them, terms would float free of context and meaning. The name "George Orwell" has become a kind of quasi-frame, as we immediately think of *1984*, Big Brother, and political double-talk in which peace means war and freedom means slavery. In another example, Lakoff examines the term "tax relief." "Relief" implies a victim (or someone who is afflicted), an evil villain who caused the affliction, and a good hero or rescuer who will save the afflicted victim. So when the term "tax relief" is used, we immediately place it in a context that assigns to the taxpayer the role of victim, to tax proponents the role of evil villain and to the proponents of tax relief the role of hero.

One of the ways negative political attacks work is they can force the target of the attack to invoke the negative frame while denying it. President Bush, put on the defensive by questions about whether he completed his service in the National Guard, cannot answer the question without raising the negative implication. When Al Gore explained that he never claimed to have invented the Internet, as his opponents allege that he said, he raised the charge anew when he refuted it.

Language as Political Practice

We have examined the structure of our political practices, looking for ways to revitalize the public sphere and restore the vigor of democracy and the possibilities for human freedom. Language counts as a political practice. While there are competing theories about how and why language evolved, most theorists agree that it developed in the context of the need for humans to devise cooperative strategies for survival. One profound paradox that language had to circumvent was this: Language depends on trust, but as the number of trusting listeners increases, so do the potential rewards for lying. Theoretically, lying would pay such dividends that lies would dominate, trust would disappear, and, with it, language. An answer to this dilemma could only be found collectively, linguists and anthropologists believe; from the beginning, language evolved along with the complexity of our social and political life. Language was the first political practice of modern man.

One way that humans reduced the payoff for deception was by developing shared ritual and metaphor, patent fictions that served to bind a group together. Membership in the group and knowledge of these shared "secrets" was reserved for those who had earned trust. If the development of complex syntax might reward lying, lying would be controlled by language's remarkable ability to operate on multiple levels of understanding. The "truth" of a group's solidarity was embodied in the symbolic fictions its members shared that distinguished them from outsiders. "In the final analysis, people are on speaking terms only with those who 'share the same gods.' The magic of words is the collusion of a ritual ingroup. Withdraw the collusion and nothing happens—the speaker's words are empty sound," wrote anthropologist Chris Knight. So when the complexity of social organization led us into the public sphere, we were lured away from prehistory and the exclusive concern for survival for its own sake. At the same time, we confronted the possibility of history and of a humanly produced future, and brought with us the communal domains of our imaginations as embodied in language. Two kinds of frames were paramount—those involving the organization of family, and those shaping the myths and legends that bonded us together and the rituals by which we celebrated them. These frames inform political discourse to this day.

Interestingly, both orthodox religious conservatives on the Right and so-called postmodernists on the Left believe these frames have lost their force in contemporary life. The former would restore authoritarian frames of god and family by decree; the latter note that the language frames of god and family are merely instruments of power. They urge us to adopt an understanding of life's radical contingency. We might think of our ancient linguistic heritage as the elephant in the room that everyone has taken for dead. The zealots and the postmodernists begin to look like the Burmese in Orwell's elephant story, who, after Orwell fired his gun, "were bringing dahs and baskets even before I left, and I was told they had stripped his body almost to the bones by the afternoon."

But the ancient linguistic frames have not perished, although their contents suffer from the twentieth-century assault on metaphysics. They are human inventions, after all, invested with transcendent qualities and designed to provide trust among people and a framework for answering the unanswerable questions that historical man confronts. Jan Patočka spoke to their continuing power when he urged us to remember that these quests—for transcendent meaning and human solidarity—would always be with us because they are essential to moral evaluation. What we find, however, is that the Right is not bashful about utilizing these powerful frames to enforce its worldview. The Left, on the other hand, believing that the power of the ancient linguistic frames has waned and that they are authoritarian in principle, has largely dismissed them. This has weakened the understanding of the Left's moral positions and ceded an advantage in political conversation to the Right. The Right, by and large, cynically uses the language of religion and family to enhance its own power, while the Left vainly points to the deception and asks citizens to join them—but where, exactly?

Political Language and the Metaphors of Family Life

In our examination of language, our first political practice, we turn to Lakoff's understanding that our political worldviews are based on models of ideal families—an authoritarian, strict parent family, and a nurturant parent family. We then consider the persistence of the spiritual linguistic frame as found in the covenantal tradition and in the messianic, savior model so dominant in contemporary political conversation; it is a tradition in which a figure like President Bush poses as the lone, selfless hero standing for us—the good against a world of evil. We conclude by looking at some of Bush's messaging and the ways his speechwriters take advantage of the cognitive patterns that determine meaning in much of our social and political conversation. When Bush says, "I am a war president," he is invoking frames of the strong parent who commands ultimate obedience as he stands alone against the dark forces of evil that are loose about the world.

Misused by the Right and misunderstood by the Left, our linguistic heritage has suffered. It is just another way our cultural and social practices facilitate the politics of deceit. Ralph Waldo Emerson, writing in the essay "Nature" in 1836, was already keenly aware of the debilitations of language. Believing that primordial language was intimately tied to humanity's place in nature, he urged us to overcome our decadent use of words and "pierce this rotten diction and fasten words again to visible things; so that picturesque language is at once a commanding certificate that he who employs it, is a man in alliance with truth and God." Emerson approached something like contemporary linguistic understanding of frames when he said, "A man conversing in earnest, if he watch his intellectual processes, will find that a material image, more or less luminous, arises in his mind, cotemporaneous with every thought, which furnishes the vestment of the thought." It is in this very sense that our cognitive frames provide context and meaning to words.

Lakoff identifies distinct conservative and progressive worldviews, mapped onto cultural and political language from different family models. He is, of course, speaking of ideal families; most people fall somewhere in between the extremes. There is the strict father model and the nurturant parent model. Each comes clothed in a moral system, or, as Emerson put it, its own "vestment of thought," or frame.

In the strict father model, authority of the parent must be maintained above all else. The family is a hierarchy, with the strong parent supporting the family and protecting it from a world full of danger and evil. Children are expected to become self-reliant, and parental discipline is key to developing this self-reliance. Competition and the pursuit of self-interest are encouraged; this is how individuals become moral beings. Children are not to be coddled. If they fail, it is because of a failure of character. Once a child in a strict parent family reaches adulthood, he is on his own. The strict father has completed the job of protecting and securing the child.

Translated to politics, the worldview of the strict parent morality demands that the authority of the political leader be maintained in all circumstances. This is how criticism of President Bush's policies can be painted as immoral. It also explains that misleading statements of fact from Bush are not recognized as such by followers of the strict parent worldview. A certain infallibility adheres to the authority figure. When no weapons of mass destruction were found in Iraq, only the immoral would accuse the Bush administration of lying. In his role as protector, Bush did what he believed was best to protect the American family. In his interview with NBC's Tim Russert on *Meet the Press* in February 2004, Bush remained squarely in the strict parent role, dismissing suggestions that he had misled the nation into war; he invoked images of a dangerous world that required a strict father's authority and guidance. "I'm a war president. I make decisions here in the Oval Office in foreign-policy matters with war on my mind . . . And the American people need to know they got a president who sees the world the way it is. And I see dangers that exist, and it's important for us to deal with them," Bush said. Russert tried several times to question the accuracy of American intelligence. Each time Bush responded by talking of his decision-making prowess.

In politics, the strict parent model divides the citizenry into two categories: disciplined, self-reliant competitors, and immature, undisciplined and irresponsible "children," who expect to be coddled by government programs that reward laziness and keep them in perpetual childhood. Lakoff undertook his analysis in 1994 as he tried to identify a coherent philosophy behind the Newt Gingrich era's

"Contract with America." From the perspective of strict father morality, "conservative policies cohere and make sense," Lakoff said. "Social programs give people things they haven't earned, promoting dependency and lack of discipline, and are therefore immoral. The good people—those who have become self-reliant through discipline and pursuit of self-interest—deserve their wealth as a reward."

The nurturant parent model grows from a more optimistic view of human nature. Nurturing parents must be empathic and responsible, two values they try to pass along to their children. Empathy implies interconnectedness, honesty, dialogue over monologue, understanding, and fairness. Responsibility means that parents must protect their children and provide for them. We are responsible to ourselves and to others. Cooperation is valued over competition. Instead of strict rules, nurturing parents define an ethical approach that insists we should help others and not harm them. "The obedience of children comes out of their love and respect for their parents, not out of the fear of punishment," said Lakoff. A sense of responsibility extends to all and to the natural resources that sustain us all.

Applied to politics, this family model extends these core values to government. Government should help those who cannot help themselves. All must be able to share in political power, and so the protection of civil liberties and democracy itself is key. Government should protect our freedoms, and provide for our security. But it must also help guard against injustice and economic unfairness. When any of these values are threatened, the worldview itself is threatened. Mutual responsibility takes precedence over absolute authority. In this model, criticism of those in authority is encouraged. It is critical to the health and stability of the nation. The nurturant model is visible throughout the history of liberal democracy. It was articulated during the progressive era, the New Deal, and the Great Society. Even President Bush tries to simulate the nurturant approach when he speaks of "compassionate conservatism." The fact that Bush's policies are contrary to the nurturant moral vision is disguised by the use of the term.

A good example of the ascendancy of the authoritarian model over the nurturant model can be found in the educational fad embodied in the Bush administration's education reforms, known as the "No Child Left Behind" Act. The nurturing educator has been replaced by an authoritarian overseer, in this case embodied by the federal government as disciplinarian of educational achievement. It is sold to the public as a commitment to "accountability" and "standards." But it is exactly the kind of inflexible, authority-at-all-costs approach that marks the authoritarian family. We used to get tough on criminals. Now we get tough on schoolchildren and their teachers, as many observers have noted. Replacing cooperative learning with high-stakes testing, school personnel are reduced to the kind of mindless, bureaucratic functionaries the right wing used to decry. Here, says the Bush administration, take these tests, and we'll decide which students will fail, which teachers will be fired, and which schools will be closed. The Bush administration means this in a literal sense. Without funding to meet the mandates of the "No Child Left Behind" Act, educators throughout the country fear many public schools will simply have to close. This is, of course, the goal of the act. Destroy (in reputation, if not in fact) enough public schools, and taxpayers will be persuaded to let their money be used to fund private, Christian schools. Bush's cold and cynical education reform is the politics of deceit at its most disturbing level.

How Conservatives Have Out-Talked Progressives

In recent years progressives have hesitated to articulate their powerful moral vision. Instead, progressives concentrate on specific programs or policies, and it is assumed that everyone should share the moral vision that the programs and policies are meant to serve. The Right, however, has not made this mistake. Conservative followers of the more authoritarian model do not hesitate to articulate the moral vision behind their policy suggestions. They have been so successful at this that Democratic campaigns often simply mimic their approach. Campaigns become Ironman contests in which candidates try to "out-tough" one another.

Lakoff points out that about one-third of the electorate favor the progressive moral worldview, about one-third favor the conservative worldview, and about one-third believe in both, employing different moral outlooks in different parts of their lives. For instance, this last group may be more authoritarian at the office and more nurturant at home. The problem for progressives is that these so-called swing voters do not see a candidate or party speaking to the nurturant moral vision. They see the authoritarian version demonstrated by conservatives, while their nurturant side is all but ignored in the public conversation.

We should resist the reduction of this analysis to simple confirmation of social stereotypes. This is not a question of strict versus permissive morality. Both recommend discipline. But the nurturant approach promotes responsibility over blind obedience to authority. Behind the two moral outlooks are radically different views of the world and its opportunities and dangers. And the two approaches lead to different outcomes as well. In the authoritarian approach, for instance, maintaining authority becomes the supreme commandment. If it should be allowed to falter, all that it stands for falters. In the nurturant model, empathy and responsibility are paramount. Ignore or displace these values and the viability of the moral system is endangered. This is why conservatives and progressives always seem to be talking past one another.

For instance, in a February 24, 2004, speech to the National Governors Association, widely viewed as his reelection kick-off, President Bush cast himself as the strong, disciplined leader while painting his Democratic opponents as weak, irresponsible children. The 2004 election, Bush said, "is a choice between an America that leads the world with strength and confidence, or an America that is uncertain in the face of danger." Bush said his administration was determined to make every American responsible for themselves, while Democrats wanted to raise taxes and make choices for people. "They seem to be against every idea that gives Americans more

authority and more choices and more control over their own lives."
This is a way of playing the strict father. In effect, Bush said, "We're
going to teach you some standards and then you are on your own.
Good luck." Bush was explicit with his strict father theme: "We're
changing the culture of America from one that says, 'If it feels good,
do it,' and, 'If you've got a problem, blame somebody else,' to a culture in which each of us understands we're responsible for the decisions we make." Bush's rhetorical trick here is to not only advance a
strict, authoritarian leadership model, but to distort the definition of
the nurturant model at the same time.

Senator John Kerry, on the other hand, explicitly evokes concepts
of both empathy and responsibility in his stump speech.
"Everywhere I've been in this campaign, I've seen the wreckage of
the Bush economy. I've met working Americans who are getting the
short end of the stick. Jobs on the run. Wages and salaries dead in
the water. Health care unavailable and unaffordable. A sense of pow-
erlessness—people waking up every day worried that their job is
about to disappear and a lifetime of dreams will be destroyed.

"I've met those workers over and over again. They have touched
my conscience and my heart. I will never forget them. And I will be
a president who fights for them," Kerry said. The contrast is clear, as
is the visceral appeal of both the authoritarian and nurturant models. But it is evident that Kerry sees a leader's role as remaining in a
partnership of sorts with those he leads. Bush believes leadership
means setting rules, disciplining those who will not or cannot follow
them, and dismissing all failures as the result of personal deficiency.
The issue is not government coddling versus responsibility, as conservatives would like to portray it. Instead, the nurturant model
speaks of our ongoing responsibilities to one another, while the
authoritarian model believes responsibility extends no further than
"follow the leader."

We can use Abraham Lincoln as an example of a nurturant
leader, one who was unafraid to return to the nation's covenantal
roots, which rely upon empathy and shared responsibility—hallmarks
of the nurturant approach. Lincoln, in one of his debates with

Stephen Douglas in 1858, said that the nation's founders ". . . meant to set up a standard maxim for free society, which should be familiar to all, and revered by all; constantly looked to, constantly labored for, and even though never perfectly attained, constantly approximated, and thereby constantly spreading and deepening its influence and augmenting the happiness and value of life to all men of all colors everywhere." Lincoln speaks of a free society in which all citizens share a responsibility for building and maintaining. Mention is made of our common, covenantal understanding that all of us are created equal. There is an understanding that the perfectly just nation will never be achieved; rather, there is the absolute necessity of ongoing struggle toward that illusive perfection. In other words, we must nurture the nation together.

President Bush can do a photo opportunity on the deck of an aircraft carrier named the USS *Abraham Lincoln*, but that is as close as he comes to the spirit and political philosophy of America's sixteenth president. At every turn, Bush uses the rhetoric of an authoritarian out to rid the world of evil. Lincoln spoke of an unfinished democratic project, acknowledging that we must continually struggle with uncertainty and ambiguity. Bush, however, speaks constantly of absolute good and absolute evil. "This will be a monumental struggle of good versus evil, but good will prevail," Bush said. Famously, Bush was reported telling Senator Joseph Biden Jr. of Delaware and CNN's Candy Crowley that he does not "do nuance." There is no room for nuance in a Christian nation.

In a speech given in September 2002, Bush referred to a passage from the Biblical prophet Isaiah: "And the light has shone in the darkness, and the darkness will not overcome it," Bush said. Aboard the USS *Abraham Lincoln*, Bush told the troops, "And wherever you go, you carry a message of hope—a message that is ancient and ever new. In the words of the prophet Isaiah, 'To the captives, come out! to those who are in darkness, be free!'" Stam, who mentions these two quotations as examples of Bush's religious rhetoric, notes that the President does not hesitate to identify God with his own mission. By painting himself as the leader of a divine mission, by asserting that he has "been called" to lead the war on terror, Bush attempts to cast into rhetorical darkness anyone who disagrees with him. Relying on the strength of the authoritarian moral view, he asserts that only the enemies of America would try to weaken his leadership and thereby weaken the nation's resolve to fight terrorism.

Immoral Certainty

Bush's mythological presentation of his role in God's history will fail him sooner or later. The world is too complex to be divided into black and white or good and evil. Too many facts will not fit the picture Bush presents. This was apparent in his February interview with Tim Russert on NBC's *Meet the Press*. A reading of the transcript of that interview "suggests that Bush's most critical quality—certainty—has oozed from him like helium from a balloon," said *Washington Post* columnist Richard Cohen, who added that Bush's certainty was undone by the failure to find Iraq's weapons of mass destruction. "It is a massive reversal of fact, hot turned into cold, tall into short. Bush's inability or refusal to come to grips with the new facts is not the product of a poor performance or an errant tongue, but of a troubling insistence that his beliefs cannot be wrong."

This insistence is required by the authoritarian view that power must be maintained above all. Bush's inarticulate appearance on Russert's show gives us a kind of morality play demonstrating the power of Vaclav Havel's observation that a post-totalitarian regime becomes captive to its own lies, myths, and legends. A simple acknowledgment of facts challenges its authority at its root. It cannot abide such a challenge. When Bush's certainty is shaken, he has nothing to fall back upon, because his rigid certainty is his only strength. This kind of moral certainty is deeply embedded in American culture. But we should remember that a similar certainty once accompanied the defense of slavery and the slaughter of Native Americans. One cannot imagine Clint Eastwood's film character Dirty Harry doubting for one minute that his violent—and solitary—defense of his moral view was certain. But it is also interesting to note that Clint Eastwood, in 2003, directed a movie about violence, *Mystic River*, in which the certainty that surrounds so much of America's obsession with violence as a redemptive act is deeply ambiguous. In other words, Eastwood accomplished what Bush cannot. By confronting his own certainty, Eastwood located redemption in the very expression of uncertainty and ambiguity.

What Bush does not say can be as revealing as what he does say. Two cornerstones of his so-called compassionate conservatism are the "No Child Left Behind" Act, and Medicare reform, which protects the profits of pharmaceutical companies while promising additional benefits to Americans. But when he describes these programs, he abandons religious language and reverts to economic justifications. Bush is quick to invoke Christian principle when it justifies military action and America's mission in the world, but Christian principles that speak of assisting the poor, the meek, the less fortunate, are absent from a description of his domestic policies. The only exception is his interest in providing government funding for faith-based initiatives, which will turn over to churches the nation's responsibility for looking after all of its citizens. But even that program is defined in pragmatic, not moral or religious, language.

Examining his 2004 State of the Union address, we find the words of the policy wonk, not the religious zealot. On health care reform: "Our goal is to ensure that Americans can choose and afford private health care coverage that best fits their individual needs." On education reform: "We are regularly testing every child on the fundamentals. We are reporting results to parents, and making sure they have better options when schools are not performing. We are making progress toward excellence for every child in American."

I think there is an explanation for the different rhetorical strategies. Bush believes he is on an international mission for God when it comes to asserting the United States' power across the world. It presents no challenge to his Christian beliefs. However, the profound call for social justice and equality we find among Old Testament prophets and in the New Testament does not conform to the conservative, authoritarian worldview. Bush cannot employ this language because he knows his policies are compassionate in name only. He cannot bring himself to justify them with the language of his faith. Bush's speechwriters are not going to advance—really advance, with rhetorical power—a worldview that acknowledges our responsibility to one another, that calls on us to empathize with the less fortunate and to act to restore justice and equality.

The traditions that lie behind our political practices remain powerful forces. As Lakoff demonstrated, our political thoughts are in many ways conditioned by language frames in which ideal family organizations are projected onto the larger world. Failure to understand the contemporary influence of these language frames is a kind of willful blindness. Some might prefer that citizens of a democracy engage in more sterile, rationalistic dialogue in which correct policies emerge from mathematical proof. But this is not the nature of our lives together, and it is not in the nature of language to provide this kind of certainty. Conservatives who would advance moral certainty in the face of life's ambiguities and uncertainties betray their own weakened moral position. We grow stronger when we face uncertainty. We are weakened by pretending uncertainty is evil. As with so many of our political practices, contemporary use of language—our first political practice—advances the politics of deceit over an honest, cooperative exploration of solutions to the many dangers and uncertainties of our common life. When conservatives attempt to lead by dividing the nation into two groups—believers and nonbelievers—they engage in the most cynical manipulation of all, sowing discord and division. They have, in the words of Thomas Paine, "joined Lucifer in his revolt." So to speak.

9

FREEDOM AND RELIGION

The Visions of Jacob
and Orestes

*Suspicion is the companion of mean souls, and the bane of all
good society. For myself I fully and conscientiously believe, that it
is the will of the Almighty, that there should be diversity of religious opinions among us...*

Thomas Paine
Common Sense

Imagine two legendary heroes separated by a wide, blue sea called
the Mediterranean Ocean. Near the southern shore, the Old
Testament's Jacob lays his head on a stone to sleep and dreams of
angels descending and ascending a ladder to heaven. Near the northern shore, the Greek hero Orestes lays his head on a stone to sleep
and is briefly free of the devilish Furies who torment him. Each of
these heroes has a vision of freedom made possible by their spiritual
yearning and their human circumstances. Each figures in a tale of
the founding of a people. Jacob, the patriarch, father of the Twelve
Tribes, is renamed Israel. Orestes, led by a compassionate Athena, is
the first defendant in the founding of the Greek court, in which rea-

soned human judgment supplants the mad retribution of the gods. Central to their journeys are spiritual experiences of freedom, of new possibilities opening from their uncertain, guilt-ridden pasts.

Now imagine Jacob and Orestes meeting to discuss the meaning of their various adventures. Orestes would insist life's meaning is found in escaping the wrath of gods. Jacob would insist life's meaning is found in earning divine blessing. Their stories appear to be theologically irreconcilable. But they have been reconciled—by the history of the people who came after them. And so it goes with a pluralistic approach to human freedom and religion. Jacob and Orestes are legendary characters with prominent roles in the traditions that lie behind social, cultural, political, and spiritual practices in the West. Their stories are compatible, or at least they were held to be by the ancient storytellers who found it easy to elaborate such different tales from parallel motifs. It is not without irony that many religious people more than two thousand years later pursue religious exclusionism, unaware of the pluralistic past of their own traditions.

Religious Pluralism

The exclusionist view has always been the invention of those in charge of religious hierarchies. It remained influential with post-Enlightenment academics of the nineteenth century, who time and again managed to discover pure racial or religious lineages that confirmed the superiority of their own tradition or race. But two centuries of archeology and linguistic analysis have eliminated the exclusionist view. Traditions swapped stories and practices freely. There were Semitic and Indian influences on early Greek traditions and philosophy. The Greek skeptic Pyrrho of Ellis (circa 365–275 BCE) studied with Indian yogis when at age 35 he traveled to India on Alexander the Great's expedition. The Roman Pyrrhonist Sextus Empiricus lived at the same time as the Great Buddhist scholar Nagarjuna; both developed a skeptical, deconstructionist method of thought and practice. Socrates was influenced by Eastern traditions. Jesus was influenced by early Greek thought. Along the Old Silk Road, Christianity, Taoism, Buddhism and Confucianism blended practices. Islam's pursuit of knowledge of the natural world sparked Western natural philosophy.

The nineteenth-century European imperialist drive took scholars to tragicomic extremes as they tried to explain away philological discoveries that Sanskrit, Greek, and Latin sprang from a common Indo-European source. If that was so, how then could they justify Aryan hegemony throughout Asia and India? Easy. The first Indians were white, it was magically discovered, and only later were they absorbed by a darker-skinned population. So, whites remained superior. In fact, the concept of race as a determinant of human capacity was invented as part of this effort. Among scholars, the exclusionist view has gradually given way. We should avoid a simple-minded "we are the world" kind of syncretism, which diminishes the unique contributions of separate traditions, and we should not fall victim to an extravagant exaggeration of diffusionist theories of a shared past. The controversy that surrounded Martin Bernal's unconfirmed claim in the 1980s of African influence on Greek thought fueled a conservative political backlash against multicultural studies. Exaggerated claims aside, we were pluralists before we were exclusionists. We were multiculturalists before we were cultural chauvinists.

It is testimony to the genius of the founders of the United States' constitutional democracy that the dangers of religious coercion and oppression should be recognized. Decades before nineteenth-century classicists were inventing elaborate justifications for European world dominance, James Madison, Thomas Jefferson, Benjamin Franklin, and others were busy protecting the nation's civil and political practices from domination by any ecclesiastic authority. Church and state should be separated, neither encroaching upon the other's sphere of influence. But the separation is easier on paper than in reality. Politics is about the business of negotiating different moral points of view. Morality springs from spiritual belief and practice. Religion is essential to the pursuit of freedom, which civil institutions are intended to protect.

In *Democracy in America*, Alexis de Tocqueville wrote, "Religion in America takes no direct part in the government of society, but it must be regarded as the first of their political institutions; for if it does not impart a taste for freedom, it facilitates the use of it." In the course of the examination of our contemporary political practices, spiritual traditions have come up regularly. It is impossible to ignore the role of religion in our civic and political life. Spiritual practices and moral viewpoints are inextricably bound to our political practices. More fundamentally, spiritual practice is a personal and communal exploration of what it means to be free. The history of organized religion makes this easy to overlook, as religious institutions have often become absolute enemies of liberty. Tolerance of the spiritual pursuits of others does not come easily to religion's institutional hierarchy, who depend on the allegiance of their followers for their own power and prestige. It is easier to lead a people when you have made them fear some perceived threat. So we humans, who want only to be happy and free, find ourselves on the front lines of crusades and jihads, civil wars and holocausts, ethnic cleansings and inquisitions.

The role of religion in American civic life is a troubled one. The framers of the United States Constitution were personally familiar with religious persecution. But they were also aware of religion's role in the pursuit of freedom. They prohibited the establishment of a national religion not because religion is unimportant to civic life, but because it is so important. The moral fervor of religious reformers helped end slavery. Activists in the Social Gospel movement brought the nation's attention to the plight of the poor and underprivileged, to the cruelties of the forced labor of children. Martin Luther King's deeply spiritual calls for change fueled the Civil Rights movement. The efforts of a progressive clergy helped end the unjust Vietnam War.

But religion has also been used in America to oppress or manipulate others for political ends. No sooner had the Pilgrims escaped persecution for their beliefs than they turned upon those in their new home who believed differently than they. Witches were hanged. The Bible was quoted to defend slavery. A Christian's duty became one of warring against alternative political solutions. Communists were executed. Protestant dread of immigrants' Catholicism bred hatred and economic bigotry. The so-called Religious Right became the breeding ground of the kind of intolerance our nation was, in principle, founded to overcome. In our time, confrontations among Muslims, Jews, and Christians, among Protestant and Catholics, among Chinese Communists and Buddhists, have led to mass murder and the potential for worldwide catastrophe. It is not hard to understand the desires of many that humankind somehow overcome the superstitions that lead to so much unnecessary tragedy.

Reinhold Niebuhr, the twentieth-century theologian who championed human rights and social justice, lost hope that spiritually-based collective action would succeed in overcoming prejudice, bigotry, hatred, and economic exploitation. He said it was sadly true that human groups were unable to achieve the moral discipline of individuals. It is "one of the tragedies of the human spirit: its inability to conform its collective life to its individual ideals," Niebuhr wrote. As we contemplate religion's influence upon our political practices, it would be wise to fully understand Niebuhr's warning. Because humans live a finite, limited existence among one another, what we may individually hold to be the highest moral good is difficult to project or extend to group behavior. Social and political arrangements will likely continue to be based on group self-interest and relationships of power. A nation goes to war to protect its self-interest, proclaiming that it is on a mission from God. Such self-deceit is common to collective human action, despite the deep moral convictions of individuals within the group. Individuals who would not murder to promote their individual self-interests reach a different conclusion with regard to group self-interest. No spiritual insight can overcome this collective limitation. Niebuhr was impatient with religious and rational idealists who believed this collective human weakness could be absolutely overcome. Coercion and force often rule our collective lives, Niebuhr believed, although some group actions can have high moral purpose.

"If we contemplate the conflict between religious and political morality it may be well to recall that the religious ideal in its purest form has nothing to do with the problem of social justice," Niebuhr wrote. For instance, Jacob and Orestes privately achieved their experiences of freedom. Both, in fact, were in exile from the communities of their birth. There is an obvious contradiction present in any effort to impose these private experiences upon others, to urge social cohesiveness upon the group by reference to individual, inner experience. How then, is the collective pursuit of freedom to be conducted? The question raises the dangers inherent in earlier suggestions that we return to covenant tradition, that we more freely use the religious language of morality in a restored public sphere. "We cannot build our individual ladders to heaven and leave the total human enterprise unredeemed of its excesses and corruptions," Niebuhr said. Individuals understand ethics out of personal, inner experience. But we cannot successfully project onto social or political practices the moral lessons of inner experiences. The paradox seems unsolvable.

Speaking from his Christian perspective, Niebuhr said, "Pure religious idealism does not concern itself with the social problem. It does not give itself to the illusion that material and mundane advantages can be gained by the refusal to assert your claims to them." He pointed out that "Jesus did not counsel his disciples to forgive seventy times seven in order that they might convert their enemies or make them more favorably disposed. He counseled it as an effort to approximate complete moral perfection." Jesus, like Buddha, understood that spiritual practice was the pursuit of human freedom. But that individual pursuit would be corrupted if it were undertaken for purposes of material gain, even if that gain were, say, perfect social justice.

In the advanced meditative practices of Tibetan Buddhism, students are urged to overcome attachment, or habits of thought, and then to overcome the overcoming of those habits. Otherwise, the student would simply have transferred older habits to a new one, specifically, to taking pride in just what a skilled spiritual practitioner he or she might be. Such pride would stand in the way of the practice of freedom. Furthermore, in this tradition, as in Christianity, the issue of religion versus social justice is directly addressed. Spiritual perfection is possible only if undertaken for the benefit of others. The legends of Jesus and Buddha confirm the social nature of the religious pursuit of freedom. Jesus died so that others may seek spiritual perfection. Buddha refused to ascend to nirvana, choosing instead to remain and teach those in samsara, or the imperfect human universe.

There is an inescapable conclusion to be drawn from these observations. A deeply pluralistic tolerance of the religious practices of others is fundamental to the moral consistency and integrity of all religious traditions. A religion subverts its own moral foundation when it claims a unique transcendent status or earthly power over others. First, taking these traditions that acknowledge as primary an individual's experience of freedom (God) or the divine (nirvana), it is illogical to assert that such freedom can be coerced. Second, most traditions contain a version of the prophet Amos's recognition that all are people among people, that no person or group can claim divine status for themselves. Third, it is self-defeating for religious exclusionists to claim that respect for all traditions undermines the moral authority of any one tradition. William R. Hutchison called such a belief nonsense, "...because, if I do concede your right to hold firmly to your beliefs, it makes no sense at all for me to deny or compromise that same right in relation to myself." Hutchison concluded, "Pluralism in its leading contemporary meaning—support for group identity and the integrity of competing beliefs—emphatically does not imply 'lack of all conviction,' either for historically dominant American faiths and their adherents or for the society at large."

The practice of religion, of course, has also served as a handy reference point for drawing distinctions between group members and outsiders. This is a profoundly adolescent attitude, dating from the adolescence of humanity. While often employed by children on middle school playgrounds, such exclusionist practices are out of place among mature adults. But they are there, and they should be confronted. When Pat Robertson or George W. Bush claim some kind of unique status with the divine, they are behaving no differently from the schoolyard bully who looks down upon a schoolmate for wearing the wrong kind of tennis shoes. Children have murdered one another over such trivial differences. Presidents have ordered the military invasion of other countries over such differences. Because such chauvinistic behavior subverts the internal logic of the actor's religious tradition (or schoolyard code), the actor, in the name of religion, becomes the irreligious barbarian he seeks to overcome.

The possibility of perfect justice is an illusion, but, as Niebuhr pointed out, it is a necessary illusion. "It is a very valuable illusion for the moment; for justice cannot be approximated if the hope of its perfect realization does not generate a sublime madness in the soul," Neibuhr said. "Nothing but such madness will do battle with malignant power and 'spiritual wickedness in high place.' The illusion is dangerous because it encourages terrible fanaticisms. It must therefore be brought under the control of reason. One can only hope that reason will not destroy it before its work is done." The framers of the Constitution, by their prescient insistence on the separation of civil and religious authorities, opened the possibility of just such a partnership between reason and faith. Those who would subvert this separation are the true enemies of freedom.

Freedom and the Practice of Religion

It is important to emphasize clearly just what is meant by saying that spiritual practice is the practice of freedom. Prayer, meditation, chants, and rituals of all kinds are intended to open the individual mind and heart to new possibilities for thought and action. They provide pauses, or resting places, that lift us out of determined courses of action. There is a strong similarity between such practices and the desynchrony of neural assemblies that divides one conscious thought from the next. They, too, are resting places intended to multiply possible courses of action. As we discussed in the earlier exploration of freedom, there would be no such thing as free will without the physical and spiritual ability to interrupt habitual patterns of thought and behavior. We are bound together in religious traditions not because we focus upon the same idols or beliefs, but because we collectively share in the possibility of freedom. This, as James W. Carey noted, is the essence of ritual communications.

When we understand that the moral integrity of a religious tradition is maintained through a pluralistic respect for practices other than its own, and when we recognize the role of religion in the pursuit of human freedom, we are able to call upon the moral traditions that inform our own civic religion, our own democracy, without fear that we will open the door to the manipulations of "spiritual wickedness in high places."

Early in the Democratic presidential primary of 2004, at least one of the candidates made an awkward effort to employ spiritually-based moral language. Howard Dean mistakenly placed the Book of Job in the New Testament. Later, Senator John Kerry made the legitimate observation that Bush does not practice what he preaches. "The Scriptures say, what does it profit, my brother, if someone says he has faith but does not have works?" Kerry said. "When we look at what is happening in America today, where are the works of compassion?" Kerry was immediately attacked by the Bush campaign for exploiting Scripture for political gain. Quite a charge when it comes from an admittedly faith-based president. But there remains a hesitancy to speak of religion in the public sphere. This nervousness could be overcome by directly addressing the role of religion in human freedom and the necessity that different traditions respect the practices of others. Many people rely upon their spiritual backgrounds in making moral or political decisions. It makes no sense to ignore this fundamental fact of life in our political rhetoric. But if the use of such language appears artificial—as it did when Howard Dean talked about the importance of religion in his life and then erred in a Biblical citation—the power of the language will be lost. Democratic candidates should be willing to use Christian language, for instance, to explain the moral justification for caring for one's neighbors. Similarly, most religious traditions call on their followers to respect nature. We are stewards of the garden. We should not hesitate to call upon these traditions in discussions of environmental policy.

At the same time that these traditions can play a larger role in our political discussions, the separation of church and state becomes all the more important. Negotiations between the two spheres are complex, and, at times, outcomes are quite illogical. The Mormon practice of polygamy was outlawed in 1862 and upheld by the

United States Supreme Court in 1879, reinforcing government as the supreme arbiter of correct and lawful marriage. The debate over same-sex marriage revolves around issues of equal protection, not religious liberty. If President Bush believes what he says when he describes marriage as a "sacred" institution between a man and a woman, government has no business holding forth on it. But a government that can ban certain kinds of spiritual unions is not free to allow prayer in schools.

The answer, of course, is not to buy consistency at the cost of the separation of church and state. Prayers are specific to specific religious traditions, and government has no business endorsing one kind of prayer over another in a public setting. Of course, it is also true that government has no business endorsing one kind of spiritual union over another, but then, the United States government has long done that. African-American slaves could not marry. Racially mixed marriages were once banned. Polygamy fell to federal government intervention. And currently, federal law does not recognize marriages between people of the same gender. Marriage would probably not attract such attention from government if there were not so much money wrapped up in the execution and dissolution of marriages. It is the fate of property that government cares about. This concern is exploited by those who would impose their own religious beliefs upon others. Nonetheless, the wall between church and state has been breached on the subject of marriage. Still, if people could become a little less absorbed in their own piety, if they understood that their righteousness depended more on their tolerance of others than it does upon the number of people they can control, politicians would have a much harder time exploiting our religious differences for their own gain.

The great majority of Americans do not want to impose their religious views on others, but the terms of the debate offer them little room for compromise. On the right, Christian fundamentalists seek to establish their own dominion. On the left, too many are afraid to speak to the spiritually based moral outlook of Americans, spooked as they are by the theocrats waiting for any opening to establish their own beliefs as the law of the land. Progressives are also much more aware of the oppressive, murderous excesses of many of history's religious institutions and, consequently, suspicious of religiously oriented conversation. However, all but the most theocratic could agree that the deceptive manipulation of a people through divisive exploitation of our fears and our religious differences may be the lowest and most despicable example of the politics of deceit. It also happens to be the most common.

Niebuhr was right about the difficulty that groups of people or nations face in attempting to live by moral views that come more easily to individuals. But he was also right when he held that the promise of the perfectly just society was enough to keep us striving for it, however distant a possibility it proves to be. This possibility will be enhanced by the elevation of a true religious pluralism. Society may remain less tolerant, but it should not be difficult for individuals to practice tolerance when we understand that a true religious pluralism—the recognition of the absolute importance of others' spiritual practices to our own—is the guarantor of our own freedom.

There are hopeful signs that a more pluralistic outlook is beginning to emerge, despite the political revival of the Christian Right and a president willing to refer to police actions to track down Islamic terrorists as a "crusade." The release of Mel Gibson's religious epic *The Passion of the Christ* has occasioned an unprecedented interfaith dialogue. Despite how one feels about Gibson's manipulation of prerelease publicity—previews restricted to those who share Gibson's religious views, controversy surrounding a private screening for the Pope—the national conversation that developed regarding the relationship of Christians and Jews should be seen in a positive light. From what I've read of Gibson's private religious views, I can say that I do not share them. But Gibson has the right to express his views in film, and I learn more about his outlook from seeing his work. However, concern that the film unfairly blamed the Jewish people for the death of Jesus of Nazareth led to fears that a new anti-Semitism would be provoked. I, too, fear that anti-Semitism lurks beneath the surface in certain quarters, and I am sensitive to public events that might stir it. Growing up in Houston, Texas, I heard religious bigots refer to Jewish people as "Christ killers."

It may yet develop that anti-Semites will crawl from under their rocks and point to the movie to justify hateful acts. But the initial public reaction seems to have been a healthy curiosity. There has been an openness to exploring what modern scholarship has revealed about the true circumstances of Jesus's execution, and about the intimate relationship of Christianity and Judaism. Shining light on these issues can lessen religiously driven political tensions and create new openings for understanding. Discussions of the film and its cultural impact in national news magazines, newspapers, and on television seem to be aimed at creating new grounds for such understanding.

Barbara A. McGraw has argued that the Founding Fathers provided a two-tiered public forum to accommodate religious and civic dialogue. There is a Conscientious Public Forum in which discussions involving voluntary acceptance of moral principles is proper. And there is a Civic Public Forum in which legally binding agreements are discussed. This is a handy theoretical approach to understanding the concern for protecting the individual conscience and the health of the democracy. But in the context of our deteriorating public sphere, it is doubtful that either forum enjoys much vibrant activity. The lines between the voluntary and the mandatory are blurred, and with it the separation of church and state. But the debate over Gibson's film did indicate that conversations with possible political implications can take place in some kind of protected forum. It was probably in a similar kind of commercial setting that the storyteller from the Ancient Near East encountered a trader or traveler familiar with Greek legend. Stories were swapped, motifs discussed, and two remarkably parallel traditions were constructed. In later years those traditions were separated, combined, separated, and combined again in a renewed understanding of the shared traditions of Amos's "people among people" in a truly pluralistic universe.

10

IN AMERICA

*Immediate necessity makes many things convenient, which if
continued would grow into oppressions. Expedience and right
are different things.*

Thomas Paine

Common Sense

There is something desperate in the way we pin our hopes on
political practices we know are harmful to the health of
democracy. In this we are like Sarah and Johnny Sullivan, the
Irish immigrant parents in Jim Sheridan's lyrical and haunting film
In America. The Sullivans and their two daughters have come to
America looking for a new beginning. After their youngest daughter,
Ariel, falls in love with the lovable movie alien E.T., Johnny tries to
win for her an E.T. doll at a carnival side show. The game is rigged,
of course. To win, Johnny must keep doubling his bet until he has
tossed enough balls into a can. The sideshow hustle depends on
rubes who underestimate the ultimate cost of doubling bets again
and again, and they simply run out of money before winning anything. Soon every cent the Sullivans have, including their rent money,
is riding on one last toss. Sarah and Johnny know this is folly, but
their motivation is pure. They simply do not want to disappoint the
young Ariel.

In just such a way we bet the future of democracy and freedom on political practices that rig the game against our success. We forget that the game is ours, that we make up the rules, and that we can change them if we muster the collective will to do so. But we are locked in a spiral of diminishing returns, a spiral reinforced by those who exploit our inaction, knowing that they will benefit from the determined outcome. As we have seen, such is the inertia of our political system that we, like the Sullivans, forget there may be much less risky and much more productive ways to secure a future for our children. We have almost forgotten what freedom and democracy are.

The title of Sheridan's film, *In America*, is evocative. It is a little like Lakoff's elephant. The short phrase comes with conjured visions of the nation's promise, although what comes to mind is likely to vary from person to person. Nonetheless, it is safe to say that Americans feel a certain hopefulness about the possibilities for their future when they see or hear the words "in America." Many years ago composer Randy Newman used the phrase to open "Sail Away," his beautiful, bitter song of slavery in which a slave trader sings to Africans, "In America, you get food to eat/Won't have to run through the jungle and scuff up your feet/You'll just sing about Jesus and drink wine all day/It's great to be an American." The power of the song comes from the fact that some part of us believes in the myth without recognizing the irony. We want to believe that freedom and democracy bloom in America like wild grapes. We just have to pick them. Ours is a blessed nation, a paradise in which "every man is free/to take care of his home and his family," as Newman sang later in the song.

The trouble with this dream is that it invests the promise of freedom with a divine invulnerability. So long as we remain in the blessed garden, we are free. Whatever our true condition, we remain free, because after all, this is a free country, and we were taught that we do not have to scuff up our feet to keep it that way. Our political practices, then, become irrelevant. Our freedom and the democracy intended to promote it are immune to their deprivations. But only a part of us believes this myth. Like Sarah and Johnny Sullivan, we know in our hearts that we are making a mistake, even if the mistake is not at the moment fatal. Still, we cling to the illusion, desperately.

When, after September 11, 2001, President Bush advised us to defy terrorists by shopping, he was promoting the illusion that Dad will take care of the emergency while Mom and the boys and girls sit, safely it is presumed, on the sidelines. Motivated by darker visions than Johnny Sullivan, Bush keeps doubling the expenditures and the risks while assuring us that he will get one more baseball into the tin can. But Bush plays two roles, for he is also the hustler behind the table, urging us on in a game he knows the people will ultimately lose. The Bush administration is skilled at playing the political games that threaten freedom and democracy, and it has figured prominently in the exploration of those practices not only because it is the most recent administration, but because it owes its existence to a rigged game.

Americans have settled on a concept of freedom that denies our responsibilities to ourselves and to one another. In this way we are isolated, and our satisfactions come largely from private expressions of will. We are free to choose what television shows we watch, what color clothes to wear, what restaurants to visit. Like magic, our freedom-to-will is fulfilled. But the more expansive freedom, the freedom-to-experience, requires that we step into the messy world and share with others the responsibility for improving our condition. We cannot magically impose our wills on others. Rather, we negotiate our differences and arrive at common strategies or solutions. The covenant tradition, which produced the Declaration of Independence, declares that all are created equal. The freedom-to-will denies that covenant, holding instead that "what's mine is mine." But freedom cannot be mine and it cannot be yours. It can only be ours.

We choose our political leaders in a deadly serious version of reality TV. Although, as is the case with these recent programming successes, there is little reality presented. Instead, what passes for political debate takes place in a virtual sphere that bathes us in its otherworldly light while growing more and more distant from the necessary role of citizens who produce political outcomes rather than consume political products. Most Americans get their political information from advertisements that are manipulative by design. We know we are being hustled, just like the rubes at a carnival side show. But, we say to ourselves, there is information available in the ads, and, well, nothing terrible has happened yet, and, it's really just other, less sophisticated people who are fooled. Each of us believes we see through it all. But we do not and cannot. If we did or could, it would not cost so much to advertise on television. Follow the money.

Those citizens who do try to look beyond the advertisements and search for balanced political information in the mainstream media are not that much more informed. Political strategists have become so skilled at manipulating press coverage that the press rewards the best tricksters with their happy admiration. A successful political journalist must have a sophisticated understanding of how the game works. The best journalists do a good job of reporting on the game. But news is based on conflict, and conflict is best represented in "horse-race" style coverage that tells us who is ahead, who is behind, and which strategists have done the best job of manipulating voters. I still believe that many reporters struggle to report important, meaningful, political news. But they are, after all, observers of the side show. It is we, the voters, who pay our money and take our chance. If we do not try to change the rules of the game, it is hardly the fault of the press.

What important, balanced information we receive through the free press is threatened by the corporate consolidation of media outlets. Driven by the need for profits, these corporate media outlets cannot always tell us what we need to know, which in many cases would be unpleasant, hard to watch, and enough to negatively impact ratings. Instead, they tell us what we want, or what they think we want. And this is when they are not overtly carrying water for a special interest, as Fox News does for the Bush administration.

Many citizens are excluded from the process, a condition everyone calls a scandal while doing little to alleviate it. About half the potential American electorate is permanently disenfranchised for one reason or another. Apologists for this embarrassment argue that they are not truly disenfranchised or legally prohibited from voting. Besides being inaccurate—we have seen how conservatives have mastered the art of purging voter rolls—the apology completely misses the point. It is our political practices that intentionally or inadvertently drive voters from the public sphere. Nonvoting is not a genetic condition. It is a condition produced by the sociopolitical environment. When antidemocratic and power-mad politicians are not aggressively trying to frighten poor and middle-class voters from the polls, others are not doing enough to improve conditions so people feel like their votes could make a difference.

As we have seen, Orwell was right all along about political language. It is intended to turn lies into truths. Conservatives are the more masterful manipulators of language, never failing to remind us that they are the parents and that we are the children. But at least they provide a working—if destructive—model for moral thought and action. Progressives have been less successful at articulating their truly moral vision, a circumstance that must change if democracy is to be saved and freedom realized. Progressives can no longer avoid speaking in a strong moral voice based in spiritual and worldly experience. As Jan Patočka made so clear, the search for meaning will always be with humanity. There is no value in pretending otherwise, hoping for a value-neutral language on which to base rational decision-making. Such a tongue does not exist, and never will. The real way to guard against a theocratic ascendancy is to make an authentic democratic alternative understandable to the minds and hearts of the people, and the way to do this is to speak a language that honors human aspiration.

There are signs of life in the public sphere. Internet activists—or interactivists, as we termed them—have successfully involved millions of Americans in public debate, citizens once sidelined by one-way communications that spoke loudly, but did not listen. The costs of information exchange on the Internet are minimal. Citizens can easily contribute to candidates or causes, express their own opinions, and solicit the opinions of others. Interactivism is in its infancy, as movement leaders like Wes Boyd understand. Because so many potential voters are not on the Net or are not accustomed to its use, the energy so well captured within cyberspace needs to move beyond our isolated offices and living rooms and into the neighborhoods of the millions of Americans with no effective political voice in their own futures.

Ernie Cortes's Industrial Areas Foundation gives us a strong and effective model for renewed grassroots activity. That organization's Iron Rule—Never Do For Others What They Can Do For Themselves—should be adopted by all grassroots leaders. The disenfranchised must be empowered. It will take resources, but the returns will grow exponentially. As more people gain access to political information, they will find it easier to engage in conversations with their friends and neighbors. Information exchanges of this sort are the most important and most likely to bring citizens back into the public sphere. It will not be enough to continue conducting annual or semiannual voter registration drives followed by waves of one-way political communications through the mail, the telephone, radio, or television. We need people talking to people. We need new relationships of trust. We need commitments of time and resources that extend beyond the immediate needs of any single candidate.

The absolute dependence on advertising as the vehicle for authentic political information delivery needs to be reexamined. The ads are lies. Sound and images are manipulated, the messages are irresistible, and even those candidates most devoted to honesty are unlikely to present balanced information in advertisements they pay to produce and broadcast. Once again, none of us with a need to communicate with voters can avoid using radio and television today. It is like the Cold War arms race. Unilateral disarmament is not an option. It would create an even greater information void, which those who are little concerned with truth and honesty in politics would simply exploit. But we have to ask ourselves if our political decisions should continue to be formed through media that the experts tell us can alter our very memories and so change the very makeup of our individual selves. At the very least, an aggressive movement or movements that would restore the vitality of the public sphere will provide powerful alternatives to the current advertising monopoly on political information. Independent sources of news, street papers, Internet blogs, email, neighborhood discussions, small living-room groups like Walter Mosley recommends—all of these and other creative and original ways of sharing political information are critical to restoring the public sphere.

Following Thomas Paine's advice, we should wake up and understand that our long habit of not thinking our political practices wrong does not make them right. Our political practices are the cause and the symptom of the politics of deceit. Their very structure lends advantage to those who would mislead rather than lead, to those who believe their own power is more important than the health of democracy, of those who believe freedom can be franchised like a fast food restaurant to those they consider worthy.

We need a revolution, no less urgently than the American colonists whom Paine sought to rally to the cause of the American Revolution. We are now subjects of the most right-wing regime in the nation's history. For the first time in history, a sitting president has recommended a constitutional amendment that would take away by fiat the rights of millions of Americans. The Bill of Rights is considered a liberal document true patriots should burn. Citizens can be imprisoned for life without access to a court, a lawyer, or knowing even what they are charged with. Federal law enforcement can search our homes without our consent or knowledge. The upper class, no less than King George III of England, is demanding that the middle class pay the costs of its luxuries. The Bush administration has all but eliminated taxes on the wealthy, and asked working Americans to pick up the tab. All the while it strips what meager benefits working Americans might expect in return. For instance, the Bush budget deficit will require deep cuts in Social Security benefits that we have spent a lifetime working to guarantee.

Although Bush lacked the courage to join his peers in Vietnam, he cavalierly sends young Americans to be killed or injured in imperial military adventures that rival those of ancient Rome. Millions of Americans die at home because they cannot afford health care, although insurance company executives, who run the nation's health care system without fear of government interference on behalf of its citizens, grow wealthier and wealthier. The Bush administration has made great progress in destroying what is left of our system of public education, substituting ridiculous high-stakes testing for real learning, hoping to so frustrate parents and taxpayers that the right wing can finally achieve its long-sought goal and turn all education over to conservative religious leaders. The environment is treated as little more than a waste bin for Bush's wealthy court.

All of this is made possible by political practices that favor the privileged over the underprivileged, liars over seekers of truth, authoritarian hustlers over those who struggle to help others, the unprincipled over the principled, and the mean-spirited over the kind-hearted. This is the legacy of the politics of deceit. It is a time of crisis for democracy and for freedom. But the crisis can be overcome with what are, relatively speaking, small reforms. We could deploy an army of young people into the neighborhoods of America, engaging political discussions, helping empower the disenfranchised, for a fraction of the cost that is spent on advertising every election cycle. Major progressive contributors would be astonished at how little it would require. Alternative sources for valuable political information are multiplying.

Vaclav Havel, Jan Patočka, and other Eastern European insurgents brought down their Soviet masters with far fewer resources than we have at our disposal. If we do not act, we will have no one to blame but ourselves. We can stand shoulder to shoulder with the Sarah and Johnny Sullivans of the country and together smash the tables of a game that is rigged against us. This is the way it should be in America.

REFERENCES

Introduction

Brown, W. *Politics Out of History*. Princeton: Princeton University Press, 2001.

Dennett, D.C. *Freedom Evolves*. New York: Viking, 2003.

Havel, V. "The Power of the Powerless," in *The Power of the Powerless*. New York: Sharpe, 1979, reprinted in 1985.

Nancy, J.L. *The Experience of Freedom*. Stanford: Stanford University Press, 1988.

Niebuhr, R. *Moral Man and Immoral Society: A Study in Ethics and Politics*. Louisville: Westminster John Knox, 1932, reprinted in 2001.

Paine, T. "Common Sense," in *The Thomas Paine Reader*. London: Penguin, 1987.

Zaltman, G. *How Customers Think: Essential Insights into the Mind of the Market*. Boston: Harvard Business School Press, 2003.

Chapter 1: The Madness of King George III and Our Contemporary Political Dilemma

Berlin, I. "Two Concepts of Liberty," in *Liberty*. New York: Oxford, 1958, reprinted in 2002.

Calvino, I. *Six Memos for the Next Millennium*. Cambridge: Harvard University Press, 1988.

Havel, V. 1979, reprinted in 1985.

Lippman, W. *The Phantom Public*. New York: MacMillan, 1925, reprinted in 1930.

McGerr, M. *A Fierce Discontent*. New York: Free Press, 2003.

Miller, N. *New World Coming: The 1920s and the Making of America.* New York: Scribner, 2003.

Posner, R. *Public Intellectuals: A Study of Decline.* Cambridge: Harvard University Press, 2002.

Posner, R. *Law, Pragmatism, and Democracy.* Cambridge: Harvard University Press, 2003.

Zukin, S. *Point of Purchase: How Shopping Changed American Culture.* New York: Routledge, 2004.

Chapter 2: Freedom

Breakspear, M. "Nonlinear Phase Desynchronization in Human Electro-encephalographic Data," *Human Brain Mapping.* 2002.

Bezruchka, S. "Are the Rich Making Us Sick?" *Washington Free Press; Free Thoughts.* http://www.washingtonfreepress.org///46/free _thoughts.html, 2000.

Dennett, D.C. 2003.

Foner, E. *The Story of American Freedom.* New York: Norton, 1998.

Findlay, E.F. *Caring for the Soul in a Postmodern Age: Politics and Phenomenology in the Thought of Jan Patočka.* Albany: State University of New York Press, 2002.

Herzen, A. *My Past and Thoughts.* Trans. Constance Garnett. Berkeley: University of California Press, 1982.

Kane, R. "Free Will: New Directions for an Ancient Problem," in *Free Will.* Oxford: Blackwell, 2002.

Kelly, A.M. *Views from the Other Shore: Essays on Herzen, Chekhov, and Bakhtin.* New Haven: Yale University Press, 1999.

Lewis, Anthony "Security and Liberty: Preserving the Values of Freedom," in *The War on Our Freedoms: Civil Liberties in an Age of Terrorism.* Eds. R.C. Leone and G. Anrig, Jr. New York: Public Affairs, 2003.

Lom, P. "East Meets West—Jan Patočka and Richard Rorty on Freedom: A Czech Philosopher Brought into Dialogue with American Post-modernism," in *Political Theory,* 27:4, 1999.

Nash-Marshall, S. *What It Takes to Be Free.* New York: Crossroad, 2003.

Patočka, J. *Heretical Essays in the Philosophy of History.* Ed. James Dodd, Trans. Erazim Kohak. Chicago: Open Court, 1996.

Phillips, K. *American Dynasty: Aristocracy, Fortune, and the Politics of Deceit in the House of Bush*. New York: Viking, 2004.

Roosevelt, F.D. "The Four Freedoms," Address to Congress, http://www.libernet.org/~edcivic/fdr.html, 1941.

Schiller, F. *On the Aesthetic Education of Man*. Trans. E.M. Wilkinson, L.A. Willoughby. Oxford: Clarendon, 1967.

Slevin, P. "The Word at the White House: Bush Formulates His Brand of Foreign Policy." *The Washington Post*, June 23, 2002.

Von Foerster, H. "Ethics and Second Order Cybernetics," *SEHR Constructions of the Mind 4:2*, http://www.stanford.edu/group/SHR/4-2/text/foerster.html, 2002.

Chapter 3: Shaking Bugs Bunny's Hand at Disneyland: Democracy Will Not Be Televised

Bates, Stephen. "Political Advertising Regulation: An Unconstitutional Menace," *Cato Policy Analysis*, no. 112, http://www.cato.org/pubs/pas/pa112es.html, September 22, 1988.

Borradori, G. *Philosophy in a Time of Terror: Dialogues with Jürgen Habermas and Jacques Derrida*. Chicago: University of Chicago Press, 2003.

Braun, K.A., R. Ellis, and E.F. Loftus. "Make My Memory: How Advertising Can Change Our Memories of the Past," *Psychology and Marketing*, 19:1, 2002.

Gallese, V. "The Shared Manifold Hypothesis: From Mirror Neurons to Empathy," in *Between Ourselves: Second-Person Issues in the Study of Consciousness*. Thorvert, UK: Imprint Academic, 2001.

Habermas, J. *The Structural Transformation of the Public Sphere: An Inquiry into a Category of Bourgeois Society*. Trans. Thomas Burger and Frederick Lawrence. Cambridge: MIT Press, 1969, reprinted in 1991.

Noggle, G., and L.L. Kaid, "The Effects of Visual Images in Political Ads: Experimental Testing of Distortions and Visual Literacy," *Social Science Quarterly*, 81:4, 2000.

Lakoff, G., and V. Gallese. "The Role of the Sensory Motor System in Reason and Language," Power Point presentation. Email to author, February 12, 2003.

Perloff, R. "Elite, Popular, and Merchandised Politics: Historical Origins of Presidential Campaign Marketing," in *Handbook of Political Marketing*. Ed. Bruce I. Newman. Thousand Oaks, CA: Sage, 1999.

"Political Ads Dominate Local TV News Coverage." News Release. *The Lear Center Local News Archive*, www.localnewsarchive.org/pdf/LCLNA110102.pdf, November 1, 2002.

"Roll Over, Jefferson. (Devil in the Details)." Editorial. *The American Prospect*, October 12, 2002.

Schacter, D.L. *The Seven Sins of Memory: How the Mind Forgets and Remembers*. Boston: Houghton Mifflin, 2002.

Squire, Bob. "The :30 Second Candidate." Interview. *PBS*, http://www.pbs.org/30secondcandidate/q_and_a/squier1.html, 1999.

Wray, J.H. "Through a Glass Darkly: Television and American Electoral Politic," in *Handbook of Political Marketing*. Ed. Bruce I. Newman. Thousand Oaks, CA: Sage, 1999.

Young, Chuck. "Brain Waves, Picture Sorts®, and Branding Moments," *Journal of Advertising Research*, 42:4, 2002.

Zaltman, G. 2003.

Chapter 4: Dead Pope Music: The Press and American Politics

Alterman, E. *What Liberal Media: The Truth About Bias and the News*. New York: Basic Books, 2003.

Beckerman, G. "Edging Away from Anarchy: Inside the Indymedia Collective, Passion vs. Pragmatism." *Columbia Journalism Review*, issue 5, http://www.cjr.org/issues/2003/5/anarchy-beckerman.asp, 2003.

Burwell, C. "Music at 6," in *Esopus*, 1:1, 2003.

Corrigan, D. "Civic Journalism Played into Right-Wing Media Bashing." *St. Louis Journalism Review*, 33:258, 2003.

Doherty, T. *Cold War, Cool Medium: Television, McCarthyism, and American Culture*. New York: Columbia University Press, 2003.

Doherty, T. Interview with Robin Dougherty. *Boston Globe*. Transcript at http://www.boston.com/ae/books/articles/2004/01/11/getting_the_picture_about_tv_and_the_cold_war/, January 11, 2004.

Figueroa, M., D. Richardson, and P. Whitefield. "The Clear Picture on Clear Channel Communications, Inc.: A Corporate Profile," report prepared for the AFL-CIO by Cornell University, 2004.

Gitlin, T. *Media Unlimited: How the Torrent of Images and Sounds Overwhelms Our Lives.* New York: Henry Holt, 2002.

Hawley, K. "A Poverty of Voices: Street Papers as Communicative Democracy," *Journalism*, 4:3, 2003.

McChesney, R.W. "'High Noon' Independent Media Summit," *The Public i*, 2:2. httpy://publici.ucime.org/mar2002/32002_1.htm.

Mitchell, Greg. *The Campaign of the Century: Upton Sinclair's Race for Governor of California and the Birth of Media Politics.* New York: Random House, 1992.

Moyers, B. "Keynote Address to the National Conference on Media Reform." Madison, Wisconsin. Available at http://www.commondreams .org/views03/1112-10.htm, November 8, 2003.

Sinclair, U. *The Brass Check: A Study of American Journalism.* Urbana: University of Illinois Press, 1928, reprinted in 2003.

Chapter 5: The Threatened Habitats of Democracy

Aldashev, Gani "Electoral Participation Based on Social Exchange: Theory and Evidence from Britain." Chapter 2 of PhD dissertation. Milan, Italy: Bocconi University, 2003.

Berry, Rachel. *"Democratic National Committee v. Edward J. Rollins*: Politics as Usual or Unusual Politics." Washington and Lee University School of Law. Available at http://web.archive.org/ web/20010611033355/home.wlu.edu/ ~real/vol2/Berry.htm, May, 1996.

Borger, G., M. Cooper, S. Minerbrook, and M. Barone. "New Jersey: An Election Controversy." *U.S. News & World Report*, November 22, 1993.

Brown, Jeff. "Testimony Claims Dean OK'd Signs." *Dallas Morning News*, March 9,1983.

Crenson, M.A. and B. Ginsberg. *Downsizing Democracy: How America Sidelined Its Citizens and Privatized Its Public.* Baltimore: The Johns Hopkins University Press, 2002.

Mitchell, Greg. 1992.

Mueller, D.C., and T. Stratmann. "The Economic Effects of Democratic Participation." *Journal of Public Economics*, 87, 2003.

Nichols, J. "Apathy, Inc.: Republicans Aim to Drive Down Voter Turnout." *The Progressive*, October, 1998.

Oberholzer-Gee, F., and J. Waldfogel. "Electoral Acceleration: The Effect of Minority Population on Minority Vote Turnout." National Bureau of Economic Research, Working Papers No. 8252. Available at http://econpapers.hhs.se/paper/nbrnberwo/8252 .htm, 2002.

Skocpol, T. *Diminished Democracy: From Membership to Management in American Civic Life.* Norman: University of Oklahoma Press, 2003

"Sup-Uh, Support! That's Right! Voter Support!" Column item. *Time*, December 6, 1993.

Winston, J.L. "Comments of the National Association of Black Owned Broadcasters, Inc. and the Rainbow/Push Coalition, Inc." Filed before the Federal Communications Commission, January 2003.

Chapter 6: Lantern Bearing and the American Covenant Tradition

Allen, B. "Martin Luther King's Civil Disobedience and the American Covenant Tradition." *Publius: The Journal of Federalism*, 30:4, 2000.

Carey, J.W. "A Cultural Approach to Communication." *Communication as Culture: Essays on Media and Society.* New York: Routledge, 1992.

Chambers, E.T. *Roots for Radicals: Organizing for Power, Action, and Justice.* New York: Continuum, 2003.

Crenson, M.A. and B. Ginsberg. 2002.

Elazar, D. *Covenant and Constitutionalism: The Great Frontier and the Matrix of Federal Democracy (Covenant Tradition in Politics, V3).* New Brunswick, NJ: Transaction Publishers, 1998.

Elazar, D. "Jacob and Esau and the Emergence of the Jewish People." *Judaism: A Quarterly Journal of Jewish Life and Thought*, V:43, 1994.

Everett, W.J. "Recovering the Covenant." *Christian Century*, November, 1998.

Greider, W. *Who Will Tell the People*. New York: Simon & Schuster, 1992.

James, W. "On a Certain Blindness in Human Beings." *The Writings of William James*. Ed. John J. McDermott. Chicago: University of Chicago Press, 1967, reprinted 1977.

King, M.L. "The Ethical Demands for Integration." *The Essential Writings and Speeches of Martin Luther King, Jr.* San Francisco: Harper, 1986.

Madison, J., A. Hamilton, and J. Jay. *The Federalist Papers*. London: Penguin, 1987.

Mosley, W. *What Next: A Memoir Toward World Peace*. Baltimore: Black Classic Press, 2003.

Patočka, J. 1996.

Putnam, R.D. *Bowling Alone*. New York: Simon & Schuster, 2000.

Scocpol, T. 2003.

Stevenson, R.L. "The Lantern Bearers." *Across the Plains*. Gainesville: Blue Unicorn Editions, 1997.

Chapter 7: The Other Superpower: The Internet's New "Interactivists" and the Public Sphere

Aldashev, Gani. 2003.

Boyd, A. "The Web Rewires the Movement." *The Nation*, August 4/11, 2003.

Boyd, W. Interview, February 16, 2004.

Carey, J.W. 1992.

Corritore, C.L., B. Karcher, and S. Wiedenbeck. "On-Line Trust: Concepts, Evolving Themes, a Model." *International Journal of Human-Computer Studies*, 58, 2003.

Elazar, D. 1994.

Havel, V. 1979.

Huang, H., C. Keser, J. Leland, and J. Shachat. "Trust, the Internet, and the Digital Divide." *IBM Systems Journal*, 42:3.

Pariser, E. "Power—Whose Planet," Remarks to Panel Discussion, Environmental Grantmakers' Association retreat, http://www.moveon.org/info/eli-ega-texas.html, August, 2003.

Schell, J. "The Other Superpower." *The Nation*, April 14, 2003.

Shah, D.V., N. Kwak, and R.L. Holbert. "'Connecting' and 'Disconnecting' with Civic Life: Patterns of Internet Use and the Production of Social Capital." *Political Communications*, 18.

Skocpol, T. 2003.

Wertheim, M. *The Pearly Gates of Cyberspace*. New York: Norton, 1999.

Chapter 8: Shooting Elephants: The Language of Politics

Bush, G.W. Interview with Tim Russert, *Meet the Press*, http://www.msnbc.msn.com/id/4179618/, February 8, 2004.

Bush, G.W. "State of the Union Address," Joint Session of Congress, http://whitehouse.gov/news/releases/2004/01/20040120-7.html., January 20, 2004.

Cohen, R. "Bushes War Against Nuance." *Washington Post*, February 17, 2004.

Emerson, R.W. "Nature." *Ralph Waldo Emerson: Essays and Lectures*. New York: The Library of America, 1983.

Lakoff, G. "Framing the Dems." *The American Prospect*, September, 2003.

Lakoff, G. *Moral Politics: What Conservatives Know that Liberals Don't*. Chicago: University of Chicago Press, 1996, republished in 2002 as *Moral Politics: How Liberals and Conservatives Think*.

Knight, Chris. "Ritual/Speech Coevolution." *Approaches to the Evolution of Language: Social and Cognitive Bases*. Cambridge: Cambridge University Press, 1998.

Orwell, G. "Politics and the English Language," http://www.resort.com/-prime8/Orwell/patee.html., 1946.

Orwell, G. "Shooting an Elephant," http://whitewolf.newcastle.edu.au/words/authors/O/OrwellGeorge/essay/shootingelephant.html, 1936.

Stam, J. "Bush's Religious Language." *The Nation*, December 22, 2003.

Chapter 9: Freedom and Religion: The Visions of Jacob and Orestes

Burkert, W. *The Orientalizing Revolution: Near Easter Influence on Greek Culture in the Early Archaic Age*. Trans. Margaret E. Pinder and Walter Burkert. Cambridge: Harvard University Press, 1992.

Carey, J.W. 1992.

Hutchison, W.R. *Religious Pluralism in America: The Contentious History of a Founding Ideal.* New Haven: Yale University Press, 2003.

McEvilley, T. *The Shape of Ancient Thought: Comparative Studies in Greek and Indian Philosophies.* New York: Allworth Press, 2002.

McGraw, B.A. *Rediscovering America's Sacred Ground: Public Religion and Pursuit of the Good in a Pluralistic America.* Albany: State University of New York Press, 2003.

Niebuhr, R. *Moral Man and Immoral Society.* Louisville: Westminster John Knox Press, 1932, reprinted in 2001.

Noonan, J.T., Jr. *The Lustre of Our Country: The American Experience of Religious Freedom.* Berkeley: University of California Press, 1998.

Index